Strong Women
Four Generations
1858 - 1982

for Sylvia and Phil -
life has been enriched
knowing you — hope
I'm up for one more
dinner at my place
before I leave for
Oklahoma —
let's hope.

Virginia
S. Jones

Strong Women
Four Generations
1858 - 1982

Virginia S. Jones

iUniverse, Inc.

New York Lincoln Shanghai

Strong Women Four Generations 1858 - 1982

iUniverse books may be ordered through booksellers or by contacting:

iUniverse
2021 Pine Lake Road, Suite 100
Lincoln, NE 68512
www.iuniverse.com
1-800-Authors (1-800-288-4677)

Because of the dynamic nature of the Internet, any Web addresses or links contained in this book may have changed since publication and may no longer be valid.

The views expressed in this work are solely those of the author and do not necessarily reflect the views of the publisher, and the publisher hereby disclaims any responsibility for them.

Pictured on the cover: Cornelia Prentiss

ISBN: 978-0-595-36675-0 (pbk)
ISBN: 978-0-595-67404-6 (cloth)
ISBN: 978-0-595-81097-0 (ebk)

Printed in the United States of America

I DEDICATE THIS BOOK TO MY MOTHER

CORNELIA FITCH PRENTISS SHRAUGER

Who gave me unconditional love
Who is my memory bank

THE EVENTS IN OUR LIVES HAPPEN IN A

SEQUENCE IN TIME, BUT IN THEIR

SIGNIFICANCE TO OURSELVES

THEY FIND THEIR OWN ORDER,

THE CONTINUAL THREAD OF REVELATION.

—EUDORA WELTY

Cornelia Fitch Prentiss Shrauger

(FAMILY GENEALOGICAL CHART TO THE 4TH GENERATION)

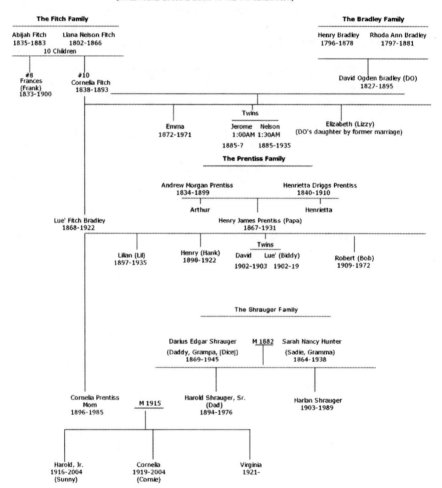

The Fitch Family

Abijah Fitch 1835-1883

Liana Nelson Fitch 1802-1866

10 Children

#8 Frances (Frank) 1833-1900

#10 Cornelia Fitch 1838-1893

The Bradley Family

Henry Bradley 1796-1878

Rhoda Ann Bradley 1797-1881

David Ogden Bradley (DO) 1827-1895

Emma 1872-1971

Twins
Jerome 1:00AM 1885-?
Nelson 1:30AM 1885-1935

Elizabeth (Lizzy) (DO's daughter by former marriage)

The Prentiss Family

Andrew Morgan Prentiss 1834-1899

Henrietta Driggs Prentiss 1840-1910

Arthur

Henrietta

Lue' Fitch Bradley 1868-1922

Henry James Prentiss (Papa) 1867-1931

Lilian (Lil) 1897-1935

Henry (Hank) 1898-1922

Twins
David 1902-1903

Lue' (Biddy) 1902-19

Robert (Bob) 1909-1972

The Shrauger Family

Darius Edgar Shrauger (Daddy, Grampa, [Dice]) 1869-1945

M 1882

Sarah Nancy Hunter (Sadie, Gramma) 1864-1938

Cornelia Prentiss Mom 1896-1985

M 1915

Harold Shrauger, Sr. (Dad) 1894-1976

Harlan Shrauger 1903-1989

Harold, Jr. 1916-2004 (Sunny)

Cornelia 1919-2004 (Cornie)

Virginia 1921-

Contents

ACKNOWLEDGEMENTS

Because of the teaching, guidance and support of
these people, this book has come into being.
Thank you.

Finvola Drury, poet, teacher, and memoirist
Colonel Ken Weber, U.S. Air Force (Ret.), novelist, friend, teacher, devoted
mentor, and editor
William Trotter, historian and novelist—for courage
William Least-Heat Moon, novelist, nonfiction writer, for confidence in the
material
James Laise, writer and teacher, for 'Use of Story'
Joyce Lackey, novelist and friend, for first reading, and constant support
Luther Gillet and Philip Chinitz of Atlantic, Iowa for local research
Louise Hunt and Deb Herbert for Atlantic, Iowa pictures
Len Messenio, writer and teacher, Writers and Books, Rochester, N.Y. whose
classes critiqued my material
Angela Bradley Jones for many hours of technical help, computer
Prentiss Mann Jones for technical help, archival photos

For the continual interest and love my four children Angela, Dennis, Cornelia,
and Prentiss have shown me during the many years of the assembling of
STRONG WOMEN—FOUR GENERATIONS I am deeply indebted.

Virginia S, Jones

GLOSSARY

	Given name:	Always known as:
FITCH	Abijah Fitch m	Abijah
	Llanah Nelson	Llanah
	Cornelia (and 9 siblings)	Cornelia
BRADLEY	David Ogden Bradley m	D.O.
	Elizabeth Neeley d ?	
	Elizabeth	Lizzie
	Cornelia Fitch, 2nd wife	Cornelia
	Lue'	Lue'
	Emma	Emma
	Nelson & Jerome, twins	Nelson, Jerome
PRENTISS	Henry James Prentiss m	Dr., Papa, Grandpa
	Lue' Bradley	Lue', Mama
	Cornelia m	Cornelia
	Harold Frances Shrauger	Dad, Harold
	Henry James m	Hank
	Marion Chase	Marion
	Lilian m	Lil
	Frank Schwarz	Frank
	Lue' m	Biddy (David, deceased)
	Marquis Childs	Mark
	Robert Jerome m	Bob
	Alice Pogemiller	Alice
	Henrietta, Papa's sister	Aunt Nettie
	Cousin Elsie Thornton	Papa's cousin

GLOSSARY CONTINUED

SHRAUGER   Darius Edgar Shrauger m   Dice, or Grampa
    Sarah Nancy Hunter   Sadie or Gramma

    Harold Francis Shrauger, Sr.m Harold or Dad
    Cornelia Prentiss   Cornelia

    Harold F. Shrauger, Jr. m   Sunny, Harold
    Frances Kephart   Fran

    Frances Cornelia m   Cousin Francie
    Edward Snow

    Jennifer   Jenny

    Cornelia m   Cornie
    John Robert Day   Bob

    Dennis   Dennis

    Virginia m   Virginia
    Joe Allen Jones   Allen

    Angela   Angela
    Dennis   Dennis
    Cornelia   Cornelia
    Prentiss   Prentiss

    Harlan Shrauger m   brother of Harold
    Gladys Anderson   Gladys

    Phyllis
    Donna

INTRODUCTION

These women, Cornelia Fitch Bradley, Lue' Bradley Prentiss, and Cornelia Fitch Prentiss Shrauger are some of the strong women in my maternal line. My children know little about them; This memoir is an introduction to them. All the material for this memoir is based on family oral history, letters, diaries, journals and my experience.

Chance has played a part in delivering the stories and papers to me. First, my mother, Cornelia Prentiss Shrauger, was, as were her mother and her grandmother before her, inveterate story tellers. Since I was closely bonded to my Mom, a constant listener to her never ending stories, I became a repository. Later, when my Mom's sister, Lue' Prentiss Childs, died, I was the recipient of a large box filled with written items she had stored away for years. Her husband, Marquis W. Childs, and daughter, Malissa, gave them to me.

When my Mom and I were offered a five week stay in Florida to furnish a condo, during our cocktail hour we reviewed her repertoire of family stories. I wrote them down; after dinner I typed the notes; the next day she read them. She told me this process stirred up many more memories. In this way we enjoyed our early evenings on a little porch in Naples, Florida overlooking a small swimming pool. When we returned North, I had over one hundred stories regarding her upbringing, her relationships with her parents, her sisters and brothers, and about their life in Dobbs Ferry, in New York, New York, and in Iowa City, Iowa. Stimulated by this exercise, I decided to write down everything I could remember about my growing up in Atlantic, Iowa, and I did.

In assembling this jigsaw mass of material, I gained insights as personalities became clear; traumas were highlighted connecting events. This work of love I leave to my children, the story of some of the Strong Women in our family.

Virginia S. Jones

PART I

1

Being catapulted from my mother's roomy womb was not my idea of how to spend the morning of January 22, 1921. Nevertheless, I found myself being shoved and jostled out of my serene, watery ambience, muscled where, I didn't know; so I panicked, resisted mightily, twisted myself from my proper position for that adventure, and arrived for my grand entrance into the world presenting my right shoulder to the sight of the witless, substitute doctor whom my Dad rustled up at the last minute, my Mom's doctor being out of town. There he was; there I was. Mom and I needed help, but we were stuck with a man who didn't have the slightest idea of what to do about this contretemps.

Shouldering my way was obviously producing no results, so with a mighty heave and a considered turn, I righted myself and burst into the world, bald-headed, furious, and fiery red. My pragmatic turn of mind was born that day—the day of my unceremonious entry into the little cottage in La Vista Place, Atlantic, Iowa, where I made my home for the next seventeen years.

My birth accomplished, this substitute doctor commented, "Mrs. Shrauger, you should have a dozen children; you have them so easily."

Easily! Not this time! Not with him on duty! Not easily, no thanks to him! Neither my five-year-old brother, Harold, Jr., born May 26, 1917, and called "Sunny" by his parents because of his pleasant disposition, nor my sister, Cornelia, called Cornie, born May 7, 1919, eighteen months before me, had given Mom any trouble at all. But just because one has little trouble birthing children, Mom and Dad decided, is no reason to populate a whole town!

My father, Harold Shrauger, Sr., at that time earned ten dollars a week in his father's sheet metal and implement factory; Dad and Mom knew they couldn't feed a sixth mouth, so when her regular doctor returned, Mom said, "Dr. Campbell, I have three children. As my husband's salary barely keeps the five of us, we think it would be prudent not to propagate further. What do you suggest?"

After a moment's thought, he answered, "Cornelia, I suggest you put a cot on your front porch and have your husband sleep on it."

Of course that didn't happen. When Mom became pregnant a fourth time, Dad arranged for the town's female doctor to take care of the problem. She aborted the fetus.

Sometime after that unhappy event, Mom visited her younger, worldly sister, Biddy Childs, in St. Louis.

"Cornelia, I can't believe you went through all this; you didn't have to, you know," she told her. "We're going to a birth control clinic tomorrow where you'll learn how to protect yourself."

She was given instructions and a diaphragm.

"I thought all this tinkering was dreadful," Mom told Cornie and me when she was eighty-seven years old.

At the time we were visiting her, and knowing of her longtime work with Planned Parenthood, Cornie mentioned its current fund raising drive. This caused Mom to reveal the incident so that we would know why she was devoted to that organization.

"The sad event of my abortion made me realize how important birth control is," she said.

Mom produced no more children and told us she was happy with the three of us.

2

My Great Grandmother, Cornelia Fitch, the daughter of Abijah and Llanah Nelson Fitch, was born July 7, 1838 in Auburn, New York—the tenth of twelve children. She was recognized at age seventeen as queen of a spring celebration in Auburn which named her the 'beauty of the county' because of her striking form, ravishing green eyes, and Titian hair. Subsequently Cornelia became the namesake of eleven other girls in the family's future generations. Her father was a successful business man, and the family enjoyed a comfortable living.

Unfortunately her planned future was disrupted when she learned of her fiancée's death on a battlefield during the Civil War. For long months she couldn't be comforted, but finally allowed her parents and their good friends, Henry and Rhoda Ann Bradley, to arrange a meeting between Cornelia and the Bradley's widowed son, David Ogden (called by his initials D.O.). He had grown up in Penn Yan, New York, where his father owned small businesses. He was now a lawyer in New York City and a dealer in real estate. This occasion, Thanksgiving dinner in 1864, ultimately resulted in a successful courtship and marriage.

Aged thirty-eight, D.O. was eleven years older than Cornelia. His first wife and two youngest children had died some years before, possibly to cholera, which was widespread in New York State at the time. His surviving child, Elizabeth, known as Lizzie, was growing up in a private boarding school in Geneva, New York, near her Grandparents home in Penn Yan, New York.

D.O. courted Cornelia with kindness and persistence, not noticing her willfulness and extreme strength of character. She ignored or didn't realize how set he was in his ways. On February 22, 1865, they were married in the Fitch home. Immediately they set off by horse and buggy through a snow storm, headed for Lizzie's school in Geneva, New York, so that she and new wife, Cornelia, could meet. There was no plan for Lizzie to make her home with her father and Cornelia.

After many months living in New York City, D.O. and Cornelia set up housekeeping in a large Victorian home set on seven acres outside the small town of Dobbs Ferry, New York. Cornelia named their home Palavista since their mansion was perched on a hill overlooking the New Jersey Palisades.

On June 26, 1868, their child, Lue', was born, the first of the four Bradley children. Her name was a favorite of Cornelia's but was not a family name. She was a delight to her parents, a loving, cheerful and intelligent child who proved to be reliable and competent. Redheaded like her mother, with close-set green eyes, she exhibited a natural graciousness and enormous energy. Shortly after Lue's birth, D.O.'s parents, Henry and Rhoda Ann Ogden Bradley, became a part of the household, moving from Pen Yann.

Cornelia enrolled Lue' in Miss Master's private school in Dobbs Ferry. Here Lue' became a leader, and organizer. Cornelia was pleased to notice that in spite of her being the center of attention from four adults, her Grandparents and her parents, Lue' showed no sign of being spoiled.

When she was four years old, her sister, Emma, was born, followed two years later by fraternal twins, Jerome and Nelson. Mama, her children's name for Cornelia, recognized Lue's' joy in learning and willingness to be of use. She began tutoring her in the operation of the household before she was ten. Cornelia asked her assistance in meal planning, and took Lue'along when she bought groceries and supplies in Dobbs Ferry. Together they discussed the decoration of the bedrooms. They worked as a pair in the extensive gardens; gardening was a love they both shared.

After over a decade of enjoying their grandchildren in the security of their son's home, the elderly Bradleys died, Grandfather Henry Bradley just before Christmas, December 16 in 1878, and Rhoda Ogden Bradley, on August 2, 1881.

A year prior to her grandmother's death, Lue', age twelve, had been left in charge of the huge Bradley home. She was to supervise the household servants, including those assigned to care for the younger children. At that time Emma was eight and the twins were six years old.

"Lue' darling," mother Cornelia said. "I am so tired; I desperately need a rest. Your Aunt Frank (nickname for her sister Frances Fitch Case whose family lived in Auburn, New York) wants me to come to her for a spell. Do you think you could manage the house while I am gone?"

Lue' didn't hesitate. "Of course I can, Mama."

D.O. had no objections. In those days wealthy wives often left their families for visits to relatives. So precedent was set for Cornelia's frequent visits in Auburn. Immediately Cornelia packed her huge metal trunk and entrained westward for the home of Mr. and Mrs. Theodore P. Case, and their son, Howard.

The wealthy Case family lived in the high style Cornelia coveted. She thrived on being attended by the servants, savored the good food and wine, and was especially pleased when discussing intellectual subjects and her painting with her nephew.

Back in Dobbs Ferry, Lue' was enjoying being in charge of Palavista. Their outdoor man drove her in their horse-drawn carriage to the village for groceries and household supplies. In this responsibility, the tradesmen, who knew her well, made her comfortable and welcome. Lue' thrived in her role of general factotum.

During her mother's absences, Lue' became her father's companion, often on Sunday afternoons driving with him to Sleepy Hollow Cemetery in Tarrytown, a landmark he had helped establish. On many evenings she further obliged D.O. by reading to him in their library.

Approaching her graduation from Miss Masters School, Lue' found resistance to her future desires when D.O. revealed his strong feeling about women's education. He opposed Cornelia's long expressed ambition for Lue' to become a lawyer. Even though Lue' was to graduate with honors, she was not to go to college. It wasn't that D.O. was against education for women; he was against Lue's being educated. He thought he had good reason.

Lizzie Bradley, his surviving eccentric and brilliant daughter from his first family, had greatly offended him after being graduated with high honors from medical school at the Sorbonne in Paris. Filled with pride, he had given her a graduation trip around Europe, feeling her success was a positive reflection on him.

While in Moscow, her last stop, Lizzie acted as if she were royalty, demanding that all her wishes be satisfied. Refused entrance into certain buildings, she made a nuisance of herself. Her aggressive complaints created a serious disturbance—she acted as if she were Catherine the Great.

The authorities expelled Lizzie from the country, causing an account of her behavior to appear in the *New York Times* followed by a reprint in the Tarrytown, N.Y. newspaper to which D.O. was a contributing editorial writer. Because of that embarrassment, Mr. David Ogden Bradley wasn't about to have his sweet Lue' develop into a second Lizzie.

He decided, "If behaving like Lizzie is what education does to women, Lue' will NOT have an education."

And as happened in most Victorian families, D.O.'s word was final.

After a year or two, lacking a challenging occupation, bored with church—related activities and continuing household duties, Lue' made up her mind to change this deadly routine. Using the good brain she was born with and the experience her mother had foisted upon her, she gathered together her school and church friends. They developed a plan. The girls began attending the morning and evening Sunday services of all the churches in Dobbs Ferry and the surrounding towns, never missing the "Socials," as moneymaking church parties were called in those days.

After a summer of intense socializing, Lue' asked her companions to invite Dobbs Ferry acquaintances and new friends from among the young people they'd met in the towns of Ossining, Tarrytown, Hastings, and Irvington to a huge reception she was giving at Palavista.

The last of the warm summer days of 1885 blessed them. The girls, dressed in their long, frilly gowns, wearing large-brimmed hats and carrying lacy parasols, were flirting with the boys—neat in their slim-legged trousers, well-cut coats, and straw boaters. They sauntered in twos and threes over the green lawns, and along the paths into and out of the seven acres of woods of D.O.'s estate.

Lue' had arranged tables to be set on the several patios; servants served sandwiches, tea, lemonade and tiny frosted cakes. Gathered around the refreshments, sitting in the many wicker chairs, the young people ate, chatted, and enjoyed getting to know one another.

Her mother was in Auburn. Just what Lue' told her father regarding this great gathering is not known, but one can be sure he complained of the expense. His business acumen in land investments and banking, plus his parsimony, enabled him to build a fine estate from which Lue' and her siblings eventually prospered.

As a result of this garden party, several who attended became charter members of a "Social Club" complete with food, program, and party committees. In her letters to her traveling Mother and in her journal, Lue' wrote about the activities the group enjoyed: tennis; boat trips across the Hudson to the Palisades; picnics; canoe outings; card parties; dances and dinners.

During these happy days, D.O. hired Lue's lifetime friend, Rob Patteson, a distant cousin of Lue's, to work in the Tarrytown, New York bank D.O. had helped found. She had met Rob when she was a child of seven or eight on her frequent summer visits to her Aunt Mary Fitch Ross, her mother's sister, in Springfield, Ohio.

After Rob became settled in his new job, he became a member of the Social Club. Although Lue' had never been approached by Rob in a romantic way, in her heart she felt he had accepted the position in her father's bank intending, eventually, to marry her.

In those earlier years she had reveled in their annual vacation times together. Never did she meet any other boy or, later, man she enjoyed so much. So the news that he quietly married a lovely, mild, conforming young lady, a member of the Social Club, took her completely by surprise. According to her diary, Lue' knew no explanation was due her, but secretly he had been her chosen one for many years. His marriage was a devastating blow.

Shortly thereafter, a once attentive friend announced his engagement to a Social Club member saying, "I am very fond of you, Lue', but you think too much like a man."

Some time later, at one of the Bradley's tennis parties, Lue' met Henry James Prentiss, (July 22, 1867—May 17, 1931). She liked him immediately and enjoyed their subsequent meetings. He was not impressed with the elegance of Lue's large and richly furnished home, for he had known wealth in his younger days. He knew proper Victorian etiquette and was used to servants, silver, and travel.

But at this time, he was poor, and his mother was running a boarding house in New York City. His father, Andrew Morgan Prentiss, (1874-1899), had been a thriving glassmaker in Brooklyn fifteen years before; but upon returning from Belgium, where he was buying chemicals for the factory, he found his partner had disappeared, taking all the profits from their business: he left Andrew with all the debts. Instead of trying to reorganize the business, he fell into heavy drinking.

Henry's mother, Henrietta Driggs Prentiss, (1840—1910) had different ideas as to how to solve their financial dilemma. She was a sea Captain's daughter, and was educated in a school in Brooklyn. An energetic, religious, and enterprising woman, she became the backbone of the family.

As the Civil War came to a close in 1865, New York City was rapidly expanding; few hotels existed and the city was crowded. Many women responded to this opportunity to make a good living by turning their homes into boarding houses.

Mrs. Prentiss packed her silver service, linens, and substantial furniture, then moved her husband and children into a rented Manhattan brownstone and turned it into a boarding house. Experienced in handling servants, she ran the house with an elegant flair, making sure the service was excellent. Setting a rich table, using her crystal and fine linens, and providing delicious food, she attracted moneyed people who became a repeating clientele. They quickly recommended her establishment to friends. Soon she rented the adjoining brownstone, installed French doors to join the two establishments, and doubled her enterprise.

As she built her business, it became evident she could pay off her husband's debt, support the family, and, God willing, educate her three children. (Arthur, 1874—?), the oldest son, later became Oregon State's official photographer.) This prayer included her only daughter, Henrietta. Mrs. Prentiss knew how important it was to educate one's daughters, so that they could provide for themselves if necessary.

One of Henry's unpleasant duties as a very young boy was to search the streets and pubs of Manhattan and bring home his drunken father. He found him one night in a noisy, disreputable tavern. In trying to get his father's attention, he touched his arm. Andrew turned on him with a drawn knife. Terrified, Henry backed off.

The bartender interceded. "Andrew, put the knife in your pocket! That's Henry, your son!"

Henry James Prentiss was traumatized by this event. He never forgot nor forgave his father. In later life he often retold the story to his first child, Cornelia Prentiss; he always added, "I hated him from that moment on."

Henry, the second oldest Prentiss child, showed an unusual musical talent and privately studied piano from the time he was a small boy; but as he approached the end of his secondary schooling, he redirected his career, giving up his ambition to become a concert pianist after deciding he'd never be good enough to be successful. Using his excellent mechanical and graphic skills, he chose to study mechanical engineering. By the time he met Lue' Bradley, he was employed in a Boston factory.

After his first visit to Lue's tennis court, Henry came regularly to the Social Club meetings. On many Sunday afternoons, he played the piano in the Bradley parlor while the young people sat in the overstuffed furniture observed by sober portraits of Lue's relatives. He brought delight to the group by leading them in singing *Clementine, Sweet By and By,* and the popular songs of Stephen Foster. Later in the evening, those who wished stayed on to played euchre.

Perhaps sensing Lue's interest in Henry, D.O. referred to him as "that silly young man who plays the piano." But her father's attitude didn't stop Lue' from enjoying Henry. Her moderate feelings for him at that time are revealed in a note she wrote on the back of one of his photographs. "Return to H. J. Prentiss, my best friend." On this low key, they developed a deep friendship.

Henry's direction changed again after he succumbed to typhoid fever. During his recuperation, he was visited by a friend studying medicine who brought him a copy of Gray's Anatomy. Having a highly developed graphic talent, Henry was intrigued by the anatomical drawings. After his recovery, and with his mother's blessing, he left his engineering position and enrolled in Bellevue Hospital's medical school in New York City.

By 1890 the Social Club's membership was dwindling. It had become a marriage factory. First one couple, then another, married and dropped out to devote their time to earning a living and bringing up babies. Finally, the only man calling on Lue' was Henry. They enjoyed concerts and plays in New York City. They enjoyed long walks and talks in the countryside. In winter they went tobogganing with neighborhood friends, and her sister, Emma.

In 1892, during an extended trip to Europe with the Case family, Lue's mother, Cornelia, became ill. On the advice of her French doctor, she stayed through the winter in Paris much to the anger of her husband who kept insisting she return even though her doctor said a December crossing by sailing ship would kill her.

D.O. wired Cornelia saying, "Come home at once. Do you think I'm made of gold?"

He made this demand despite the fact that Cornelia's sister, Frank, and her husband were paying for everything except Cornelia's spending money.

Cornelia ignored D.O. and wrote to Lue', "If I had it to do over, I would never again put myself under the thumb of a husband."

The spring of 1893 arrived, and Cornelia sailed home, arriving safely and in fair health to find that Emma was engaged, and had set the marriage date for September. Lue', who hadn't had a break from her household duties since her mother went abroad almost nine months before, immediately departed on an extended trip. She visited her Aunt Mary Fitch Ross in Springfield, Ohio, cousins in Penn Yan, New York, and friends on Cape Cod, Massachusetts.

During her trip she wrote in her journal, "How different my life might be if I weren't so competent."

My Great Grandmother, Cornelia, still not completely well, but always challenged by big occasions, worked endlessly all summer getting ready for Emma's wedding: redoing all the bedrooms for the out—of—town guests; seeing to the cleaning and painting of the many rooms of the house; supervising the grooming of their seven acres of forest-trees and paths; working with the gardeners so that the extensive plantings were weed-free; designing and overseeing the making of the wedding dresses for the bride, for herself, and for Lue'; ordering and addressing the invitations; planning the menus; making elaborate decorations for the house; and arranging the wedding dinner.

Emma spent the summer with various friends.

When Emma was safely married and gone, Cornelia, fifty-five years old, gave up her unsatisfactory life. On November 14, 1893, she died. For many years she suffered bouts of malaria, but there's no record of what caused her death. Her final illness remains a mystery.

Lue' was again in charge of Palavista and her father's welfare. Her brothers concluded their studies at Princeton, and in 1895, two years after Cornelia's death, her father, David Ogden Bradley, on February 16, 1895 suddenly died of a heart attack. To help Lue' through this sad time, her mother's sister, Mary Fitch Ross, came to Palavista to be her chaperone while the Bradley estate was being settled, and while Lue' made plans for her future. The future included marrying Mr. Henry James Prentiss.

3

Dressed in her perpetually worn mourning clothes of black dress, black bonnet and cloak, carrying her black purse and parasol, Henry's mother, Henrietta Driggs Prentiss, now widowed, came to Dobbs Ferry from her boarding house in Manhattan to call on Miss Bradley at Miss Bradley's invitation. Lue' welcomed Mrs. Prentiss graciously, had the maid remove her cloak, and escorted Henry's mother into the gloomy parlor, darkened by the heavy wool draperies Lue's mother had designed and woven.

"Please sit here, Mrs. Prentiss," said Lue' indicating an overstuffed chair.

Lue' sat herself in a companion chair as an Irish maid brought tea in tiny porcelain cups. Neither threatening snow clouds nor the sight of Mrs. Prentiss in her mourning clothes dampened Lue's resolution. Nor did Lue's mourning clothes dampen Mrs. Prentiss's resolution. They were comfortable in the large chairs dominating the clutter of furniture scattered about the room. Beside them, small Tiffany lamps set on the marble tops of Chinese end tables lent a subtle glow.

"Your trip from Manhattan was uneventful, I trust?" asked Lue'.

"Yes. Uneventful, thank you," said Mrs. Prentiss. "Miss Bradley, I was very sorry to hear of your father's death. Henry told me it was unexpected."

A small plate of sugar cookies was brought by the maid who placed it on the table near Lue'.

"Yes, it was unexpected, but he hadn't been himself for some time. Thank you for your condolence."

Lue' passed the plate of cookies to Mrs. Prentiss. The two ladies settled down for their important conversation.

"Miss Bradley," began Mrs. Prentiss after her first small sip of tea. "My son informs me that you and he wish to marry as soon as it can be arranged. I wish to inform you that, unfortunately, Henry is in no position to marry and support a family at this time."

Mrs. Prentiss paused for another sip of tea and a bite of cookie.

"A delicious cookie, Miss Bradley," said Mrs. Prentiss.

"A favorite of mine since my childhood," said Miss Bradley. "The recipe was handed down to me by my mother."

Lue' paused for a sip of tea.

"Of your concerns regarding the future for Henry and me, Mrs. Prentiss, I am well aware. However, my Aunt Mary Ross, who has kindly been staying with me since Father died, is anxious to return to her husband in Ohio."

Lue' settled back in her chair.

"Fortunately, I have been left with a considerable inheritance, more than enough to support Henry, myself, and whatever children we might have until the time that Henry is ready to go into medical practice."

She paused, smiling pleasantly on Mrs. Prentiss.

"I am sorry that I cannot honor your request."

Mrs. Prentiss nodded, and continued sipping her tea. She had read the notice in the paper regarding the large estate David Ogden Bradley left to his children. She kept nodding. Taking another cookie, she smiled slightly.

Having finished her tea, and feeling assured concerning the welfare of her son's future, she took up her purse and her parasol, was given her cloak, and returned to her brownstone and business in New York City.

Lue' and Henry married soon after on April 18, 1895. Henry was twenty-eight, Lue', twenty-seven.

They had a long honeymoon in Europe. Lue', being of a romantic disposition, especially enjoyed their sojourn in Italy. She had a photographer take a picture of Henry and herself seated in a gondola being propelled along a canal in Venice by a gondolier. She bought fine laces, handsome Italian stationary, and Murano glass necklaces. She was delighted to find herself pregnant.

After thoroughly enjoying her six month honeymoon, she was content to return to Dobbs Ferry to take up housekeeping in her new status as the wife of Henry James Prentiss.

Three months later their first child, redheaded like Lue', was born at Palavista, January 24, 1896. This child, my future mother, was named Cornelia Fitch, honoring her grandmother, Cornelia Fitch Bradley. Little Cornelia would come to know her grandmother through Lue's storytelling.

Soon after his daughter's birth, Henry realized the commute between Dobbs Ferry and his medical classes at Bellevue Hospital was taking too much of his study time. He and Lue' rented the huge Victorian house and moved into the city. They brought baby Cornelia to an apartment on the top floor of 103rd Street and Riverside Drive which Lue' called her "Sky Parlor."

Two more children were born to them while Henry was still in school—first, Cornelia's brother Henry, known as Hank, and then Lilian, known as Lil. These two were also redheaded. All three were born within thirty-two months. Lue' liked the location of their new home because it was near a park on the Hudson River. Here her Nanny or she could take the children for their daily outing.

Doctor Prentiss was attentive to his children. On one fine Sunday, to give Lue' a rest, he took the three of them, aged five, four, and three, on a trip to Manhattan Beach via the ferry. Doctor Prentiss much preferred Manhattan Beach to Coney Island. Off they went, the doctor holding Lil's hand, Lil holding Hank's, and Hank holding Cornelia's.

Papa, as the children always called their father, liked taking the ferry because in the confined freedom of the boat he didn't have to worry about their safety. Of course they got hungry, so he had the three of them lie down on the deck, side by side. He took their bottles from his ever-present doctor's satchel.

"There you three were," Dr. Prentiss told his oldest daughter years later, "dressed in your navy blue sailor clothes, your red heads flaming—brilliant against the gray deck—each with a bottle in your mouth, each green eyed and sucking. The crowd strolling on the deck parted like the Red Sea and walked around you. Soon a large group of passengers gathered, eyeing you children, you children eyeing the passengers. Since you three were so close in age, Lue' thought she'd wean you all at once. We were waiting for baby Lil to give up her bottle."

"Now that we were living in Manhattan," Mom told me, "Grandmother Prentiss came calling every Sunday afternoon. She assumed the responsibility for my religious education, assigning me Bible passages to commit to memory. The next Sunday she'd test me. Grandmother had me bring a straight chair, and I sat exactly in front of her. If I knew the passage perfectly, that was fine. If I stumbled or got some words wrong, she'd quickly raise her hand to my forehead, put her middle finger behind her thumb and release it—giving me a great thump on my forehead. As a result of this discipline, I learned many passages from my Bible."

Twins were born to Dr. and Mrs. Prentiss in 1902, David and baby Lue', who was always called Biddy because her Mama thought she was fat as a biddy hen. Lue' knew about chickens. While she was growing up at Palavista, her father kept poultry as well as a carriage horse and a cow. Lue' welcomed twins because they reminded her of the happy days when she entertained her little sister and twin baby brothers.

Much to the family's grief, during games while celebrating David and Biddy's first birthday, an escaped bean from a bean bag being tossed by his brothers and sisters found its way down baby David's throat. He choked and died.

At her baby brother's funeral, my Mom, Cornelia, couldn't understand when her cousins, her Aunt Emma's children, teased her for crying so much.

"I thought they were mean. He was such a dear little boy. He died on his first birthday, April 30. I don't think Mama ever got over David's death as she was especially fond of children when they were babies."

Henry James Prentiss, tutored in Bible learning by his severe mother, took to heart Proverbs Xiii, 24: "He that spareth his rod hateth his son; but he that loveth him chasteneth him betimes." As a father, he was of the "spare the rod and spoil the child" variety, and use the rod he did.

The worst example of this took place in Dobbs Ferry where the Prentiss children stayed with their Aunt Emma and cousins while Henry and Lue' shopped for a house to replace the apartment they'd outgrown. Cornelia, Lil, Hank and Biddy were about seven, six, five and two at the time.

The cousins ran down to the orchard and somehow began playing the perennial game of many children, Doctor. It consisted of sniffing each other's genitalia. Aunt Emma discovered them. Since my mother was the oldest, she was punished, and intending isolation to be the end of the matter, her Aunt sent her to her room.

When Lue' and Henry returned, the cousins began chanting, "Cornelia's been sent to her roo-oom. Cornelia's been sent to her roo-oom."

Of course Henry demanded Emma tell him what had happened. In a rage he took my mother upstairs to the bathroom, and in her words "beat my bare bottom with a brush until the room was filled with feces and blood."

Aunt Emma, hearing her screaming, rushed upstairs, and seeing the carnage she shouted, "Henry stop! HENRY STOP!" He did.

Later she told him, "If you weren't my sister's husband, I'd report you to the Society for Prevention of Cruelty to Children."

Mom never mentioned whether or not Lue' took any part in this episode.

Since that day, my Mom told me, she has never eaten a banana because the penis of one of her cousins' smelled like one.

A fortunate result of my Mom's outrageous treatment by her father was that when she and my Dad decided to marry, they vowed "never to lay a hand on any children we might have." And they seldom did. They knew the terrible beating affected my Mom all the days of her life.

In 1904, Dr. Henry Prentiss, having finished his medical training at Bellevue Hospital, was working there as Professor of Practical Anatomy. He was pleased when the State University of Iowa in Iowa City, Iowa, "called" him, as was written in the New York newspaper reporting the event. Their Board proposed that he come west to head the new Anatomy, Histology, and Embryology Departments in Iowa's developing medical school.

The fledgling school was at that time staffed by doctors who struggled to support themselves and their families by both teaching and having an active practice. The university board decided this situation must end as the Medical School was not progressing as they wished. It was at this juncture that Dr. Prentiss was asked to come to Iowa City.

According to the offering letter the proposed salary of one thousand dollars a year was "what Harvard is paying a man in a comparable position." Henry accepted the offer.

Lue' immediately got out her geography book to see exactly where Iowa City was located. She learned that it straddled the Iowa River, was founded in 1839, and became the capital of the Iowa Territory in 1853. Iowa University was founded in 1855; the same year the railroads arrived allowing Iowa City to become an important outfitting center for the western trails. Two years later Iowa's Capitol moved to Des Moines. In 1904, when the Prentiss' arrived, farmland surrounded the town which contained eight to nine thousand people and some small manufacturing.

Doctor Prentiss was to begin work on September first, so the month of August found Henry and Lue' making travel plans and packing belongings. Lue' loved New York and knew she'd miss her life there, but she accepted this radical change in their lives knowing it was a fine appointment for Henry. Fully aware he did not like to deal with patients, the academic appointment was perfect for him. She knew that developing the three departments, the teaching, and having time to research would make him happy.

Together they agreed she would return to New York each summer to visit Lue's sister, Emma, and her twin brothers—one working in the Tarrytown National Bank and the other in New York City.

Just before they left, Lue' and Henry gave a farewell party for their relatives and friends. It was Sunday, a day when the entertainment for many boarding house couples was to stroll the bustling streets of New York. Fifth Avenue was expanding northward, and long-time residents filled the streets alongside smartly dressed young couples out for exercise—to see and be seen.

With the party distracting their parents, Cornelia, then eight years old, commandeered Hank and Lil, ages seven and six. The three redheads slipped out of the apartment, down the elevator, and onto the sidewalk joining the crowd. The girls wore elegant pale green party dresses with neat collars and huge sashes. Hank wore a sailor suit. The three of them managed to clear a small space among the long skirts and the slim trousers of the passersby. They loved sidewalk games, hopscotch especially, and Mama or their nanny, while accompanying them, often allowed them to play along the street. So while the adults were busy with their departure party, the older Prentiss children were busy having a party of their own.

Among the strollers they made a circle, holding hands, and merrily danced around sing-songing, "Mama and Papa are going to get mar-ried! Mama and Papa are going to get Mar-ried!"

My Mom never forgot hearing a woman, who was wearing a large, red, ruffled hat, say, "I should think so."

Henry and Lue', the four children, and two maids entrained for the Midwest, which Lue' expected to find rather primitive, unsettled, and lacking in grace. As they threaded their way down the aisle to their compartments, heads turned.

First came Lue', red-headed and elegant, dressed in her favorite eggplant colored silk suit and matching big brimmed hat set off by a long black plume. Following her was a dark haired infant being carried by a pretty, blue eyed girl. Then came a huge Swedish woman shepherding three red-headed children obviously close in age. Bringing up the rear was a small, prim, mustached and bespectacled man with a derby hat on his head, a black medical bag in one hand, and a black umbrella in the other.

A female passenger was so curious about this group that she privately inquired of Lue' what the relationships were among them.

"Oh," answered Lue' graciously, "we are Mormons. The Doctor is our husband, and these are our four children."

4

Lue' was happy in her new home in Iowa City. Built for gracious living, the large, square, frame house sat on four acres scattered with mature oaks and maples which stretched down a long hill to the Iowa River road. The leafy view reminded her of her home in Dobbs Ferry. Formal visitors came up the driveway, and walked around the house to the front door; but family and friends—and that included almost everyone—came through the back porch door and into the kitchen.

Located on the sparsely settled newer part of the city—the west side of the Iowa River—it was one of a row of large, comfortable houses. Older homes and most of the University buildings were on the east side.

The Old Stone Capitol, a handsome building of classic architecture, was now the center of the campus. Earlier it was the Capitol building of Iowa, but the seat of government moved to Des Moines, a more central location. Now it housed Iowa University's administration services; eventually when money was allotted, it was crowned with a gold dome, a beacon for all eyes.

Iowa City was a small town, asleep during the summer when most of the university students were on vacation, lively when they returned in the fall. Dr. Prentiss was reassured when he found the public school system excellent, and that the professors and their families were a stable part of the churches.

Lue' was pleased to find all the necessities were available—groceries, basic clothing, a library, household needs, and servants. She was surprised that a town of eight thousand or so people were supplied with everything needed. New York City had a population of 3,500,000 at the time they moved. After she affirmed that Iowa City was a regular stop for the Rock Island Railroad, her mind was eased. She would easily entrain to New York each summer to visit family and friends, enjoy the variety of New York City, and purchase clothes and special items not available in the small town.

What's more, she soon learned that Iowa City wasn't at all uncivilized. In fact, the professors and their wives were gracious and stimulating. They had welcomed her immediately and warmly, thus assuring her of a busy and pleasant social life. Iowa wasn't New York, but she was gratified to learn that living here promised more than the life in Dobbs Ferry.

The neighbors welcomed her with cookies and visits. The children made friends up and down the street, and found life better than living in a "Sky Parlor" where playmates weren't handy. Soon Lue' discovered that dealing with the town merchants was a pleasure; Lue' now felt completely at home with the friendly Iowans.

Dr. Prentiss's teaching quarters were across the Iowa River from the family home, past the dome, near the hospital and the nurses' dormitory. He walked there every day. His work began after meeting the University authorities.

Lue' and Henry now knew they had made a wise move and were pleased to see that they were a part of a growing institution. Everyone settled in easily.

Later in the year Henry's sister, Nettie, decided to work for a Masters Degree in Speech and Dramatics. Henry invited her and their mother to live with his family in Iowa City. It was the economical thing to do. Grandmother Prentiss, now widowed and retired from running her boarding house, was making her home with Nettie.

Nettie, for the time being, gave up teaching science at Hunter College in New York City. She would receive her Masters of Arts degree from the English department from the University of Iowa.

About this change, as published in the local paper, she said, "When I taught Science, I was teaching pure science, with crayfish, and starfish as subjects. When I teach Speech, I will be teaching applied science with human beings as subjects."

Upon completion of her degree, she returned to Hunter College and taught there for the rest of her life.

The household made room for them, and all was fine until it came time for them to gather around the dinner table. Grandmother Prentiss had something to teach her grandchildren.

She believed in Fletcherism; Mom in her memoir said, "That means Grandmother chews and chews each bite of food until it becomes a liquid mass in her mouth, and then she swallows it. Everyone else at the table is ready for dessert by the time she has eaten half her meat. Since no one ever leaves the table in our household until everyone is finished eating, we are caught.

"All the eyes of us children are upon Grandma. We silently count the number of times she chews. It takes about seventy, and we anticipate that number, waiting for her to swallow. But then Grandmother takes another bite and the whole process begins all over again."

Finally Papa got tired of all this waiting. He moved Aunt Nettie and Grandmother into an apartment.

On April 7, 1909, the last-born Prentiss child, Robert Jerome, came into the world with little trouble. He was frail and scrawny. Lue', now forty and experienced in nurturing babies, brought him along nicely with her usual loving care.

By this time my Mom was large, redheaded and freckled. She was teased unmercifully by the boys in the neighborhood. The ringleader was LeGrand Byington.

When she walked down the cinder river road to the bridge crossing the Iowa River, "he and his cohorts (Mom's word) would be waiting for me and pelt me with rocks. But one day I met LeGrand when he was alone. I grabbed him, and since I was bigger than he, I wrestled him to the ground, grabbed his hair, and banged and banged his head on the cinders."

A neighbor, Dean Gregory of the law school, witnessed this and phoned her Papa.

"Henry, your daughter, Cornelia, is on the road outside my window banging LeGrand Byington's head on the cinders. I don't know what the argument is about, but I thought you might want to be informed."

Nothing came of this since Papa knew how LeGrand was ganging up on her, and he thoroughly approved of her action and victory. He thought LeGrand's "torturing" of Mom reprehensible.

But in other matters, Papa wasn't as supporting of his daughter. Walking to school one day, she left the house late and caught up with Papa. He looked down at her and said, "What do you have on your face?"

She replied, "Well, maybe a little talcum powder."

"Go back and wash your face," he ordered.

She did. She was "trying to cover up my freckles, and since powder was the only makeup Mama used, I thought it would be all right. But Papa didn't care for reasons, and he always had the last word.

"But one thing I did get away with had to do with underwear. After I was out of sight of the house down by the shrubs next to the Burlington Street Bridge—this was a wintertime deception—I'd take down my long stockings and roll up my long underwear to my knees, then pull up and fasten my stockings again. By doing this I thought I made my legs look slimmer.

"One day those tall bushes were a hideout for a man who stepped out and exposed himself to me as I walked by. I took off at a run remembering the park where I had played in New York City. There an old man often came and watched the Nannies watch us children. He'd sit us on his lap and show us dirty pictures. I guess they were French postcards. I was one of the children.

"And, later on, a different man came to the park and began exposing himself. Some of my friends reported him to their parents; I didn't have the courage to tell Papa. The police set a trap. The man was apprehended. Papa took me to the Tombs for the man's trial as I had to testify along with my friends. We climbed up long, gloomy stairs to get to the court. He was convicted.

"But Papa refused to believe me when, during dinner that evening, I told him about the Iowa City man who exposed himself to me. I never understood why he didn't believe me. But I had learned my lesson well: 'Watch Out For Dirty Old Men.'"

Mom made another discovery one day when she went to visit her Papa in his office. In her enthusiastic entry, she banged into the door, it banged into the skeleton Papa kept on a rack behind the door, and the bones came rattling down.

Interrupting her screaming, he laughed and said,

"It's only a bunch of bones, Cornelia, nothing to be afraid of. It's the bones of men with flesh on them to beware of."

Mom told me she never forgot that admonition. When she reached dating age and a young man called for her, he never approved of any of them.

Grandpa Prentiss told Mom he invented the metal tanks filled with formaldehyde for the storage of cadavers. The lids, when opened, automatically brought up a shelf holding the cadaver; there it was, ready for the dissecting period. After the class was over, the student had only to close the lid, and the cadaver automatically receded into its liquid bath.

At that time the cadaver room was next to the animal room. All the Prentiss children knew that dogs were used for research. However, Mom wasn't prepared for the either-or proposition Papa outlined when she asked him,

"Papa, Lil and Hank and I are old enough now to take care of a dog. We want one ever so much. Can we have one?"

After considered thought, their Papa answered as they stood in their stair-step line in front of him; three pairs of green eyes stared at him from under mops of red hair. They held their breaths as they knew having a pet hung on his decision.

"Yes, you may have a dog—providing you three are prepared to care for the animal," he told them. "However, if even once you fail to provide the creature with either food or water, off it will go to the laboratory."

"We were overjoyed," Mom told me, "and promised to take perfect care of the dog, and a little brown and white cur came to live with us. But we hardly had time to name the dog when Hank forgot it was his turn to feed her. Papa, of course, found out about this (Mom never could understand how he found out about all their failures) and immediately the dog disappeared to the laboratory. We never asked for another pet."

The Prentiss house had a back stairway which connected the bedrooms and the kitchen. Mom told me about the time she, Hank, and Lil got into an uproarious washday fun—fight that began near the bedroom doors in the wide upstairs hall, and came right down the backstairs.

All day, Esther, their laundress, and her assistant were busy washing and ironing clothes, bedding, and napery. Their work was folded and placed in separate baskets. A maid put away all the flatwork, but Lue' always sorted the baskets of clothes left for her in the upstairs hall.

Mom told me, "Hank, Lil, and I were on our way downstairs to sit on the porch swing until dinner time. Hank spied the clothes baskets, grabbed one of Papa's shirts, and threw it at me. I retaliated, and then threw a dress at Lil, who threw some muslin underwear at me: and the fight was on. We were like windmills, tossing whatever came to our hands, shouting and laughing all the time, each taking a basket of our own. Clothes were all over our big hall and falling down the back stairs. Then Hank pushed me, and I pushed him. He fell into his basket, and it turned over. We all three kept tossing the clothes, giggling and yelling until, finally, Mama came out of her room. Her mouth dropped open. We stood stock still—frozen with our 'weapons' in hand—and stared at her. We had scattered almost all the clean clothes, littering the floor with the work of a whole day.

"Mama said, 'Children! How could you? What are you thinking of? Cornelia, you are supposed to set a good example.'

"Mama looked as if she were going to cry. I didn't know how to answer her. I guess I didn't know how to set a good example. We three children looked at each other, then began picking up the wrinkled clothes, putting them into the baskets.

"What shall we do with them," I asked her.

"Take them to the laundry room; Esther will see to repairing the damage tomorrow," she answered.

"With great effort we managed to drag the clothes to the basement. Esther and I were friends even though Mama told me not to make friends of the hired help. But I knew Mama had made friends of the servants at Grandmother Bradley's home for she had told me stories about her early life there."

Both Lue' and daughter Cornelia, people lovers, made friends of everyone.

Mom found Esther changing clothes late the next afternoon when she went to the basement to apologize.

"Esther smiled as she pulled up the skirt of her bright flowered dress while saying to me, 'Never mind, Cornelia dear. I can't even think about it now. I am going out on a date.'"

"Why are you powdering between your legs, Esther?" Mom wanted to know.

She said, "Honey, when you go out on a date, you've got to be ready for whatever might happen."

"With a hearty laugh, she spun out of the basement room." That was the way Mom told the story.

An occasional pleasure for Cornelia, Hank, and Lil were the evenings when Mama and Papa were entertaining guests for dinner. Cornelia, being the oldest, was asked to assist in the preparations: she got out the special sugar and creamer, and located the unusual, ornate silver cake server from the buffet. Mom told me Lue' made her feel a part of occasions.

"We were fed early, and sent upstairs to prepare for bed. We did this with no fuss, for we had some secret fun to come. We were very quiet during the time the guests arrived. When we were certain the guests were seated at the dinner table, dressed in our night-clothes we crept down the wide stairs to the point just before the landing where we could easily stare through the banisters and see the assembled party. All the faces and the bare arms of the ladies bathed in Mama's candlelight.

"Our delight was to observe the formalities—to see how Papa and Mama nodded and smiled and used words they never ordinarily used. We were astonished to learn that Papa could be charming which he seldom was at our family dinners, and how overly gracious Mama was. Sometimes we could barely suppress our giggles. Here we learned of the artificiality of company manners. Lil especially thought the adults were acting strangely. 'Pretty silly performance,' were her words. We were never caught, and this spying remained one of our favorite secret entertainments."

One day, when Mom was about thirteen, she was assigned to keep an eye on young Robert who was three.

Mom told me, "We two were playing near the bathroom in Mama and Papa's bedroom; that is, Bobby was getting into things in the bathroom, and I was sitting on the bed reading. All of a sudden Bobby let out a yelp. He found the suppository knife. I knew he knew what that was for but not how sharp it was. He cut himself.

"I scrambled to my feet just as Papa came running from out of nowhere. We both saw blood streaming down Bob's right hand (he was left handed). Papa rushed at me, pushed me into my bedroom, fury in his face. He shoved me toward my bed so violently that I lost my balance, and my head hit the brass bed-post knocking me out. Bobby had barely pricked a finger."

Besides teaching, Grandpa Prentiss's love was research, and he was an expert in the dissection of fascias. He took time to devise a prosthesis for broken jaws. He did this for his friend and neighbor, Dean Wilber Teters, head of the dental school. He also designed a brace for disabled ankles to assist in walking.

"Designing these inventions used his mechanical abilities," Mom learned from Lue'. "Papa's interest in the ankle brace was a result of his mother injuring his ankle when he was a baby. She had roughly jerked Papa's little button shoe from his left foot before she had fully unbuttoned it; not only once, but another time, too, breaking some bones."

As Mom told this story, she added, "I think Papa was a misogynist. I feel he loved only two women, his mother and his wife."

I questioned her. "How could he really love his mother when she injured him as a baby, and he walked in pain and with a limp the rest of his life?"

After a long pause she answered, "I never thought of that."

Mom continued. "Papa's foot always bothered him, especially when he and Mama took their turns in chaperoning university dances. He'd dance with her for a while and then say, 'I can't dance any more, Lue.'

"The last time they danced, Papa hobbled into the kitchen, sat down and took off his shoes and said, 'Lue', I just can't do it anymore. I'm sorry, but for at least two days after these dances the pain in my foot and ankle is so intense it inter-rupts my teaching—the most important thing I do. I have simply come to the end of it.'

"'I understand, dear,' Lue' told him. 'It's all right. I'll do my dancing in heaven.'

"Being an ardent believer in the afterlife," Mom added, "this remark carried conviction. She adored dancing, so giving it up was a special gift to Papa. Perhaps it wasn't proper for her to dance with another chaperon if Papa couldn't return the courtesy and dance with the man's wife."

But Lue' sometimes danced by herself. Mom said, "Once on a warm summer night, we three older Prentiss children, me, Lil, and Hank were with Mama in the upstairs parlor enjoying the brilliant light from a full moon flooding through the wide windows.

"We were cuddled together on the sofa, dressed for bed. Mama was telling us stories while flicking her palm leaf fan, cooling herself. Suddenly she stood up and began dancing. She had on a diaphanous pale pink nightie with a flowing skirt and lacy trimmings. The moonlight streamed into the room through the open windows, and Mama responded to the romance of the pale light. Her gown softly swirled as she turned and swayed. I was sure she was wearing a fairy gown. She loosened her long golden-red hair, and it swung and moved about her shoulders; her full breasts pressed against the light fabric as she swept the air with her fan.

"Mama smiled and her love for us children showed in her lovely green eyes as she glanced at our joyous faces. The silvery light and the pink nightdress made her seem to me like a magic being—a lovely outsized nymph. And when Mama stopped dancing, I, enamored, sprang up, rushed to her, and kissed her gently on her bottom. Mama hugged me, smiling."

Mom often told this story; and her eyes, also green, glowed with love for Lue'. I always welcomed hearing it repeated for it spoke of the strength of the connection between the two of them; and that strength and connection became part of me and made me feel rooted, loved, and full of grace.

It was during these years that Lue' finally completed her college education. She enrolled in university classes. By 1915 she gained her Bachelor of Arts degree despite her father's shortsightedness.

"Papa believed in college education as a preparation for life and better living," Mom told me.

Early in Lue's acquaintance with him, Henry had given her a photo of himself on the back of which she wrote, "A most charming friend, a citadel, whom I wish I could know better. A perfectly guarded inner self, impregnable against attack."

She came to know him very well, although she never became inured to his inexplicable, uncalled for rages. Often, while the family was at lunch, he'd lose his temper—for no apparent reason.

"And Mama," Mom recalled, "who had been whistling all morning—her way of showing her happy mood—became sober, and the light went out of her eyes."

As had been agreed, Lue' returned to New York City for six weeks almost every summer. She would visit her old friends, her brothers and sister and their families, and have evening gowns made by her dressmaker, Madam Sloat.

Lue' was adored by her children, and "one way we showed this was to go to the basement and nail kindling together to spell out WELCOME HOME. When the day of her return arrived, we wound the words with garden roses.

"After Mama's trunk was delivered, a glorious time would ensue; for in it were presents for all of us. Then she'd model her new gowns for our delight. They were elegant costumes, symbols of adult privilege, and they beautified our Mama."

One of Lil's letters survives:

(private) Sept. 28, 1909

My dear Mamma—

I hope by this time you will have safely reached Aunt Emma's house and have received my postal.... When we looked at the car you were in, train pulling out, we turned to walk uptown and had only gone a few steps when Mr. Hostetler, the cab man, called out and said he would give us a ride uptown free. So we got in and went spinning uptown ... to the interurban bridge.... ... Cornelia and I have not had any quarrels yet. The baby (Bob) has been out every day in the sunshine, and yesterday when Miss Toomey weighed him, his weight was fourteen pounds, nine ounces.

... I miss you very much, dear Mama, and there seems to be a kind of vacancy that no one can fill ... but Cornelia is as gay as a lark with Miss Toomey. If I was around it seems as if I was always in the way, so I have to keep to my room. I would like to talk and be as pleasant as Cornelia but I always do something and am reproved.

Well goodbye dear Mama. I take pleasure in writing to you. From your loving daughter,

Lilian Prentiss 1909

May I go down to the Listers now because Cornelia broke the Listers new chicken coop and we could not go down there for a month and send a letter and tell us. Your loving child, Lilian

"When Lil and I got to be adolescent, Mama went through a period of bringing us Chinese embroidery on collars and cuffs. For several seasons we received these embroideries.

At last Lil said to Mama, 'Mama, I wish you'd stop bringing me these. I just don't like them, so why put out the money.' Mama was hurt."

Finally, after many trips, Lue' said to her children, "This is my last visit to New York. Things have changed and my friends have changed."

Mom recalled how disappointed she and all the children were. For it was the end of the excitement of their mother's return, the surprise of the presents, and the thrill of seeing their Mama model her new evening gowns.

Long before, when Lue' was twelve and growing up in Dobbs Ferry, she entered a story writing contest in the St. Nicholas magazine and won the right to have it published. It was her only written story, but she was an inveterate storyteller. One day, when her daughter Cornelia heard Lue' telling a tale to a neighbor, she noticed that some of the things Lue' said weren't what really happened.

In private she said to Lue', "Mama, you were telling lies to Mrs. Smith when you told her about what happened yesterday."

"My dear girl," Mama answered, "when you are telling a story, you don't tell just the bare bones of what happened. That would make the story dull and uninteresting. Now I always embroider a little here and there to tune it up, and make it better. I cannot consider that lying."

At the age of fourteen, Lil wrote in her journal,

"A Recollection of Mama at Age forty"

"Mama is still good looking. Her hair is fluffy, no longer red, but brownish with no grey. She has a rather large Roman nose that lends to her face something serious and dignified although she certainly has her gay moments when she dances for the amusement of the children. All our little faults she takes much to heart and worries about them. She makes it a duty of great importance to see that we are correctly raised and never lets the girls go around in the evenings to parties, theatre etcetera without a responsible chaperon. She is very neat and hates untidiness. She scrubs Henry regularly and digs the 'potatoes' out of his ears. She can't play the piano but is a very light and graceful dancer. Her religion is good. She is strong on morality and she is not a gossip.

"Mama would get all of us ready for church and Papa would walk with us across the river. But more often than not, Mama stayed at home for her one chance in the week to enjoy her home in silence."

Lil's recollection of Papa is lost except for a snip, *"Papa has a strong temper."*

Once in anger Papa pushed Lil. She fell down the stairs. So I learned Mom wasn't the only Prentiss child who got into scrapes with their Papa.

5

Lue' kept the household accounts and paid the bills.

"Every month when the day of reckoning arrived, she'd write checks and end up weeping," according to Mom, "for there was never enough money to cover all the statements. On bill paying day, Lue' always sent Bob out to buy her ice cream.

"On one of those days, Lil came into Mama's room, saw her reddened eyes, saw the empty ice cream container, and said, 'Mama, I wish you wouldn't cry. It makes you look so ugly.'"

Lue' didn't possess the beauty of her mother or her sister, Emma, but to quote a favorite saying of hers, "t'ain't in the looks, it's in the woiks."

However, her prominent Roman nose and close-set green eyes didn't prevent her from having friends. Both men and women appreciated her charm and intelligence, humor and vitality. When Mom was twelve, she accompanied Mama and Papa to New York City having earned her fare by darning socks for a nickel a sock. She accompanied Lue' when she went to look up an old friend, a Mr. Becker.

Mom observed, "Mr. Becker rushed up to Mama and embraced her warmly. I was horrified at the embrace. I was shocked. Also, when Papa's assistant, Professor J. J. Lambert's wife died, and he was to marry again, Mama gave the new wife an emerald and diamond brooch that had been her mother's. I sensed J.J.'s attachment to Mama and that she returned the affection."

Lue' didn't play cards. Her entertainment was attending luncheons and teas. In the early days of automobiles, Papa bought her a Model T Ford so she could drive herself to her engagements. Until then, her transportation was with Mr. Neider and his horse-drawn cab.

Late on a hot summer morning, Mama sent thirteen year old Hank down to start the car. This required cranking. The car refused to start. He cranked and cranked as Lue' stood by. Finally she returned to the house "to avoid hearing the grinding noise." At this point Papa came home for lunch.

Mama told him, "I don't know what's happened, but Hank doesn't seem to be able to start the car."

Papa observed his sweating son for a while. Finally he said to Hank in disgust, "Why are you so stupid with something so simple?"

Hank burst into a rage, cursed, and shouted, "This car is no good. Absolutely NO GOOD!"

"What do you mean this car is no good! I bought this car for Mama so she could drive to her luncheons, and it HAS TO BE GOOD! WHY ARE YOU SO EVIL TEMPERED? WHY DO YOU BURST INTO A RAGE OVER SUCH A SIMPLE THING?" Papa roared.

"Well, dammit, if I have lost my temper over this, IT'S BECAUSE YOU'VE SET ME THE EXAMPLE ALL MY LIFE!"

Papa thought for a moment, turned on his heel, and called Mr. Neider to come with his horse and buggy to take Mama to her luncheon. Whether Lue' ever drove the Ford, I wasn't told.

Lue' Bradley Prentiss, was Iowa's DAR representative attempting to interest the Governor, William L. Harding, in supporting the acceptance of Mrs. Lucy Gebhardt's design for an Iowa State Flag. The state of Wyoming was the second to last state to consider a state flag. Iowa was the laggard. But the men in the legislature were afraid that adopting an Iowa flag would denigrate the United States' flag. Lue' was granted an interview. Dressed in a deep blue silk dress hiding her black boots, a wide brimmed blue hat sporting a long black feather gracing her red hair, she found her way to Governor Harding's office in Des Moines.

Lue' told Mom about the interview with the Governor: "As I tried to interest him in the project, the Governor lolled back in his high-backed leather chair and vigorously chewed his wad of tobacco. I heard a gurgle. I looked towards him just as he lobbed a ball of spit-and-tobacco over my skirt and into the humidor placed on the far side of my chair. I give Governor William Harding points for marksmanship but not much for manners."

As she struggled with Iowa's governor, Dr. Prentiss often repeated to Lue', "The DAR is like a potato plant; the best part of it is underground."

Three women were the signers of the petition the Governor finally sent to the legislature. At first he wouldn't accept the petition. On one of the four visits Lue' made to him, she suggested they call it a banner if not a flag, hoping to calm his fears. But eventually Lue' won him over. He agreed to influence the legislators, and the cautious Iowa representatives followed the lead of all the other states in the Union.

The Iowa State Flag became a fact. Two of the women on the Flag Committee signed the petition as Mrs. Charles A. Rawson, and Mrs. Harold R. Howell. The third signed as Lue' Bradley Prentiss, proudly using *her* given name.

Obviously, Mom's "doggedness," as she called it, her persistence when she wanted to make a point, right a wrong, or see justice done, came from her Mama, Lue' Bradley Prentiss.

My Mom, Cornelia Prentiss, was chubby as a child, by nature as well as by diet, for the whole family loved sweets and was fed them. She was a green eyed, red-headed girl, full of energy, high intelligence, and sense of fun and hi-jinks. As she matured and was well past her thirteenth birthday, suddenly it occurred to Mama that her oldest child was "going into a decline"—a Victorian idea. In front of her eyes Cornelia lost weight, developed a waistline and obvious, successful flirtatious ways—so much so that Lue' gave her Booth Tarkington's book, *The Flirt,* to read.

"Papa dealt with me more directly," said Mom. "He enforced strict rules: each night, in at ten; come home immediately after the dances; no fun at all if I wasn't getting good grades. He was being fiercely protective of me, for he felt that falling in love was "Nature's Trap" which swept away reason and was to be feared. Papa felt I needed constant reigning in. I felt the restrictions as a victim, and I struggled against him."

As a beautiful young woman, she encouraged and received more than her share of attention.

"I was tempted to 'play the game since I had the blame.'"

But she didn't, not until her final flight from the Prentiss household.

On a beautiful cool summer evening during World War I, Lil and Cornelia were on the front porch enjoying the moonlight and the shadows.

"We were thinking about Hank for he had joined the U.S. Army and was training in Plattsburg, New York. We three had never been separated before. The local militia was having a gathering of units from the surrounding towns, drilling and practicing handling their guns.

"Our peace was suddenly interrupted by uproarious and raucous sounds coming from a drop-off, a short cliff at the end of our neighbor's lawn near River Road. Lil, being inordinately curious, decided to investigate. Down the hill she went and stared into the flattened area beneath the drop-off. The full moon enabled her to see two people stretched flat, one on top of the other.

"I heard her call out, 'God sees you, and I see you!' She ran back to me and related all."

In Mom's words, "The loving couple, disturbed, scrambled up quickly. They scurried down the hill. And as Lil saw them climbing over the barbed wire fence next to the road, the young man called back in a mocking voice, 'Goodnight, Lilian.'

"Lil was silent a few minutes and then asked me, 'Cornelia, what does it mean if my beau begins to breath heavily when he's kissing me goodnight?'

"After a moment I answered, 'Lil, Papa once told me that we would understand such things if we had our genitalia on the front of our pubic bone.'"

Mom felt that Lil was a Puritan at heart and very naive.

A love of literature could have brought Papa and my Mom together. His favorite novelist was Charles Dickens, from whom he could endlessly quote. But Papa, convinced that every girl should have a profession, didn't allow Mom to study literature as she would have preferred as her major in college. He decided that she would major in Home Economics. This meant she would take science courses in high school. So she did.

Perhaps Papa had his sister, Henrietta, in mind, who went to Smith College to study science and become a teacher. Why he didn't allow Cornelia to study literature, which she loved, and become a teacher like Aunt Nettie? This was never discussed.

As preparation for her degree in Home Economics, a high school class in sewing was required. Mom couldn't knit or crochet, so the prospect of learning to sew was a terrible burden to her. Lue' did no handwork either.

"First I kidded myself through textiles. Then I worked out the sewing problem by telling my favorite teacher, Miss Donovan, I couldn't understand how to sew French seams. My accommodating teacher sat down at the machine. As she demonstrated, I entertained her. While we both laughed, the seams were quickly accomplished. In this way Miss Donovan made most of my notebook for me; I got A in the course, not learning a thing.

"Then I fell in love with the manual training teacher. He was a big, redheaded, pink-eyed man; and I enrolled in Mechanical Drawing so I could be with him. We'd go into the lumber room and spoon. He came to call on me at home. Then Papa went to the school board and told them he didn't think a teacher should be calling on a pupil. He wished they'd inform Mr. Miller that his attentions to his daughter were no longer acceptable."

Mom observed that Papa confronted only his children and his students. This occasion was exceptional—although indirect.

A day or two later, Papa came home at noon bringing the mail, which was his habit, and gave Cornelia a letter addressed to her. She opened it. Out fell the pictures Mr. Miller had taken of her in times past, all torn into little bits.

Lue' exclaimed, "Oh, I think that's the cruelest thing I could ever imagine. How could a young man do such a thing?"

Mom had to take Chemistry and other science courses and managed to get good grades by flirting with the science teacher. Papa got wind of this "unsavory" situation.

His solution: to remove her from high school and put her in college at age sixteen to "get her out of the clutches of that blaggard of a teacher" whom, Mom felt, was desperately in love with her.

Of course she had almost enough credits to enter college since she was a marathon "school-goer," as were Lil and Hank, and later Biddy. She'd be eligible to enter the University after taking Ovid in the summer. Papa firmly believed that 'The Devil Finds Work For Idle Hands To Do,' so all his children went to school spring, summer, fall and winter, and all were well-prepared and early into college.

"It was of little importance to me to lose contact with the science teacher," she told me, "for when a young man got seriously interested in me, I was no longer interested in him."

Her last year in high school, her junior year, was crowned by an embarrassing family situation. The Junior-Senior Prom, the biggest event of the year, was approaching.

"Who is your partner?" Lue' asked, and approving of the young man, she added, "Of course I will come along with you."

"But Mama, no one else's mother will be there!"

Nevertheless, Lue' planned to chaperon her. News of this sifted around school. Emblazoned on the next copy of the *Red and White*, the school newspaper, was the headline, "WHAT'S THE MATTER WITH CORNELIA THAT HER MOTHER HAS TO GO WITH HER TO THE JR–SR BALL?"

"I knew Mama was embarrassed by this, and I was humiliated and teased; but Mama went, and so did I."

The summer before her freshman year in college, Mom finally accepted an invitation to go to dinner with a young man who was twenty years old … after putting him off for some time. She was sixteen. Papa said the invitation was not appropriate; she must break the engagement.

When told of this, the young man said, "Cornelia, if you ever get the chance, just call me."

One Friday evening Papa and Mama were invited out to dinner with friends. As soon as they left the house, Mom called the young man, quickly dressed, and met her date at the Burlington Street Bridge. She was wearing a white muslin, long-sleeved summer dress trimmed with Irish lace. The two walked across the bridge and up the long hill past the Old Capitol Building to the Jefferson Hotel where the young man arranged for them to have dinner.

Led by the Headwaiter through the dining room, she walked like a queen, head held high above her lovely summer dress, her brilliant red hair and sparkling green eyes making all heads in the crowded dining room turn and follow her progress. Her 'swain' trailed behind her, hastening to catch up. The Headwaiter seated them. Menus were brought.

There was a rustle at the door. In walked a party of professors and their wives, and among them, Dr. and Mrs. Prentiss.

Petrified, Mom gasped, "Oh, my gosh, what'll I do!"

"You might begin by going over and saying hello to them," was her dinner companion's suggestion.

She did this. Papa hissed into her ear. "Leave this room immediately, and go straight home. I'll tend to *you* later!"

Up she got and home did trot, doing what she was told.

"Whatever happened to my date, I didn't know," Mom said, "but I never saw him again. I went straight to bed, planning to be asleep by the time Mama and Papa came home. I wasn't, but pretended to be. Mama came into my room and listened to my breathing, then left. Nothing happened."

At lunch the next day Papa meted out her punishment: three dateless weeks. Mom said she could never understand why she couldn't have dinner at the Jefferson Hotel as all her friends did. But since young ladies in New York City didn't go out with young men without a chaperon, the Prentiss's didn't allow it in Iowa City, Iowa.

Late on a hot and humid July night that summer, a terrible thunderstorm ripped across the Iowa cornfields. Thunder enveloped the square Prentiss house and reverberated through the neighborhood. Lightening kept the night sky bright; the red daggers threatened danger; heavy rain flooded the window panes. Not being able to sleep for all the noise, Mom took her Ovid and went quietly to the downstairs parlor and began studying.

She was surprised when Papa rushed in shouting, "What are you doing here? Get back to your room!"

"Up the stairs I went. I think Papa was frightened by the terrible storms that swept across the plains, that he had gotten up in the night, discovered me there, and exploded in fury mostly because he couldn't acknowledge his fear."

In her freshman year at the university, Mom immediately fell in love with Homer Smith.

"He gave me a big Memory Book. But when I learned he had a 'steady' in Clinton, Iowa, his hometown, I called it off."

Using her wiles to her advantage, and yet having certain standards, was a pattern which continued—for there was no lack of dates. In the first decades of the nineteen hundreds at the State University of Iowa there were more than two men to every woman.

Perhaps she learned from her experience with one "serious beau," as Mom referred to him. Ed Stevenson came to visit her at home one beautiful full-moon night.

Lue', always of a naive and romantic turn of mind, gave the young couple a blanket saying, "Here, take this blanket. Go out and enjoy the moonlight."

Of course, overcome by the moonlight and Cornelia, her date got carried away. Spooning wasn't enough. She escaped unscathed.

"A few months later, Ed took me to the senior hop and proposed marriage. I was utterly astonished.

"Why Ed," I told him. "I'm devoted to you, but I'm not even thinking of marriage at this point in my life."

She was seventeen.

Ed then wrote her a letter saying,

> *"Dear Cornelia, I want the best for you in life so I want to advise you about something. You have a way of making each of your boyfriends feel that he is the king-pin; then when they get serious, you turn them off. You must stop leading on all these young men who are devoting attention to you."*

This letter was found and read by Lil who showed it to Lue'; Mom defended herself saying, "I am always devoted most to the beau of the moment."

Lil's comment to her sister was, "You are just as bad as Dorothy Cochran."

Dorothy was the town whore.

The hidden rage Mom carried deep inside, a result of her earlier physical abuse and the present and continual verbal abuse Papa directed toward her, showed itself in unpredictable ways. While watching a girl's intramural basketball game in the crowded gymnasium, she disputed a referee's call.

"I leapt from my seat and rushed to him and beat him on the chest, all the time angrily expressing my disagreement. I couldn't stop myself. Flooded with adrenalin, I was completely out of control. The officials finally took me away and sent me home in a taxi. I was in bed for two days."

Thursdays were servants' day off. As a reward for preparing the dinner, Cornelia and her sisters were free to invite guests.

"I can't tell you how many boy friends I lost this way," said Mom. "While we ate, Papa seemed to enjoy bringing up all kinds of gruesome subjects about dissecting, or he explained how all we were was bone and muscle surrounding a tube that was spit on one end and shit on the other. This kind of table talk was not unusual for us in our family setting, but it was foreign to these unknowing young men. I never heard from most of them again."

Besides grade requirements, all the girls had duties around the house, which they learned from the servants. They took turns helping cook supper, doing dishes, cleaning house and ironing.

Lue' told her daughters, "I'm paying the price for being brought up in a house full of servants, and I want all of you to be prepared for whatever station in life you eventually find yourselves."

Lue's contribution to housekeeping was to prepare their first course for dinner—soup; according to Mom, "it was always delicious."

In addition to these duties, Cornelia was unexpectedly given another assignment. Since there was no one to take the retiring organist's position at the Episcopalian church, Papa, who directed the choir, told her, "You will be our new organist."

And so she was. She, of course, was a pianist having begun lessons in New York City at the age of six. All the Prentiss children were required to take piano lessons, but she had no training as an organist. However, when Papa said, "Do," she did. As a result, Mom was a church organist for years, until she was almost sixty.

The love of acting came naturally to Mom. To become a member of the Iowa University Dramatic Club, one had to 'read' to a committee. Mom chose a scene from Macbeth.

She began in her deepest, stentorian tone crying, "Out damned spot!"

The committee stopped her immediately saying, "That's all, Miss Prentiss. You are accepted."

During her college career, she performed in a number of plays presented in the local theaters. But it was the movie she was in that attracted Papa's outraged attention. The Superior Film Co. of Des Moines, Iowa, came to Iowa City, advertised for actors and actresses, and, of course, Mom was among the first to apply. Similar productions were shot in Burlington, Ft. Dodge, Ft. Madison, and other Iowa towns. The finished films would be shown in local movie theaters.

In Iowa City, that was to be in the Garden Theatre "just as any other film for the citizenry to pay for, see, and enjoy the full 1000 feet," said the advertisement in the local newspaper.

The cast of seven was made up of local young people. Iowa City supported this amusement happily.

From local newspaper clippings reporting the event, it appeared that the film began with a train wreck, moved on to an auto wreck, a fight involving the chauffeur, a canoeing scene on the Iowa River, shots in Iowa City's "nice new park," and a marriage in a local home. Mom was cast as the bride.

During the shooting, Papa happened to be on his way to Reichert's Drug Store on Dubuque Street in downtown Iowa City. The bride and groom, newly married, were getting into a roadster to depart for their happy 'ever-after'. Dr. Prentiss saw his daughter dressed in wedding finery standing up in the rear of an open touring car being soundly kissed in public with the gathered crowd of onlookers staring at the scene.

"… a ridiculous enterprise," Papa pronounced at dinner that evening. "And your kissing—that disgusted me!"

But she was delighted, for almost everyone in town went to see the local young people in a real movie. As it turned out, this was the only time Mom wore a wedding gown.

My razzle-dazzle Mom's career in college seemed to be one long round of dating, assembling lines of suitors, performing in plays, filling her dance card at the college dances, being selected a beauty queen, and, in general, having as much fun as possible. During rainy days when my sister and I poured over Mom's memory and college year-books stored in the crawl space off our bedroom, she became someone besides the Mom I knew. My admiration for her expanded enormously. I began to see that she was very pretty. I examined the hundreds of party programs, the dried roses tucked into envelopes, and the names of the boys she danced with. I read clippings about the plays she was in, the university clubs and organizations she belonged to, and altogether saw that she had a wonderful time in college. There were no grade reports.

Sister Cornie and I found a clipping from an Iowa City newspaper published on Valentine's Day, a poem about her by C. H. Brueckner. Her face, placed in the center of a large heart, was surrounded by the faces of eleven young men. The poem read:

"QUEEN OF HEARTS"

Cornie with the golden tresses,
Cornie with coquettish way,
Cornie gen'rous with her yes's,
Cornie sometimes saying nay,

Sought and wooed by lads a-many,
Sought and wooed, but not yet won,
Cornie, Cornie, pretty Cornie—
Full of laughter—made for fun.

6

Just why her rigid Victorian father allowed Cornelia to take a three-week automobile trip with a suitor and his family is beyond comprehension. Perhaps Lue' assured Henry that she would be well chaperoned. Certainly Papa didn't foresee Cornelia's determination to escape from him.

Cornelia Fitch Prentiss was nineteen. She would complete her Bachelor of Arts degree the next summer. Harold Francis Shrauger was twenty and in his sophomore year at the State University of Iowa. Together they would visit sites in Eastern Iowa, South Dakota, and Illinois with Harold's father, Darius Edgar Shrauger, known as Dice, a small-town industrialist in Atlantic, Iowa. His mother, Sarah Hunter Shrauger, known as Sadie, and his younger brother, Harlan, not quite eleven years old, accompanied them.

It was a leisurely tour, taking in, among other places, the penitentiary at Ft. Madison, Iowa, where they 'saw convicts at work.' In Mt. Pleasant it was their pleasure to visit the hospital for the insane. These diversions were typical of the time. Some say it was because work was worshiped and vacations were 'time stolen from work.' But if educational visits were included on the agenda, the work ethic was satisfied, and the vacationers need feel no guilt. Therefore, they were free to enjoy themselves.

Harold, however, stirred romance into the mix. Never one to miss a main chance, my future father and his Sigma Nu Fraternity brothers conspired to liberate Cornelia at a secret marriage ceremony to be conducted by a local Episcopalian minister at the home of Harold's friends in Ottawa, Illinois. On August 23rd, 1915, the young couple simply drove off in the Shrauger car on a parentally approved private evening outing. Afterwards they returned and continued to be under the aegis of Harold's proper mother and father.

Maybe it was Mom's red hair and seductive wiles which prompted her mother-in-law's perennial animosity when it became known she was her son's bride. Or perhaps Mrs. Shrauger felt guilty for not keeping a closer eye on the two young people.

In any case, as truth will out, eventually it was apparent that Cornelia was pregnant. In the winter of 1916 all hell broke loose in the Prentiss household.

Papa ranted and raved, shouting his worst convictions, "You, Cornelia, ARE NOT TO BE TRUSTED!"

Lue', true to her temperament and common sense, immediately arranged a huge reception for the young couple, and joked, saying to her friends, "You know, Cornelia is exceptional. She's going to get her MA before she gets her B.A."

Mom told me that the last course she took to satisfy the university's graduation requirements was Dostoevsky's *Crime and Punishment.*

Mr. Darius Edgar Shrauger sent Cornelia a letter of regret:

"April—

Mrs. Cornelia Shrauger,

I feel keenly disappointed that it will not be possible for Mrs. Shrauger and myself to attend the reception for you and Harold tomorrow evening. I am glad your Mother takes the Philosophical view of the matter and is providing this nice reception for you. My very choicest blessings, love, affection, best wishes and future hope rests on you and Harold. I feel proud that I have an added joy, a daughter whom I will always have the affection and love of a Father. Do not feel too keenly disappointed in our absence from the reception. I am sure everything will work out in time. Be cheerful, show the people at your reception you are happy. I am sure you are going to do your part and make yourselves worthy of each other, proud of each others achievements, happy in your love…. I am sure the outcome will be so bright you cannot help but succeed.

With Love, Daddy"

After the reception, young Harold and Cornelia departed from Iowa City and moved into a tiny house at 407 Oak Street in Atlantic: there my brother, Harold Frances, Jr., was born on May 26, 1916. Cornelia returned with baby, called Sunny by his parents, to Iowa City to take her final exams. She was graduated from the university on July twentieth.

Later that summer, Grandmother Lue' came to the new Shrauger household to inspect the progress of her infant grandson.

"She wore a copper pin spelling 'Granny'," Mom told me. "The town taxi deposited her at the door, and she saw the young father sweeping the front walk.

"Lue' rushed up to him saying, 'Dear Harold, show me the darling baby!'"

During their first hot summer in Atlantic, now and then young Cornelia and Harold would put infant Sunny into his carriage and stroll to the Atlantic Theatre to see a movie. Baby would sleep soundly in the lobby. After the movie, his mother and father would purchase one quart apiece of ice cream, stroll back to their little Oak street home, and proceed to slowly devour both quarts.

"Very cooling," Mom said, laughing, "and it seemed enough."

This turn of events, this eloping, excruciating for her Papa but not disappointing to her Mama, emancipated not only herself but also her brothers and sisters.

Mom told me, "They were allowed to follow their talents and interests as I was not. Hank wrote stories and studied journalism, an acceptable occupation to Papa. Papa was very proud of Hank. He was a fine athlete, and a collegiate championship boxer. Papa had never been able to compete in sports because of his injured foot, so he took satisfaction in being the Chairman of the University's Athletic Board. He also was the attending physician for the collegiate football teams.

"Lil, an artist, and so 'different' and obviously talented, was allowed with no question to study art. Biddy was fascinated with high achievement and languages."

In a note in Lil's diary, she says, "*Biddy's ambition is to finish high school and be in college by age sixteen.*"

And so she did, and she was. Maybe she was following her sister Cornelia's example, who was a freshman at age sixteen, but for a different reason. Both Lil and Biddy received Phi Beta Kappa Keys. Biddy, after she'd gotten her M.A. at Iowa, was sent to Paris for a year to live with a French family and study French at the Sorbonne. She became a teacher of French.

"Robert Jerome, Mama's last born," Mom said, "was eight years old when I left the household, and after Lue' died, he grew up without a mother from the age of thirteen. Biddy, at age sixteen, did what she could to be the surrogate mother, and Papa failed in his attempts to control Bob. He was already a womanizer in his late high school days, learning about sex with the town whore."

World War I was in full swing when Hank completed his sophomore year in college.

Mom told me about her brother. "He enlisted in the army. His career there wasn't a success. At first he was promoted rapidly, but he could never keep the rank he earned because he continually lost his temper.

"After training for six weeks at Plattsburg, New York, he embarked for what he and all the troops thought was a transfer to another camp. Instead, they were unloaded onto a New Jersey dock and proceeded up the gangplank of Cunard

Line *S.S. Kashmir* which became part of a large convoy. During a terrible storm while crossing the Atlantic, the *Kashmir* collided with a much larger ship in the convoy, the *Otranto*, and pierced it amidships. The Kashmir's bow was stowed in.

"Luckily for Hank and his companions, their ship managed to limp into port at Glasgow, Scotland, but the *Otranto* sank with great loss of life. He spent a few uneventful months in France, was sent home in June of 1919, and immediately returned to school."

Mom, pregnant again, was visiting the Prentiss's, the reason for which I will tell you later. Mom discovered that the army had done a lot for Hank. Before enlisting he had always been super-sensitive, often reacting in ways Mom thought were excessive. But the army had toughened him, she told me. One day when the two of them were doing the dishes, Hank ran the long-bladed knife he was drying down between the sink and the counter coming up with a blade full of white squirming worms.

"Oh, I see we have maggots," he said.

Mom explained. "In earlier days, such a sight would have made Hank throw up. He ended his army career with the rank of mess sergeant and the undesirable job of cleaning the mold from the animal carcasses hanging in wait to be cooked and fed to the troops. That toughened him up."

As evidence of his closeness to Cornelia, he confided that he was still a virgin because "Papa had put the fear of hell and damnation into him about having sexual relations before marriage," she said.

"I had opportunities to change that in France," Hank told her, "but Papa's words kept me from taking action. So I'm still pure."

When Lue' learned of this, of course through Cornelia, she said, "I wonder: if Hank had taken advantage of his opportunities to have women while in France perhaps the sexual release might have helped him control his temper."

As Mom told the story, "Before he had gone into the army, he visited his beloved Maude Adams, armed with an engagement ring which Lue' ordered made for him from a pin of hers. He asked her father for Maude's hand in marriage. When he returned, we all knew instantly he'd been rejected."

"What happened, Hank?" Lue' asked.

"Her father told Maud and me, 'You, Mr. Prentiss, are not good marriage material. I have heard of your terrible temper.'"

Mom said, "I think this grave disappointment made him vulnerable."

Shortly after Hank's return, Mom and Sunny, bringing his new sister, Cornie, born in the university hospital, returned to Atlantic and to their home in La Vista

Place. Lue' soon arrived to visit Mom and Dad, to see the new house, and visit her grandchildren.

"I had invited a few friends to meet her and, of course, used my best silver, napery, and glassware. While tidying up afterwards, I inadvertently dropped a lovely cut glass goblet from the set one of my friends had given me as a wedding present. I burst into tears.

"Mama hugged me and said, "Cornelia, don't cry over broken glass. Cultivate people, not things."

The happy visit ended unhappily. While dressing one morning, standing in front of the guest room mirror, Lue' noticed a dimpling in one breast. She left immediately, taking the four o'clock train back to Iowa City; and shortly thereafter she was diagnosed as a cancer patient. The breast was removed, and she was given the latest treatment: radium. All it did was burn her horribly.

Some months after her mastectomy, during one of Mom's visits in Iowa City to help run the Prentiss household until Lue' had completely regained her strength, Lue' sent my Mom to Papa to ask him why he no longer made love to her.

Mom told me, "She was afraid her mutilation made him unable to love her anymore. Being a dutiful child, I approached Papa and asked, 'Papa, Mama asked me to inquire why she is no longer attractive to you.' Papa was very hurt. He answered, 'Cornelia, your Mother has always required a lot of attention in sexual matters. I have tried to satisfy her during our years together. But now I am impotent and can no longer mate with her.'

"Mama accepted this and said, 'Papa was like his Mother, cold and inverted for the most part. I was surprised he ever married me. He has always been married to his science.'"

At this time Lil was teaching school in Denton, Texas. Papa was lucky that Biddy was a talented organizer and a good cook, because, now that Lue' was ill, it was she who kept the household running. Bob was nearly twelve.

After my arrival, battered, red and mottled pink, but 'none the worse for wear,' Dad had telegraphed Mama and Papa telling them I had been born at 10 a.m. on January 22, 1921, and my name was Lue', in honor of her.

Immediately my grandmother sent a telegram to my Mom and Dad which read, "WELCOME TO LITTLE VIRGINIA. I THINK LUE' SHRAUGER SOUNDS TOO MUCH LIKE A DUTCH LUNCH."

"Your Dad and I had to agreed," Mom told me. I was christened Virginia.

I was the only Shrauger child born in the new house in La Vista Place, but I was part of the Prentiss household often during my first year and a half. Lue's cancer metastasized, and she became bedridden. Mom spent at least a week of every month helping care for her. Of course she took me to Iowa City with her. Lil had given up teaching, and was now working on her Masters degree at Columbia University in New York City. She came to help whenever she could, for Papa's salary was not enough to support private nurses throughout Lue's long illness. Biddy was still in school at the University.

Lue' deteriorated.

As Mom told the story, "Papa now hired a nurse, for lifting Lue' was a struggle. Lil had come to help, and we moved Mama to the bedroom where she could see her beloved Iowa river through the French doors. One summer morning Lil and the nurse were helping her onto the bedpan, a fearful thing, because the cancer had moved to her hip. But Lil, often detached from the world, allowed her attention to wander. She was caught up by the beauty of the early morning sunrise shining through the French doors. She forgot about Mama and the duty at hand and dropped her. Mama screamed in agony.

"I remember to this day the sound of Papa's feet as he rushed up the stairs from breakfasting and into the bedroom shouting, 'What are you doing to my Lue'?'

"Assuming Lil was at fault, he impulsively slapped her across the face so hard he knocked her down. Lil, incensed, planned to leave on the next train.

"Aunt Nettie, who was with us at the time, took Lil aside and counseled, 'Lil, you must forgive your father. He is so heartbroken about your mother's condition he can't stand any additional suffering for her. His hitting you was instinctive because you caused her additional anguish.'

"Lil was persuaded to stay on."

My Mom and I traveled back and forth between Iowa City and Atlantic spending most of Lue's' last year with her.

Mom adored Lue'. I could tell by her expression in later years when she talked about her. I assumed that Lue' comforted Mom after all her many altercations with Papa, though she was powerless to interfere or change matters.

Mom's physical beatings had ceased when she matured, but the verbal abuse continued, always. If Grandpa had not been abusive, I doubt if Mom would have run off and married my father, although they were very much attached to each other. Besides, I wouldn't be here if there had been no elopement, so who am I to complain? She had many young men to compare Dad to before marriage. Papa tried to interest her in his favorite medical students, but his choices were never hers: one had bad breath; one wet hands; and so forth.

Grandmother Lue's bed was my playground during most of my first year. Later Mom told me Lue' adored babies, so I was a great joy to her during those unhappy days. Lue' watched me discover my hands and my feet; she delighted in my attempts to roll over and sit up. Later she was charmed as I clung to her bed-covers trying out my legs. Uncle Bob and I were the children of the household.

Whether or not Mom's long absences and the resulting loneliness of Dad at home in Atlantic contributed to the drinking problem he developed, was a sub-ject Mom often brought up in years to come.

I remember nothing of this first year of my life, but I often think my resilience to vicissitudes began in my babyhood, being adored by two wonderful women. That was luck. But I was unlucky in never knowing first hand my grandmother who was a gay–heart, full of fun like my Mom.

Lue' at last lapsed into Cheyne-Stokes breathing. Mom was there, waiting for the end with Papa.

"One evening Papa was being supported and comforted by his medical friends, playing cards in the kitchen, laughing and joking.

"Papa," Mom asked him, "how can you behave like this when Mama is dying upstairs?"

"Cornelia, your mother is for all intents and purposes dead. She's like a sturdy oak tree, cut down before her time. Her body is dead, and this breathing goes on because her heart is strong."

Three days later on May l, 1922, Lue' Bradley Prentiss died. She was fifty-four years old. Mom and Grandpa Prentiss took her to Sleepy Hollow Cemetery in Tarrytown, New York to be buried in the Bradley plot alongside her parents. Dr. Prentiss was now a widower with a son, Robert, to bring up.

After Grandmother's death, Mom and I came home to stay. She felt that after Lue' died Papa softened and gradually seemed to accept her as she was.

"But," she added as she told me this, "I was always mortally afraid of him."

In June of 1922, Hank was graduated from the State University of Iowa, fin-ishing with a red star opposite his name for distinguished scholarship. He imme-diately joined the *Des Moines Register* as a reporter and feature writer—working there only three months. It was a momentous three months.

Before Lue' died, Mom told me, while he was finishing college and starting his new life, an aggressive girl, Marion Chase, whom he met in classes, set her cap for him, won him, and they became engaged. Lue', in her usual helpful way, had a large diamond removed from a pair of her earrings and set as a ring for the bride to be.

In her journal Mom wrote, "But Hank soon began to realize he couldn't live with Marion. Deciding to break the engagement, from Des Moines he wrote telling her this. She was still in school. She immediately went to Des Moines, and convinced him to marry her, secretly, immediately. She was too strong for him. Even though he consulted with his best friend who advised him not to marry if he wasn't sure it could be a good marriage, Hank married Marion in a quiet ceremony at her home in Des Moines. Only her family attended. Hank later said that one of the foods served at the small meal after the wedding was pigs feet."

At this point the *Cedar Rapids Republican*, a newspaper in Cedar Rapids, Iowa, hired Hank to be their managing editor. He and Marion moved to Cedar Rapids after an 'official' church marriage was arranged by Hank who knew how Papa felt about any marriage not performed in church.

"Papa never knew that Hank was married twice," said Mom.

On the job in Cedar Rapids only three days, Hank was talking with a professor from the university, a friend of Papa's, when Hank excused himself to take an assignment downstairs to a reporter. A terrible accident occurred. Only one letter home was allowed by the army from the troops on the Otranto; Hank had written to Papa on Father's Day telling him of the collision at sea.

On the back of this letter Papa wrote an account of Hank's accident: "*He tripped on a metal protector which ran across the top cement step of a flight of five, and being a fine athlete, deliberately turned a somersault. He expected to land on his feet, Hank told me. But instead, he landed on his back on the last step, hitting his fifth cervical vertebrae and severing his spinal cord. He couldn't move at all, not even his head.*"

Mom went to Iowa City immediately. She and Papa informed his sister, Aunt Nettie, and Lil about Hank's situation by telegram. Mom said she sat by Hank for hours at the university hospital, talking, reading at his request the stories of Octavius (Roy) Cohen, or just holding his hand.

"Cornie," he said to Mom, "Please keep Marion away from me. She lays all over me and kisses my face and her breath smells awful."

He confided that their marriage was impossible, that he couldn't satisfy Marion sexually.

"She is too much for me."

"He needn't have worried," Mom wrote Lil. "He died on the tenth day."

During the three days Hank lay in state before his funeral, Dr. Henry James Prentiss did not miss teaching any of his classes.

"Duty," Mom said. And added, "The night after the funeral, Marion, who was living with Papa while Hank was dying, left on a date, her hair decorated with some flowers from a funeral bouquet."

Henry James Prentiss, Jr. died October 31, 1922 at age 24. His ashes were laid beside Lue's' in the Sleepy Hollow Cemetery, Tarrytown, New York, by Dr. Henry James Prentiss, Hanks' sister, Cornelia, and his wife, Marion Chase Prentiss.

"Lue' never knew of Hanks' death for which Papa was grateful," said Mom

Dr. Prentiss, for whom having a son to continue the family name was of utmost importance, was left with his young son Robert to bring up.

Unfortunately, in the midst of his anguish, Dr. Prentiss said to Bob, age fourteen, "I wish you were the one to die."

In later years, Bob told his youngest daughter what Papa said to him. She told me she thought this 'telling' ruined her father.

A few weeks after burying Hank's ashes, Marion Chase Prentiss came to her father-in-law, Dr. Prentiss, and said, "People are asking me why I haven't been asked by you to be your hostess?"

Papa replied, "Mrs. Prentiss, my son married you, I didn't. You will never be my hostess!"

She moved from the Prentiss home after she received Hank's $10,000 life insurance policy, and $10,000 in Veteran's insurance.

Dr. Prentiss wanted Lue's diamond returned, the one made into an engagement ring for Hank to give to Marion. Who did Papa send to Marion? Cornelia, of course.

Dutifully Mom called on Marion in "in her lovely, and well appointed apartment. I approached her with Papa's request.

"She said to me, 'Cornelia, I'm glad I can hurt Dr. Prentiss and withhold this ring and its diamond from him. The answer is NO—NEVER.'"

Grandpa's cousin, Elsie Earle, his mother's sister's child, had never married, and was living in New York City. She agreed to come west and become Grandpa's hostess.

Mom said, "She lasted two years during which time she managed to offend all the trades-people we Prentiss's had dealt with for seventeen years. One by one she antagonized all the merchants in Iowa City by talking down to them, feeling that she was superior. Cousin Elsie didn't understand small town life. So Papa sent chubby, officious Elsie back to New York.

"By the time she left, all our old associations had been terminated. Papa went around to each one of our former merchants, apologized for Cousin Elsie's behavior, and asked to be reinstated as a customer."

Luckily he then found Mrs. McGoogle to be his housekeeper and cook.

7

My Aunt Lilian and Aunt Biddy were surprised to learn that each had planned to be married during the summer of 1926. Lil wanted a quiet civil wedding in New York City, but Papa insisted she come home and have a 'proper church wedding.' During all the preparations for both weddings, he continually verbalized his disapproval of their choice of bridegrooms.

Biddy said to Lil, "We're lucky he settles for tuberculosis as Mark's and Frank's 'defect'. I remember when Cornelia told him that she'd eloped with Harold, he called him a "turd on toast."

They, exactly as their older sister had done, proceeded on their chosen paths.

Lil had now completed her Master's degree in Art at Columbia University. Her fiancé, Frank Schwarz, a handsome, exceptional artist, had been studying and painting in Anticoli, Italy, having won a Prix de Rome in 1921. He continued his courting through letters; a few years later when he returned to New York City, he and Lil decided to marry.

Always short of money, Frank Schwartz's rent was long past due. His landlady asked him to leave, but that same day the mailman saved him the trouble by bringing the good news that he had been awarded a Guggenheim Fellowship. This was in 1926. The *New York Times* published a photograph of Frank the next day with the story.

Lil sent the article to Papa, who, as he looked at Frank's picture, said, "That young man looks half starved."

Often in his courting letters, Frank had told Lil he didn't have enough to eat. Now he planned a return to Anticoli taking Lil with him as his bride. Despite this proof of talent, Papa thought Frank would never be able to support a wife and family.

Lil, however, was determined to marry her exceptional, intelligent suitor even if "he looked underfed, consumptive, all bones," as Papa said.

Marquis W. Childs, the journalist engaged to Biddy, was at that time completing his MA degree at the university. He also looked consumptive, Papa thought, and he told Biddy she'd find herself supporting him if she insisted on marrying him. She had returned from Paris equipped to teach after polishing her

49

French at the Sorbonne. She was as determined as Lil to marry whom she pleased.

So in spite of Dr. Prentiss's objections, the engagements endured, and the weddings were planned as only a traditionalist, my grandfather, Dr. Henry James Prentiss, could plan them. The small but gracious Trinity Episcopalian Church at 320 East College Street was lavishly decorated with summer flowers on the two separate dates. Invited to each wedding were the relatives and friends of the young people, and also all the academic, church, and town friends of the family. Not a seat in the charming Victorian church would be empty.

Aunt Lilian set the date of her marriage for July second. She rather enjoyed seeing that Papa was horrified when he saw the wedding bills.

My sister Cornie and I were thrilled when we were asked to take part in both of our aunts' weddings. Why Lil and Bid didn't have a double wedding I never learned.

Oblivious to adult concerns, we two paved the path to Aunt Lil's future with pale pink and white rose petals. I loved my pink beribboned basket and flung the sensuous, velvety petals high in the air, into the pews, broadly acting out my role. The ends of each pew were decorated with pink and white flowers matching the petals in our baskets, and the perfume of fresh summer flowers filled my nose. All the colors complemented Aunt Lil's red hair.

In Aunt Biddy's August twenty-sixth wedding, Cornie was assigned the role of ring bearer, carrying the ring on a pretty white satin pillow ahead of the procession. Discovering that, I felt a tinge of jealousy, but as the best man forgot to bring the ring which Mark had entrusted to him, Cornie carried an empty pillow up the aisle. Aunt Biddy and Uncle Mark play-acted as if everything was as it should be.

I preceded the bride and Grandpa up the aisle tossing at random Biddy's choice of deep blue-red rose petals. I was joyful at the sight of them winging their way upward, coming to rest wherever they may. Some fell on the women's hats, some on the men's dark trousers. Here they showed their color especially well; and I forgot everything including why I was doing this. I also forgot about my sister's privilege, but later thought, "she is older than I and deserves precedence." I was five, and she was seven.

My wedding dress—I suppose my sister had an identical one—was the loveliest dress I ever had; it was my first party dress. If I twirled, the full skirt flowed like a cloud about me, for the pale blue material was thin. Our seamstress and neighbor in Atlantic, Minnie Smoller, had cut small rounds of the same fabric in colors of pink, brighter pink, and bright blue.

Mom explained how she stitched near the edge of each circle, then pulled the thread which gathered the rounds into poufs and finished by tying off the threads. After the poufs were pressed flat, they looked like tiny balloons. Mrs. Smoller had strewn them carelessly over the skirt, then blind stitched them on. A wide bright-blue sash was tied into a fluffy bow behind me. Altogether I felt as lovely as both brides.

After the late afternoon weddings, identical receptions were held in Grandpa's backyard. Long tables were set near the back porch and laden with small cheese and ham sandwiches, nuts, olives, celery and little cookies frosted with pastel sugar, and fruit punch. As I was completely ignored, I saw to it I had my share, or more. There must have been wedding cakes too: I didn't notice.

As the last of the day's light disappeared, Grandpa turned on the electric lights threaded through many Japanese lanterns. They were strung along the porch, over the tables and through all the trees by the driveway, and the other side of the lawn.

In the soft magic light I floated among the adults dressed in their suits and short party dresses. The weather for both weddings was perfect, the evenings cool. As I drifted over Grandpa's well-kept lawn among the trees, my precious shiny new patent leather shoes got sprinkled with evening dew.

On each occasion, when the newly married couples were about to depart on their honeymoons, my Grandpa set off rockets. Then he lit a wonderful firework: a little balloon with a miniature basket attached, and in the basket were a tiny bride and groom dressed in their wedding clothes. Many of the guests crowded around Grandpa as he saw to the heating of the air. Gradually the balloon fattened; and then slowly, slowly it rose carrying the wee bride and groom, safe in their little basket, away and away, high above the tops of the apple trees, over towards the quadrangle, where university students lived. The guests sighed when it disappeared. Then everyone cheered.

I heard one say, "This is a fine way to launch a marriage since no one ever knows what the final landing will be."

Unfortunately, while the wedding preparations were being made, Lil discovered she had infected tonsils.

Papa insisted she have them removed before she and Uncle Frank left for Europe. Her surgery was scheduled to take place after their three-day honeymoon in the Wisconsin Dells where they planned to spend their days painting.

"While Lil was in the hospital," Mom told me, "an old beau of Biddy's wanted a last good time with her since she was to be married soon. Her friend brought some booze and Biddy cooked her usual delicious meal. Frank Schwarz and I rounded out the party. Quite unexpectedly, Mr. Neider, who transported us around in those days with his horse and buggy, brought Lil home a day before scheduled. Papa was out of town. Bid and I consulted; we decided to go ahead with the planned entertainment.

"The four of us were laughing and joking in the kitchen when our gaiety was interrupted by the clop clop clop of slippers on the back stairs. It was Lil. Frank ran from the room and hid."

Lil, appearing in the doorway, said, "I hope you're having a good time while I'm lying in bed, utterly miserable."

"She returned upstairs, and Frank returned from his hiding place. Bid and I gave him hell for neglecting his bride, and Frank retorted hotly, 'Nobody is telling me what I'm to do. I'll go up there when I'm ready.'

"Neither I nor Biddy cared as much for Frank after that. However, Lil got her revenge. She wrote from Anticoli, Italy, where they were honeymooning and painting, 'I took care of Frank on the boat over. I refused to sleep with him.'"

In later years I realized Grandpa arranged these lavish weddings for his beloved Lue' as well as for his daughters. During his courtship of Lue', he had seen how Lue's mother staged gala celebrations in Dobbs Ferry. He knew what was required.

It was after Grandma Prentiss died that Dr. Henry Prentiss had invited his three daughters to spend each August with him whenever it was possible. The invitation marked the beginning of adventures for my family. Mom, having Duty ingrained in her, felt her Papa's invitation a command. Even if it weren't, from then on we were driven by my Dad to Iowa City every August—until Grandpa's death changed everything.

My earliest memory occurred during one August day when we were visiting Grandpa Prentiss. I see myself in a light summer dress, skirt moving in the gentle breeze, the soft material feeling good against my three year old legs. I could see through the fence I was standing by. My brother and sister were in a swimming pool. I wasn't upset that I was excluded from getting into the icy, blue water of the Big Dipper, the City Park pool in Iowa City, Iowa. I was too little; I knew, when I was older, I would get my turn.

Aspens, which stood around the egg-shaped pool, spread their heads high above me, their delicate, light green leaves twisted and turned, dancing. The morning sun pierced through them and twinkled on the surface of the Big Dipper, making moving diamonds. I breathed in the rich, delicious smell of hot dogs coming from the nearby food stand, and knew that we'd all have one when the swim was over. I felt happy, just being, and knowing that one day, I too would be taught to swim.

That same summer I often sat on Grandpa's front porch swing and looked down the long sloping hill to the Iowa River, charmed by the poetic stand of three white birches growing to the left of his porch. On mornings, the sun would glint on the tiny, trembling greenish leaves. To me the trees were the most beautiful in the world with black lined bark curling back from the speckled white boles. I resolved to have a pair of them in a yard of mine one day.

If Mom called me to hurry to the upstairs sitting room, I'd struggle with the heavy porch door with its beveled, glass pane, etched with frosted leaves and curly-cues and push my way into the intimidating, huge and scary front hall. I immediately wished I had gone around to the back door, for the hall was dark and noiseless, light barely sifting into it from the bay window in the music room on my right and through a window on the stairwell landing at the end of the long hall. As I stood on the enormous oriental rug covering the hardwood floor, I could see a faint outline of myself in a large mirror hanging on the wall at the far end of the hallway. This hall opened into a gloomy parlor, the dining room, and Grandpa's music room. The smell of something sweet usually came from Googie's kitchen in the mornings, and that helped me put down my fear.

The first thing I found out about Grandpa was that he played the piano to amuse himself. His music was complicated, nothing at all like Mom's. I loved to hear him play; and when I'd hear the piano, I'd run to the hall, stand out of his sight, and listen. There was no door to the room, just a wide, open space. He never invited me to come into the room, so I decided he didn't want an audience. He couldn't have known how much I loved to hear him play.

When he wasn't home, and there was nothing special going on, I'd go to this room and sit on his beautiful piano bench. It had delicate curved legs and a dark-red, cut velvet cushioned seat which was soft to sit on and nice to run my hands over. Wooden upright arms, short and curving out a little, were at either end. I thought they were handles. These were inlaid with lighter colored woods in the shapes of leaves and vines. Mom called it marquetry. I felt enclosed and happy when I sat on the bench.

Grandpa's upright Steinway was loaded with piles of yellow music books labeled with the word Schirmer. The books were squeezed between a metronome and a funny, squat, square yellow lamp. These things sat on a strange mirror cloth, black with small disks of mirrors stitched onto it. I learned it came from Morocco. There was always music spread out ready to play. I liked to stare at the black notes spiraling up and down and across the black lines, wondering if I would ever be able to read so many notes. I had just begun music lessons.

Often I'd go to the little bay window in this room and look out over the driveway to the Teters' house. When Grandpa was at work, I sat on the red cushions there reading or watching the squirrels sniffing around the shady backyards.

Sunday dinner at Grandpa's was a ceremony. No matter how hot the day was, we always ate in the dining room, not on the airy back porch. Since we went to church each Sunday, we were in our best clothes. Harold, Cornie, and I were expected to speak only when spoken to. We sat silently while Mrs. McGoogle brought in the food. Grandpa served and talked with the adults who were at the table that day.

Even though the high-backed mahogany chairs and table were heavily carved like the furniture I'd seen in the in the parlor, I didn't mind them here for they seemed suitable to the occasion. And besides, this room was made cheery by a big bay window stretched across the wall behind Grandpa's chair. The starched white linen tablecloth caught the light and brightened everyone's face. Small in stature, Grandpa stood up when he ladled the soup and when he carved the meat.

The matching buffet, like the table and chairs, took up a lot of space. In between Sundays, centered on a long linen runner, sat a sterling silver soup tureen guarded by two elaborate silver candlesticks. The buffet stood behind Mom who always sat opposite her Papa.

Set back in the bay window, the teacart held the sparkling Prentiss silver tea and coffee service. From there, on these August Sundays, Mrs. McGoogle would serve the grownups their coffee. It had been Mom's Thursday job to clean the silver when she was growing up in this house. I supposed it was Googie, as everyone called her, who polished the silver now. To begin our meal, Googie brought in the soup tureen, for every dinner began with a delicious homemade soup.

To Grandpa's left was an oval serving table full of gleaming silver serving dishes and also the small sterling silver carving set engraved with a P. The sharp little knife and fork just fit Grandpa's small hands. He was an elegant carver, for he had a lot of practice with his dissecting tools. His hands knew just how to cut the slices, all even and smooth, and place the meat, potatoes and vegetables just so on each plate. For some reason our Sunday vegetable was never changing green peas—canned tiny Le Seur brand peas.

I noticed when it came time for second helpings, Grandpa never asked, "Do you want more lamb, Virginia?" He always said, "Would you care for some lamb, Virginia," as if I hadn't already had a helping.

I guess he didn't want to call attention to my greed, or anyone else's. On Sundays it was always the mouth-watering smell of lamb filling the house as we came in from church. Since my Dad loved beef, and it was the meat of choice for many of our meals in Atlantic, lamb with its accompanying mint sauce was new to me and a treat.

Googie, coming and going from the pantry and kitchen, would squeeze carefully between our chairs, the buffet, and side tables when she cleared away the plates, or brought the next course. Of all her delicious desserts, my favorite was a miracle of raspberries or apples and pastry with just the right amount of cinnamon sauce, its soothing perfume filling the air.

Opposite the wide dining room door was the equally wide stairway to the bedrooms. Just past the large landing, a black and white print of three figures, Laocoon and his two young sons, hung on the wall. He and his sons had come to make an offering to Poseidon at the seashore, but were being crushed in the twining of two sea serpents. Mom said Laocoon was a priest of Apollo at Troy who had warned the Trojans not to touch the Greek's wooden horse. But the Trojans decided Laocoon's and his son's deaths meant the warning was false. So they brought the Trojan Horse into the city, and tragedy followed. Whenever I went up or down those steps, I looked at the picture. Mom told me their story was a Greek myth—my introduction to mythology.

My favorite place for meals at Grandpa Prentiss's was the back porch. It was across the back wall of the house, adjacent to the kitchen. Except for Sunday dinners, Googie served all our meals there in the airiness of the long and narrow, screened-in porch, cooled on three sides by the many deciduous trees growing in Grandpa's and his neighbor's backyards.

Grandpa's place of honor was at the end of the narrow table right next to the kitchen door, and my place was on his right—why I never knew; I certainly didn't cause any trouble when Grandpa was around. Sister Cornie was on my right. One of the adults sat at the far end of the table by the window leading into the kitchen. It was used as a pass-through. For breakfast Googie made wonderful four-inch-high popovers which would appear magically because all I could ever see were her hands at the open window. Whatever dish came next, there were those hands passing it.

We ate a substantial breakfast, as Mom called it, for Papa believed that was the way to start the day. So along with the popovers, we had scrambled eggs, and hot cereal, fruit, milk, and juice. For the popovers Googie made delectable homemade jams: raspberry, blueberry, and marmalades. And for our luncheon salad, she made a pale dressing that I can still almost taste, just oil and vinegar and herbs. Perfection!

I was well aware that she was a wonderful cook, but whenever I think of Googie, and how everyone liked her, I see only a short, round body, a smiling face, and a pair of hands.

Once, soon after we had arrived for our August visit, sister Cornie hadn't put her napkin on her lap.

"Cornie, unfold your napkin," prompted Grandfather.

"Oh, I'm sorry, Grandpa. You see, we don't use them at home, and I didn't think to."

Mom almost collapsed. This was a blatant lie. She was furious with Cornie, for Mom carried deep inside, glued to her guts, a dread fear of her father and his disapproval. Our regimentation about manners was almost as strict in our Atlantic home as it was at Grandpa's. He knew that, but he admired Cornie's spunk and said nothing more. One time, however, he did correct her severely. It was when she called him Gramps. This was much too informal for Grandpa. It was all right for us to call Dad's father Gramps, but never Dr. Prentiss.

As for me, I was afraid of the man. Sarcasm was the art that he must have used with me, but I can't recall just how. I overheard that he was ruthless with his freshmen students. Perhaps it was his tone of voice: I sensed he was dangerous, at least for me. I avoided him. I never talked with him at all. But I watched him.

He fed the squirrels that lived in the huge trees in the back yards. With them he was patient and had trained them not to be afraid. Some evenings he'd come home from work with a sack in his hand. Out in Dean Teters' yard, which was more open than his, he'd kneel down, and offer peanuts from his hand. The little beasts would appear as soon as they saw him, advancing a foot or two at a time, red tails twitching, and gradually they'd come near Grandpa, bounce skittishly to his outstretched hand, snatch a peanut—race away—then stop and nibble off the shell. Oh! How I wanted to try that, to see what it was like: but he never offered to help me. And I was too timid to ask.

All the bedrooms in Grandpa's house were upstairs. His impressed me most because his bed was so high. I had to run, jump, then pull on the bedspread and scramble to get up on it. Of course, I wasn't supposed to be in his bedroom at all, but 'when the cat's away....' The tall bedposts were topped with carved pineapples. At the bottom of the posts were little plugs that pulled out, so I saw how the bed was screwed together.

Grandpa hid candy under his pillow; and when Mom was a little girl, she'd secretly come and take a piece or two. I learned this one afternoon at home in

Atlantic when she was lying on our guest room bed reading, a little bag of peanut brittle beside her. Into the bag would go her hand, as regular as the tick tock of a clock. She told me Grandpa did that too, but he liked peppermints. Much later, Mom's sister, Biddy, told me that she, too, always kept a bag of candy under her pillow. I don't know what her favorite was. Maybe chocolate?

The bathroom for children and mothers was at the end of the wide upstairs hall that ran from the front to the back of the house. One night the hall was the scene of a bat hunt.

All of us children were in our nightclothe; Mom and Aunt Biddy were supervising. I was in the bathroom brushing my teeth when someone let out a blood-curdling cry.

"Bats, bats—a bat came down from the attic!"

I rushed from the bathroom. Everyone rushed out to the hall. A huge bat careened back and forth dipping up and down from ceiling to floor, and sometimes just above our heads. Cornie and I ran to and fro, hands holding our hair down, yelling and screaming just for the fun of it. Now pursued by Mom, her long red hair undone for the night and flying about, the bat escaped the broom she had in her hands. The yells must have been heard all over the neighborhood. Mom's aim wasn't good. The bat continually avoided her wild, slashing lunges. This was a great delight, and we kids exaggerated our screams much to Aunt Biddy's annoyance. Finally the creature flew back up the attic stairs. Mom slammed the door shut; we all paused for breath.

Biddy said, "Enough of this nonsense. Bats don't hurt you: he's simply lost."

"We'll let Uncle Bob take care of it later," added Mom. His room was in the attic, and we were forbidden to go up there. After this incident, I lost my desire to do so.

One frigid Thanksgiving eve after Grandma Prentiss died, Grandpa Prentiss came by train to our house for the holiday. Dad drove all of us to the railroad station to meet him. Sheltered from the cold wind, we crowded together to keep warm against the railroad station, shivering in spite of our winter coats. Long before we could see the train, we heard the woo-woo-ooooo of the whistle and felt vibrations trembling beneath our feet.

Then the rumble began. Coming around a slight curve, the engine raced toward us on two silver ribbons made by its huge headlight shining on the railroad track. On came the black beast growing enormous as it closed in on us, not seeming to slow at all. The bricks below our feet shook as the roaring engine passed by, surrounding us with a blast of soot-filled air, pinning me up against the brick wall of the station. Would it stop? Suddenly, surprisingly the train slowed, then gradually came to a halt.

As far as I was concerned, the excitement was over. We stood waiting to see from which car Grandpa would exit. Who could miss him? He had on his long black wool coat, his black Homburg hat square over his stern face, black gloves, and in his hand his black medical bag. I knew there were no instruments in it. Mom told me he was bringing the turkey—it had to be in the bag. He didn't greet me in any way, and since he always intimidated me, I put a lot of space between us.

During this visit, Mom took her Papa out for a ride around the countryside, showing him what the November cornfields looked like. She got lost and ended up on a bumpy, frozen dirt road, stalled the car, and then had trouble turning around to go back the way she came.

Grandpa said to her, "I see, Cornelia, that you drive about as well as you do anything."

8

La Vista Place, Atlantic, Iowa: that was my address for seventeen years. Why was a town of 5000 people located near the western edge of Iowa, 1000 miles from the east coast and 2000 miles from the west coast, named for one of the great oceans cradling the United States? As I was told, the first pioneers flipped a coin thinking they were standing on the mid-point between the Pacific and Atlantic Oceans; it seemed suitable to name the fledgling town after one of them. But which—heads or tails? Heads won. The town was named Atlantic. It thrived and grew on the Midwestern plain known to the Indians as *Iowa*, meaning "Beautiful Lane."

The farm land surrounding Atlantic was not flat or rolling like most of Iowa. Southwestern Iowa was hilly. But in spite of the hills, and because of deep, rich soil developed through eons of rotting prairie grass, Cass County eventually produced plenty of corn for hogs and cattle.

Mom told me that Mr. James Whitney, who owned the land on which Atlantic was built, had a friend, a Des Moines man, who was influential in choosing where the railroads crossed Iowa. Through their efforts the Rock Island Railroad made a new survey, ran the tracks twenty miles south of Exira and adjacent to Atlantic at the northern edge. Mr. Whitney wrote into the contract that every train that came over these tracks had to stop in Atlantic. I suppose it was his foresight that Atlantic became the county seat of Cass.

One fed the other: Atlantic became the home of the county fair grounds, a center for farmers to shop and from which to ship their products, and the location for several small industries. Since they traveled by rail in the early days, Atlantic became a good location for salesmen to live. More to my interest, it was an accessible and central location which attracted circuses and other traveling entertainments.

My Dad was enchanted by vistas. Lovely views fed his fantasies and freed his soul. Shortly after my Mom told him his second child was on the way, he built a cottage on the southern edge of Atlantic which was laid out on a grid as were many Iowa towns. If you stand on the northern edge of Atlantic at the Railroad Station where Chestnut Street begins and then walk through the main shopping section and up the fourteen blocks of a long sloping rise to the top of a hill, you arrive at a flat area to the East named La Vista Place. Further south, in the distance as seen from the backyard of the lot he bought, was a high rounded hill. Dad thought this was his longed-for vista. But the true vista was in his mind's eye. There he could see the hilly farmland of Southwestern Iowa spreading endlessly. He was sure of his vision for he'd lived in Atlantic during his high school years, hunting the countryside, and driving his father's Ford far and wide. He knew Southwestern Iowa.

Bordering on the north of what became his one-story cottage was a street with no name and no view whatsoever except for vacant lots, two older houses, treetops and sky.

To me La Vista Place seemed a romantic name regardless of views, and a curious location because none of the houses had numbers. All of us neighbors were thrown into one address which neither increased our intimacy nor caused confusion. The postman knew who lived where, delivered the mail twice a day, and that was all anyone cared about.

Around 1918 Sears & Roebuck and others sold pre-cut houses, costing only a few hundred dollars, to people all over the United States. But Dad preferred to plan and build a house in his own way—with Mom's assistance of course.

World War I was under way. Mom and Dad were living in their new home when Mom's brother, Hank Prentiss, signed up with the army having finished his sophomore year at college. My grandfather Prentiss decided his son-in-law should do the same, even though Dad was a father of one child, and soon-to-be father of another.

Mom told me, "Your Dad was in Mitchell, South Dakota selling farm implements for his father. But he enlisted and was supposed to be called up within four weeks. I rented our house so as to have money while he was away.

"Then Sunny, (Harold Jr.) and I joined him in Mitchell. Mama and Papa agreed that once he was called up, Sunny and I should stay with them in Iowa City while he was overseas.

"We had no idea the winter temperatures in South Dakota would be as frigid as thirty degrees below zero or that our tiny rental house was not insulated. I could walk no more than three blocks before the freezing weather forced a retreat to the icy house, myself cold to the bone and Sunny, frozen to tears."

When it seemed as if pregnant wife and Sunny were about to be frozen solid, Dad wired Henry and Lue' Prentiss asking if Mom and Sunny could join them immediately and stay until the rental of the La Vista house expired. Papa and Momma welcomed them. Mom turned over the La Vista house-rent money to her parents during their stay, while Dad continued selling farm machinery in South Dakota. He was never inducted into the army. And the Shrauger family was adrift for a year.

A month before Hank's return from France, my sister, Cornie, on May 7, 1919, found her way into the world, caul-covered, and in the splendor of the State University Hospital in Iowa City where Grandfather Prentiss taught his would-be medical students. Sister Cornie (now we had two Harolds and two Cornelias in our immediate family) was an unusually beautiful baby, and born, unlike her brother, in sterile circumstances.

Grandpa Prentiss visited Mom in the hospital every day, and on the seventh day she told him, "My nurse says I mustn't get out of bed at all today."

"Why not?" he asked.

"She says my organs will go back in place today, so I must be very quiet."

Instantly furious, Dr. H. J. Prentiss shouted, "IF THAT'S WHAT SHE BELIEVES, IN SPITE OF WHAT I'VE TAUGHT HER IN THE NURSES' CLASSES, I'LL NEVER AGAIN TEACH NURSES!" And he never did. He turned that job over to a colleague.

After the war ended Dad brought little Sunny, infant Cornie, and Mom back from Iowa City to the little house he'd built in Atlantic.

Little Cornie adored her big brother. Following him everywhere, she gave him no rest, her bright green eyes always focusing on him.

Her constant tagging brought peace-loving Harold to shouts of, "Go find something to do," or "Mom, make Cornie leave me alone."

Harold was now almost five years old; Cornie, two.

It all came to a head one summer morning when Harold went from the kitchen to the toilet. Cornie toddled after him never letting her brother out of sight. He slammed the bathroom door. Little Cornie howled. Mom, cleaning up the breakfast dishes, felt her temper coming to a boil. She rushed to the bathroom and gave her daughter a sharp slap on her diapered behind.

"Cornie, you've got to stop annoying your brother!"

Then she noticed Cornie's hand was caught in the door. Mom quickly freed the little hand, scooped the wailing child into her arms, and rushed to the icebox for ice. Balancing her over the kitchen sink, she could see that the bloody little hand was cut and scraped, but not broken.

My Mom repeated this story so often through the years that I wondered if she were doing penance. Cornie's extreme devotion to her brother touched Mom, but later on, when learning of Mom and Dad's decision "never to lay a hand on any child of theirs," I began to think the event reinforced her resolution never to be provoked into losing her temper by any action of her children.

After I joined my brother and sister on January 22, 1921, our house in La Vista Place became a fun house for three kids. The enclosed stairs to our bedrooms were in the center of the house. This allowed us to make a full circle running through all the rooms and small hallway. During one happy session of Hide and Seek, Cornie hid behind the half-glass door that led from the kitchen to the small room at the back of the house where we kept our icebox and breakfast table.

Harold came racing through the kitchen, and Cornie jumped out shouting, "Boo!"

Startled, Harold shoved his arm through the glass and tore a two-inch gash on the inside of his left arm. The doctor left a piece of cotton in the wound as he sewed it up, causing an infection, a reopening of the wound, and eventually a scar worth talking about.

We had two different dining rooms at different times. One was on the north of the house adjoining the pantry. The second dining room was adjacent to the kitchen on the south side of the house. I later learned that this evolution had to do with my Gramma Shrauger's disposition.

An example of Mom's problem with Gramma interfering with her life had to do with white boots. After Mom, Dad and we kids were settled in our in La Vista Place house, whenever Mom walked downtown she could be sure Gramma was watching her progress down Chestnut Street. One day Sadie saw this ravishing, redheaded young woman, her daughter-in-law, tripping down Chestnut Street on her way to town, wearing her apparently new, white, high-topped buttoned boots. How Gramma knew they were new, I don't know.

Cornelia saw Sadie walking to the edge of the hill on which her house perched.

She said, "Cornelia. How dare you spend Harold's hard earned money on expensive boots!"

"Mrs. Shrauger. My father sends me a check every month for my special things."

And with a nod, Cornelia continued her walk to town.

Of course Dad had to have a fireplace in his house, for he grew up with one in Grampa Shrauger's house. Unfortunately it never became the source of pleasure he had in mind. It was on an inside wall opposite the front entrance and tiny foyer. A mistake was made planning the width of the house: so what was supposed to be a cozy place to sit around a fire became a dark red brick fireplace with dark red tiles on the floor in front of it scrunched in by parallel walls just two feet on either side of it. The tiles stopped at the living room. The fireplace was nothing but a narrow, useless alcove. The two-foot spaces on each side of the fireplace failure were occupied by Dad's smoking stand and a few logs.

The adjacent dining room, which soon became our music room, was the scene of a memorable first-and-last-of-its-kind family Thanksgiving dinner. Gramma and Grampa Shrauger, Uncle Harlan, ten years younger than Dad, and a table full of Dad's relatives whom I didn't know, sat down for a delicious turkey dinner. Our oval, claw-foot oak table filled the entire room. We crowded all the straight chairs we owned around it.

Dad helped Mom spread her largest white damask cloth over the enormous table. As they shook it out, it floated aloft, folding and unfolding like flapping wings of an enormous fat bird. With her guidance, I arranged the silverware in proper order. She placed her oval, cut-glass bowl filled with orange flowers at the table's center, green candles guarding it: very pretty.

Everyone wedged themselves into the chairs, thigh to thigh, and Dad carried in the browned and steaming twenty-five pound turkey. My mouth watered. I knew it was filled with Mom's good bread dressing. She basted the bird every half hour, never leaving the kitchen. Because Dad always insisted on having more than enough, Mom prepared not only mashed potatoes and her perfect gravy, but also candied sweets. These were for brother Harold, she said, at the last minute scattering tiny marshmallows on the top of that icky, syrupy dish. But I think Mom made that for Mom. She dearly loved sugary things.

Silver serving dishes held heaps of buttered green peas, pickled beets, and Brussels sprouts—a tradition in the Prentiss household. Celery sticks, which looked pretty with their leafy tops spreading beyond Mom's long, oval, cut-glass serving dish, the big pieces being stuffed with cheddar cheese mashed with onion and mayonnaise, was salad.

Dad carved the enormous turkey perfectly—he made an art of it. How he did it so delicately was a wonder, for his hands were huge. First he served all the adults with tender breast slices and succulent cuts of turkey thigh. Cornie and I, being the youngest, were singled out for what Dad told us was the best part of the turkey: drumsticks. All kids prefer drumsticks, don't they? Well, not I. The dried-out drumstick completely filled my plate with its bone and tendons sticking out; but I didn't whine or complain. That wasn't permitted: Dad saw to that.

I envied the adults. But "Oh well," I thought, "Someday I'll be the grownup, and it will be my turn to get the best parts."

Anyway, after the guests were gone, for supper our menu always was delicious leftover breast of turkey sandwiches on soft white bread with lettuce leaves and mayonnaise, so I knew that there was some fooling going on.

Mom's homemade cranberry sauce was a bright spot of red on the table. I often watched her make it. Put the cranberries into the saucepan with water just peeking through the berries. Bring to a boil. Listen for the pop of the berries, first one, then two, and soon the whole pan-full goes poppety pop; the race is on for the finish! Silence tells you it is time to put the berries through the Foley Food Mill. Taking equal measure of pureed cranberries and of sugar, stir to dissolve the sugar and bring again to a full boil. Boil exactly one minute. Pour into a pretty bowl. It always jelled, was tangy sweet, and never failed to please.

For dessert Mom served flaky-crusted pumpkin pies smothered with whipped cream, and mincemeat pie made especially for Dad. Who among us could stuff dessert into a full stomach? All of us.

It was after this last sumptuous Thanksgiving dinner with Dad's relatives that we stopped having holiday meals with Gramma and Grampa. I wasn't aware of how Gramma kept interfering with Mom's life, verbally attacking her about this and that, but it must have been her only means of communication. Sadie simply resented Mom. Mom could stand up for herself, but Dad was tired of being a buffer between the two. He decided he couldn't be congenial with his mother any longer.

He severed the family relationship. No more socializing. He followed the admonition in Genesis 2-24; "*There for shall a man leave his father and mother and shall cleave unto his wife and they shall be of one flesh.*" In this way Mom was emancipated from the second test life threw her way. My life changed too, in ways I didn't understand for years.

But we kids were always welcome to stop in for a visit whenever we wished. We stayed with them when Uncle Hank was injured and dying. Both Gramma and Grampa continued to have open hearts as far as their grandchildren were concerned.

Never dismayed for long by unexpected mishaps, my parents didn't allow the stopping of family dinners deter them from making the best of a disturbing event. From then on Mom and Dad invited all their childless friends to join us for a jolly evening on Christmas night. Dad built a roaring fire in the fireplace, and the tree stood in splendor surrounded by our new toys. Their friends Mabel and Roy Hedges, Jenny and Owen Meredith, Harry and Gwen Swan, Rae and Arthur Lee, Jane and Percy Chase, and others came.

We three Shrauger kids triumphed at those parties. All the grownups came bearing gifts for us. The skinny men got down on their stomachs pushing Harold aside so they could run his toy train around the sparkling tinseled tree decorated with lights and glittering, fragile glass Santas and fruits which, Mom said, came from Germany. The women and the men with big stomachs sat on chairs placed here and there in the living room and settled for drinks and food. Some played Parcheesi with Cornie or me on an unstable tin game board brought by the Swans.

When game time was over and the grownups were laughing and chatting, I sat on the bench near the fireplace studying the red and white of the leaping flames and enjoying the warmth of Dad's fire built only on this yearly occasion. Then I concentrated on one of the items from Mom's entertainment menu. She always made, among other things, small ground cheddar cheese, onion, and mayonnaise sandwiches and heated Vienna sausages, pierced with toothpicks, then placed on a large, round, silver tray. These sausages, which I dearly loved, were beside me on the bench waiting to be passed to the guests.

I was quietly eating one after another until I heard Mom's voice saying, "Virginia, please pass the sausages around." So I stopped being piggy and became an exemplary hostess.

The Christmas after Dad's no-more-family-dinners ultimatum, knowing our family pattern had changed, Rae and Arthur Lee invited us to their home for the holiday dinner. They didn't have children but they did have alcohol. The dinner was fine, and I was happy to be introduced to pickled walnuts, 'an English idea,' Mom told me. Mom called Arthur, "The Duke." Maybe it was because he came from the gentility of England, as she put it. In spite of his protruding belly, his bloodshot eyes, pale skin, and bulbous, venous nose, I somehow knew he was a friend. He had a way of turning his head and looking down at me over the top his glasses. He never smiled, except in a slow-motion way, was stiff necked, almost bald, and, maybe, this made him seem regal.

Rae was different. She was not gentle. Having been raised in the woods of Canada, the daughter of loggers, she knew every four-letter word which had been invented (Mom told me this), the names of all the birds in the woods, and had read hundreds of books on history, politics, novels, poetry, everything.

Also she could cook. The turkey was as beautiful and tasty as Mom's, and the mashed potatoes dripped with butter. All went well until dessert.

Mrs. Lee (we children were trained to never use first names of adults) came from the kitchen balancing a fine English pudding on a platter that just skimmed her protruding belly. The pudding was on fire! A sweet scent drifted to our noses.

We impatiently waited, staring at Rae, mouths salivating. Mrs. Lee, tossed her unkempt, uncurled, course white hair while talking and talking; she seemed to me to be awfully slow in serving. Finally she gave each of us a large helping of crumbly looking fruited cake floating in a brown liquid. A bite—ugh! What was that acrid sharp taste!

"Oh, Rae," said Mom seeing our grimaces. "The children aren't familiar with the taste of whisky, so don't mind if they can't eat your delicious pudding."

"I'll get them something else," she said. And off she went to the kitchen and returned bringing mince pie. It, too, was floating in a sauce, a thin sauce, and ah, the deep, wonderful rich smell. A taste of the sauce—heavy with rum! Dessert suddenly became uninteresting.

Rae was engrossed in conversation when we three asked to be excused. Later Mom and Dad decided we would have all holiday dinners at home from then on. And we did.

In late spring, 1925, Mom and I walked to Jackson School for a very important interview. Just what that meant, I didn't know, but Mom was taking me, so I was comfortable. I suppose she told me we were going to see if I could go to school in September. My brother and sister already went to school there; but this was the first time I'd been in the tan-brick building. Jackson School and I were the same age. The cornerstone said it was built in 1921.

We had a long walk down a slippery, wide hall to a little flight of stairs at the very end. A tall man met us. Maybe it was the enormous desk in the middle of the little room that made it feel small. Stuffed bookcases lined the walls. Two chairs sat in front of the desk. I could see the leafy green treetops outside the big window.

"Good morning, Mrs. Shrauger. Please sit down. And here is Virginia. Hello, Virginia."

Mom had told me we were going to talk with the principal. His face was smiling as he scooped me up, and we sat down in his desk chair, me on his bony knees. Before I had a chance to answer his hello, he put a board in my hands that had a triangle, a circle, an oblong, and other shapes cut out of the surface. I saw a pile of green, red, purple, and yellow blocks on his desk.

"Virginia, can you fit these blocks into the spaces where they belong?" he asked in a kind voice.

I placed the pieces quickly. Whether or not there were other tests, I don't recall: but if so or if not, I was at age four mature enough, the man told Mom, to begin Kindergarten in September.

Jackson became my beloved elementary school. It was on Cedar Street between eighth and ninth on the west side of Chestnut Street. Grant School also on the west side, was open only for Kindergarten and the first four grades. The kids who began there moved to our school for fifth grade. Lincoln was the elementary school for the kids who lived on the east side of town.

We learned that we'd join the Lincoln eighth graders after we finished eighth grade to become one class as freshmen at the Atlantic High School; but that didn't mean much to us Kindergarteners. The red brick Atlantic High School was built in 1885 on the corner of seventh and Walnut, just a few blocks from my Grampa's sheet metal factory. I could see the High School every Sunday for it was right next to the First Presbyterian Church at seventh and Chestnut where Mom played the organ and where I went to Sunday School. So in the back of my mind, I knew where my future lay.

In September, when I began school, I was surprised to find the Kindergarten room was half underground. We kids looked out the windows and knew Cedar Street was there, but it was hidden by the rounded drop-off of the yard. The gymnasium and the furnace room were down the hall at the other end of the building near the boy's entrance, but we exercised in our room or outdoors.

I liked being half underground because, when I stood up, I could see the lawn out the big windows at eye level. There was the grass, green in the fall and spring, snow-covered in the winter. It seemed odd that we sat below the lawn. If I looked up, I could see the tree boles shining in the sun, waving their huge leafy heads laced with electric wires. From the outside, above the kindergarten windows, two rows of tall windows marched across both of the upper floors where the big kids disappeared every morning.

The back of our school looked like the front except there were no wide entryways with four steps and no balustrades.

Boys and girls had their own playgrounds. The girls' was on the south side of the school, and the boys' on the north. They were identical, each having three swings made of boards suspended from chains and hung on triangular metal supports. This was a popular fixture on both playgrounds, long lines forming for turns before and after school and at recess. If the swinger took too long a turn, verbal harassment began.

"Get off! Now!" "Your turn's up," "Don't be a pig."

There were twice as many kids in our class than were in my neighborhood, about twenty, so tag during recess on the playground was livelier. Under our feet was a firm surface of small stones; that meant if anyone fell down, a trip to the office was required for a cleansing of the wound and an application of iodine.

In good weather we'd stay out there until the first bell rang. That was the signal to line up by grade in twos. Jostling and scrambling to stand by our favorite friend brought a loud clap from the supervising teacher: we quieted; then she marched us into the building.

Kindergarten was special. I felt privileged because all the older kids had to go upstairs to get to their rooms while we Kindergartners went downstairs. All was lightness and joy as we began the day seated in a circle on the floor. Some of my classmates, Dorothy Hupp, Charlie Hunt, Armelda Welch, Billy Kelso, and Bobby Britton went through all the grades in Jackson School with me, and High School too. In our cozy circle we sang songs, and listened to our teacher read stories. Except for her dark hair I can't recall what she looked like or what her name was, but I do know how much I loved her. She let us lay on our bellies on the floor, to draw and color. I was enchanted with the movable chairs and little tables, just the right size for me and my new friends.

Above the blackboards, all the printed letters of the alphabet were displayed, small and capital, black on white. The black board, and it was black, was memorable for a favorite story our teacher repeated again and again at our request.

At the beginning of it, her chalk rested on a spot on the board. As the words came flowing from her mouth, she moved the chalk in a line, each move prompted by the story. We gradually saw a cat's head and ears appear, then its back, its long tail curling down under its rump, for it was seated, and then the chalk moved up and down the front legs. Voila! A cat! It was magic! To me, no high-tech computer-assisted visual effect has ever seemed more dramatic, more memorable, than those simple, elegant strokes of chalk.

Perhaps I loved school so much because neither Cornie nor Harold were in my class to tease me. In later years Mom told me that Harold and Cornie teased me all the time. If she or Dad tried to alter circumstances, I didn't notice. But I was very aware of the fruits of teasing—my pouting and whining—for Mom made me aware and did help me, not by demanding the teasing cease, but correcting its exterior affect on me. I'd be with her in the kitchen.

She would turn to me, see me pouting, and say, "Virginia, if the good Lord had intended for horses asses to be on people's faces, He would have put them there."

Every time she spotted me wearing the pout, I'd hear that sentence. Even now, as I think of those words, I feel my face straightening in and up. It was a very effective method, for eventually she ceased having to say it to me. The whining ceased as I grew a little older and had more of a life with my friends.

Often I ran to Mom after the fun of the day, school and play, was over. I was avoiding my brother and sister since this was their chosen time to pick on me. I didn't exactly cling to her skirt, but I felt her presence as armor. I stood in the corner between the door that led to the basement and the adjacent doorjamb that led to the pantry. Out of Mom's way, I'd quietly enjoy watching her prepare dinner.

She'd be cutting up vegetables, making salad, or her delicious and famous oil dressing. She first assembled her tools: from the icebox she brought an egg, the eggbeater and bowl where they had been cooling along with the Mazola oil; into the bowl went the egg which she beat into foam; slowly, she added one cup of oil—drop by drop—beat each in well, another drop until all was used and thickened; then into the mixture went a dash of dry yellow mustard, and some salt and pepper. Last of all, Mom shook in lots of paprika making it a pretty pink. This hang-around hour taught me some rudiments of cooking.

I'd watch as she wielded a large and wicked looking triangular knife slicing onions and carrots right on the counter. She often cut herself with this knife, once horribly—in the thumb joint while dismembering a chicken—just after Dad had sharpened it for her. He said he'd never sharpen a kitchen knife for her again. He kept his word.

Mom was my constant instructor. From the time I was old enough to hold a coin, she taught me to save money. The Atlantic State Bank, where we did business, furnished slick and shiny, chrome, ovoid savings banks. As I put my pennies in and watched them disappear down the slot in the top, I paused to stare at my reflection on its surface: both events gave me great pleasure. Grampa gave me pennies, and now and then, when giving amused one of my folk's friends, I'd be the proud possessor of a nickel or even a dime. Into my beloved bank I popped them.

Occasionally Mom took me with her to the bank downtown. Off we'd go, I clutching my precious bank, marching down Chestnut Street to the imposing stone building that had bars on the small side windows.

Guided by Mom, I rushed up to the cashier. Hardly able to reach the marble counter even on tiptoe, with an outstretched arm I placed the treasured ovoid there, watching it teeter back and forth as I struggled. Standing back, I could see the lady—who kept glancing at me—put a small key in the slot on the bottom to open it. Letting the coins spill out with a clatter she counted them, and then wrote in the bankbook Mom kept for me. I enjoyed these excursions, and, since there wasn't any place near home where I could spend the pennies on candy, what I was given ended up in my much loved, smooth and shiny bank.

I wonder how much I accumulated before all the banks closed October 24, 1929. I never saw my bank book. Harold thought we each had about a hundred dollars. Everything anyone had entrusted to the bank was gone after that day. I learned more about the closing by listening to the adults talk and reading the headlines in the *Atlantic News Telegraph*.

That momentous event made me aware that the grownup world wasn't all that certain. I don't recall saving again in a bank.

When I began stamp collecting, I hoarded my coins and bought commemorative stamps. But the idea of saving spilled over into college days where I worked for tuition, board and room money. I faithfully bought World War II ten-cent savings stamps each payday. I put them in books that, when filled, were worth twenty-five dollars. All these books were later turned into government saving bonds, which, much later, helped to buy a house. Small beginnings....

Since Dad worked in Grandpa's sheet metal factory, he naturally thought of having a metal kitchen counter. Made of some kind of soft metal, it eventually had knife cuts and dents all over it. Long and narrow, it ran along under the bank of windows. Dad liked his house full of light. I could see the back wall of our neighbors, the Smoller's, house. It sat just twelve feet away; we looked out on their backyard.

Our sink was on the far left of the counter. On the far right was our little pantry, a walk-through to the dining-then-music room. There was just enough space in it for Mom's Singer Sewing Machine, used for mending.

In the pantry cupboards she stored her Haviland china, a Greek Key design below its green and gold edge, all her crystal goblets, the big-sized, silver-plated turkey platter with the same Greek Key design on its edge, and her treasured pare-point sterling trays. She told me these were wedding presents from her friends, but mostly from friends of her parents.

My favorites, which came from Grandma Prentiss's pantry after she died, were the eight-inch blue-green ceramic plates with large, raised and carved yellow dandelions on them, and the deep five-inch fish-shaped ramekins whose curved fish heads were elevated a bit over the flat bottom that stretched to a flipped up tail. Pale blue lines drawn on the outside made sure I knew it was a fish. Mom served creamed tuna in them when she had lady's luncheons.

I'd be in the kitchen with Mom, she, chopping. If I'd been a thumb sucker, I would have been in limbo staring at her. But no, I was seeing that the little counter-cuts were full of dirt.

How I loved my protector, and how I wanted to please her. She really didn't do much to protect me, for she thought children should fight their own battles.

But just to be near Mom discouraged teasing. All Mom had to do was make a gesture, and I'd try to conform.

Once I was standing near the cast-iron stove, which she used before the gas line was put in. The stove stood opposite the sink. Mom was preparing supper. I was barely tall enough to look over the edge and see the pulsing, fiery red coals outlined and misted in black. To get the heat up she'd scoop more coal from the bin with the scuttle and spread it on the bed of embers.

On this particular evening I was pressing my genitals through my light summer dress. Mom noticed this, never said a word, but catching my eye she waggled the index finger of her upraised right hand, shook her head, "No," and made tsk tsk sounds.

Disappointed, I learned that this little comforting pleasure was not allowed. I never again touched myself. It is hard for me to believe the strength and power that woman had over me: good and bad.

However, when I was old enough to give myself a bath, I, for some reason, decided to look inside the crack between my legs. Maybe Mom prompted me to give that place a good scrubbing too. I curled my back over, spread the outsides, and discovered a funny little point near a little hole. A lot of creamy white stuff was there too, so I soaped myself and let the matter rest.

9

In September of 1925, I left my babyhood behind in the basement of Jackson School by climbing up a flight of stairs. Miss Bell, my first grade teacher, welcomed us as we arrived at her door. I didn't realize it at that moment, but the only certain thing about my destiny was that I'd spend six hours a day, nine months a year, for the next eight years in this two-story, tan-brick building.

Harold, Cornie, and I walked to and from Jackson School in good weather. We wandered home on different routes, depending on our fancy or which friend we were with. But in frigid frostbite-threatening weather, Dad drove us to school in the morning, and picked us up on Chestnut Street at noon on his way home for lunch. We looked forward to Mom's hot and tasty meal awaiting us. My favorite was creamed beef on toast, a chunk of iceberg lettuce smothered with Mom's homemade mayonnaise, a glass of milk, and warm chocolate pudding. She made the pudding in a double boiler. The rich smell of chocolate was mouth watering as we rushed through the door, shook off our scarves, hats, mittens, boots and coats, making a pile of them on the floor in the foyer. Clambering over it, we rushed to the kitchen, and shouted in chorus, "What's for lunch, Mom, what's for lunch?"

Short, chunky Miss Bell covered her thick body with dark colored print rayon dresses which terminated just below her calves and revealed slender ankles, the uneven hem hovering over her practical low heeled, black, lace-up shoes. She cheerfully taught us how to read, sounding out each syllable, always with a smile on her face. Graying, fuzzy hair stuck out from her head like a bird's nest, and her small eyes sparkled behind her little, round lenses. We all knew she loved us; her kind face told us so. We never caused her any trouble. If she bent over you to check your work, a faint smell of lavender wafted down.

Having done our time in the half-basement and its movable chairs, we now were in a room full of stationary desks. Our chairs were joined to the desk of the person who sat behind us. All of the desks in the school were like that, even the ones in the assembly room on the top floor where the big kids sat. All the rooms from grades one through five were identical except for some extras the teacher brought in—a bookcase or table—and placed near her. The tall wall of windows was on our left, and the coat closet was in the rear of the room. As we went along from grade to grade, everything was familiar, nothing different or distressing.

Recess was a favorite time for most of us. Even in cold weather the class went outdoors. Miss Bell saw to it that we found our hats, mittens, and galoshes, then helped us button up our coats. Out we'd march to play, two by two. Pristine snow covering the playground was what we hoped for. I thought it was an adventure to mark out a huge circle with cross walks, and then stamp down the snow in the center for Home. This was the preparation for a game of Run, Goose, Run. After fifteen minutes, all rosy cheeked and full of fresh air, back inside Miss Bell marched us. We were ready for another lesson in phonics, writing, or arithmetic.

In spring and fall, before classes started in the morning and at noon, our group games of Drop the Handkerchief, or London Bridge always made me feel I was at a birthday party. Some of us girls polished our skill in jumping rope, or we raced around in a game of tag. One day a racer took a short cut through the swings and got bonked on her head. A school lecture followed.

If a wise teacher sensed her class was not paying attention, (all of our teachers in grade school were women) she'd ask for a volunteer to open the windows. A wild flailing of arms erupted as the competition to be the one chosen brought everyone to attention. It took skill to put the hook into the little metal nook at the top of the window, for the top of the windows were more than half way up to the ceiling, and the pole was long. How I wanted to be chosen for that job; but I never was.

School policy insisted we get fresh air at mid—morning and mid—afternoon. If weather didn't permit us to go outdoors, we raised the windows and then stood by our seats. To Miss Bell's measured clap, we raised and lowered our arms, taking in deep breaths to a count of eight.

Seldom did we sit and talk during recess. Most of us preferred active games. In later years, during Physical Education class, we organized into teams, softball being our favorite. Often I was chosen to be captain, and it made me proud. I decided I was chosen because I knew how to hit the ball well. One day, as I was tearing into home plate, the next hitter made a practice swing with her bat and hit me in the solar plexus. Down I went, couldn't breath, struggled—learned what it was like to die. Slowly, slowly my middle relaxed, and I came to life again for the good of the world.

In winter we filed to the gym in the standard double lines for calisthenics to strengthen our bodies, we were told, and to improve our balance. Here we had running contests. I was surprised to discover I was the fastest runner of all the boys and girls, so I took great pleasure in the races.

Every morning after we got settled at our desks, certain kids in our first grade class picked up a carton of milk from a box set on a table at the front of the room. Mom told me that those children weren't lucky like I was—to be sent to school with a good breakfast in my stomach. But I wanted to be one of those chosen few.

Mom inquired. One day she gave me a nickel. I gave it to the teacher who allowed me to join the line of special classmates and have a half pint of milk. But I felt conspicuous not really needing the milk. However, my curiosity was satisfied. Once was enough. Later I learned from Harold that Mr. Pellet, our neighborhood farmer, gave the milk to Jackson School kids during the Depression and wouldn't accept any payment.

Mrs. Bell taught me to read, and that was a good thing, for reading was about the only quiet thing I ever did. We sounded out the syllables in a method called phonics. That was fine for me. I found learning to read easy and fun. Socializing with the kids in the class was the other joy for me in first grade.

At times my usual restlessness would subside, and I'd fall into a staring, quiet fantasy world. This I associate with having my periodic haircuts. Mom would take me to the Preston brother's downtown Barber Shop. Outside was a Barber Pole, Mom called it, which had red, white, and blue stripes running diagonally up and down. It turned and turned, and you certainly couldn't miss seeing where the barbershop was. The long, narrow room inside contained five special chairs in front of huge mirrors, and behind the chairs and opposite the mirror were a coat rack, chairs to sit on while waiting, and a table covered with sports magazines.

I always sat in one of the two front chairs where either full faced, round nosed, solid Roy or his brother, thin faced, sharp nosed, skinny "Skeet" would put the kiddy seat in place resting on the arms of the grownup's chair. Then with a little help, I'd scramble up and look at myself in the mirror while being swathed in a great white cloth.

Rigidly I'd sit and stare into the mirror looking at myself while calm, blue-eyed Roy or fidgety dark-eyed Skeet snipped my hair in a nice, straight line across the back of my neck, evenly, to exactly under my ears. Last was the cutting of my bangs, straight across over my eyebrows. I didn't like that; bits of hair came tickling onto my face and eyelashes that were long like my Dad's.

This style, best for straight-haired kids, Mom said, was called the Dutch Bob. Sure enough: my picture book about the little Dutch Boy who put his finger in the dike showed his hair was cut like mine.

My sister and I had these haircuts for years. I liked the hum and buzz of the electric razor as it whisked off the hairs that grew far down on the back of my neck. When I returned to school, it was the stroking of this stubble that sent me off into dreamland. I loved to go over and over those sharp ends, a solace to my fingers, a general soporific. I'd be calmer for a few days until the hair grew softer and became uninteresting.

Our second grade teacher, whose name I can't recall, one day gave us our choice of colors from a pile of construction paper. After we'd drawn a flowerpot and the outline of a hyacinth, she showed us how to curl crepe paper. We cut it into quarter-inch strips and inch-and-a-half lengths. Holding a strip between thumb and a finger, we took our round-nose scissors and ran the cutting edge firmly along the strip. This produced lovely little curls.

My color choice was purple crepe on light lavender paper. I chose these colors because they were Mom's favorites, and this was our present for our mothers in celebration of Mother's Day. We put paste on one end of each curl and placed them close together within the outline of the hyacinth. For once I was so careful I managed to make a really pretty present for Mom without smears of paste in the wrong places.

We began to learn cursive writing in the last six weeks of our third grade in Jackson school. This made me sure I was on my way to being a grown up. Our desks had an inkwell, a small hole in the upper right hand corner into which would fit a bottle for ink. The hole was just beyond where the desktop was hinged enabling us to raise the top so we could store our books inside.

"Dorothy," I whispered to my neighborhood friend who sat next to me. "Look: ink bottles are in the inkwells!"

She nodded. Soon we'd learn to write with pen and ink.

On a sunny spring day Mrs. Margaret Linn announced, "This is the day to learn how to hold your pen and fill it with ink. It's been a surprise for me to watch how hard you've worked on penmanship lately. As a reward you'll now begin to learn how to use your pen for writing."

She went to her cabinet and brought out a tall thick bottle with a strange, short curved pipe coming out the center of its rubber stopper.

"Class, attention please," she announced, looking from under her gray bangs balanced by a short, stubby haircut. "Please get your pens from your desks while I come around and fill your ink bottles."

Up went our desk tops and out from among the papers, erasers, pencils, books, baseballs, and maybe apples, gum, candy, handkerchiefs, wadded up paper, or even a doll came the pens: down slammed the lids.

"Quietly, please. Now, look at your nibs, the point on the pen, and be sure it isn't broken. If it is, come to the desk, and I'll show you how to take out the old one and replace it. Bobby Britton, take the paper you'll find on my desk on the big blotter, and give one sheet to each of your classmates."

Soon we were settled. We began our first lesson. Now we would learn to write like big people wrote, "a sure sign I'm growing up," I thought to myself.

Although I never could write with much grace, I loved learning how to do it. I don't know how the left-handed kids managed, having to cross their left arm in front of themselves over to the ink bottle. Maybe they had to learn to write with their right hands and risk stammering or some other horrible fate, as rumor had it. Mrs. Linn was soon letting the careful students take turns at refilling our little bottles. I wasn't given a turn to pour the ink. I never found out why.

One day, as the chosen one came around with the big ink bottle, I took my little bottle from its well to check the level. Did I need a refill? I quickly brought it up to arms length against the light of the window to look through it. The half broken cork stopper flew up, the ink in the bottle flew out pouring onto my desk, then onto me drenching my favorite gingham dress, one with tiny orange flowers on a white background.

Dismayed, I was holding back tears when Mrs. Linn said, "Virginia, go straight home. I'll call ahead so your mother knows you're coming."

Down the steps I ran, straight up Locust Street hill, over on fourteenth to Chestnut, and home to La Vista Place. Mom was at the door. She took me right to the kitchen. There she pulled the dress over my head and dunked it into the dishpan of milk she had waiting. Miraculously the stains began to disappear, or at least I thought they did. Maybe she did something else to the stains, but they did come out.

"There, Virginia. Now wash the ink off yourself, then run to your room and put on something else. You can go back to school after lunch. The milk will take out the ink, and by tomorrow I'll have it all ready for you to wear again."

Knowing Mom was rescuing my favorite dress and that she was taking time to have it ready for me the next day returned my spirits to normal. It was a special favor. From then on, I never was in a hurry to check my ink supply. And even though I didn't understand it, I had experienced my first lesson in the magic of chemistry.

My dear, dear Mom. She knew how I loved that dress. She bought it at Sam Marshall's clothing store for ninety-eight cents. Every time it reappeared in my closet I chose to wear it. And dear, dear Mrs. Linn. She knew how hard clothes were to come by, how precious each school dress was. Missing a couple of hours of school was nothing compared to having a ruined dress.

The Parent Teacher Association hadn't presented itself to my mind, but I became aware of it when, at one of the assemblies in our gymnasium, my Mom was up on the stage talking to us. She had an office in the PTA, was on the board, or something. I was proud to see her up there, just like a teacher, talking. About what, I didn't register.

In the gym one day we were shown a moving picture about a giant steel mill. We saw the molten metal in the furnaces being poured from giant ladles into forms, (for I-beams we learned), which were refired, and then pulled, hot and glowing, red and orange (the teacher told us this, the picture was in black and white) by men through a groove which they straddled. All the men wore hard hats, and the place looked as if it might be very hot and very dangerous. Steel wasn't anything we met up with in our lives, living in the midst of farm land, so it made a deep impression. It was the only movie we were shown at school.

One of my teachers was Miss Alma Beckwith. She was dark skinned and thin boned with a deep parenthesis enclosing the slight smile always present under her narrow, rather long nose. She wore little wire-framed glasses. Her almost black hair was done up in a small tight bun and loose strands came straggling over her cheeks. I thought she must spend a lot of time at her desk for her shoulders hunched forward.

One morning she made an announcement to the kids who brought their lunches to school and ate together in the gym. I hadn't been aware that there was a lunch club meeting during the noon hour. I wanted to be included. I always wanted to try anything I hadn't done. Even though Mom told me that the children who ate in the gym either lived in the country or couldn't go home for lunch because no one was home to provide a meal for them, I insisted. I had to do it. So one day she gave me a sandwich in a bag. I sat with the kids in the gym, missed the usual pleasant walk home with my friends, missed Mom's good hot lunch, and missed the family noontime chat. Eating with the kids who lived on farms around town wasn't enough.

In fifth grade, an explosion in my sensibilities occurred on a marvelous day when a special teacher, who traveled from school to school, came to teach us something about music. The janitor trundled the school's Victrola into our room, so we were all curious and eager to know what the surprise would be.

The visiting teacher told us she would play special records she thought we'd enjoy. This got our attention. When she placed the needle on the record, we heard a woman's voice say the name of a musical instrument, and then we heard the instrument being played.

First were the stringed instruments. "This is the sound of the violin," the voice said; and we heard an ethereal sound one would never forget or mistake for any other instrument. The viola followed.

As the Victrola's voice took us through all the instruments, the special teacher showed us a picture of each one. Next were the mellow sounds of the cello, and the deeper voice of the bass viol. We were enchanted by the voice of angels—the harp. We learned that the piano was a stringed instrument.

Then the Victrola lady said, "These are the sounds of the woodwinds. They are played by blowing through a reed and pressing down keys against little holes."

As we heard each one, we saw pictures of the flute, piccolo, oboe, clarinet and bassoon. Then came the brasses, from the piercing trumpet to the bass tuba. The record ended with the clatter of the snare drum, the soothing silver-voiced chimes, the tinkley xylophone, and, finally, the resounding clash of the cymbals.

For once I paid absolute attention; I didn't notice when the music teacher left. From that day on, I was able to identify any instrument I heard. It was a revelation, and a great joy to me.

My fifth grade teacher, Mrs. Clara Ergenbright, and I didn't get along very well, that is, she got along, but I had my own destiny to fulfill. She was as tall as a great gray mountain, six feet or more it seemed to me, topped with coarse, rather wild, curly steel-gray hair.

In her class, it was my misfortune Marjorie Fouts sat behind me, or maybe it was her misfortune. Even though Marjorie was not a close friend of mine, one day she asked me to come home with her after school. That was nice, for her mother welcomed us with one cookie each. But Marjorie's idea of fun was to play the piano for me. I was invited to sit on the sofa and listen. After sitting and listening ten minutes or so, I decided it was more fun to walk on home and play outdoors with my neighborhood friends. I stayed for what I thought was a polite interval, thanked her, and excused myself. I admired her skill but didn't care to be like her. I was a member of the legion who took piano lessons but avoided practicing.

My seat was attached to Marjorie's desk. One day we were in the middle of our Palmer Method writing class. Making large ovals and putting diagonal lines through them wasn't what I was cut out to do in life. However, this day it was my turn to go to the blackboard to draw a cursive capitol D. I managed to draw it perfectly: a one-time event. I was elated. For some reason this success made me restless. I shifted around in my seat so much it disturbed Marjorie and Marjorie's desk.

"Sit still, Virginia," Marjorie whispered.

I responded with a jerk. Since I didn't hear another word from her, I made a violent, side-ways lunge.

Now came the order from behind: "Sit still!" in a louder whisper.

This time I jerked around several times, until Marjorie's desk was rocking.

"Virginia, I can't write when you do that! SIT STILL."

For pale-faced Marjorie, this effort was a major happening. I decided to honor it in the only way I could think of. I turned around in my seat and shook her desk, hard. Suddenly I felt myself shaking faster than I was shaking Marjorie's desk. I lost my grip. Someone was shaking me! Was my head going to fly off?

Finally, all shaking stopped. I turned around and met the stare of my tall-as-a-beanstalk, blue eyed, bespectacled fifth grade teacher, Mrs. Clara Ergenbright, her gray hair in great disorder, her mouth open a little, sagging, the lower jaw slanted showing her large discolored teeth, and her face aflame with anger and effort. Mesmerized by the fury in her face, I felt my face become as red and hot as hers.

Somehow I broke our gaze and looked down at my desk, intense shame overcoming me. I didn't say a word, nor did she. She didn't have to. Nor was any more punishment meted out. That was enough. I couldn't believe I had misbehaved like this, for my object was to be a model of decorum. Marjorie, as well as all my friends, and all my other classmates were kind enough never to mention the incident. Mrs. Ergenbright moved Marjorie to a front seat. I never did learn to write Palmer Method well.

Years later I was surprised to discover, upon coming across some report cards from these early years, my idea that I was a quiet, orderly school girl was absolutely wrong. I had been given Cs and Ds in Conduct.

In the space on the cards for comments I found my Mom's scraggly writing, little notes saying, "I'm sure Virginia's behavior will improve this next six weeks."

Now I ascribe my restlessness to boredom since I always completed my assignments quickly. But who knows.

By the time Valentine's Day rolled around, my conduct had improved, and I think Mrs. Ergenbright had either forgiven or forgotten me. I came trudging to school snug in my brown wool coat and blue stocking cap, bubbling with happiness because in my hand was a brown paper sack jammed with homemade valentines. The air was nippy, even though we were having a February thaw. I kept a tight hold on the sack with my mittened hand, thinking of the special one I'd made for Donald Baker, the boy who sat next to me—one of the kids who moved to Jackson from Grant School. He was my favorite, and the first boy I'd ever really noticed. Mrs. Ergenbright said the Valentine Box would be ready when we came back from lunch.

After school the day before, sister Cornie and I had gone to Woolworth's, carefully selected stickers of hearts and flowers, angels and cherubs, and sayings asking and telling: "Be My Valentine," "I Love You," "Will you be mine?" We found a pack of red and white construction paper, and had to make a mad search for envelopes and paper doilies. We hoped the laciness of doilies would make the valentines look store-bought. We planned this fun for a long time and saved our five cent a week allowances. Mom reminded us to be sure to give one to each classmate.

That night after doing the supper dishes, we brought our sack of Woolworth purchases to the dining room table, spread newspapers on it and laboriously cut out hearts from the construction paper, and matching hearts from the doilies. I went to Mom's funny, huge pull-out-and-down door that hooked to the cabinet at the floor. It contained a fifty-pound sack of flour into which I stuck my hand and filled a cereal bowl with the soft, soothing white stuff. I then let a little water gently flow into the flour and stirred it to make a just-right paste.

Cornie had cut and folded little red tabs to elevate the doily hearts over the red and white hearts. While we were assembling, I got paste on my fingers and inappropriate places on the valentines—smearing too much on the little tabs, and dribbling on the hearts. I was gratified to see that the doilies camouflaged my messiness.

While we waited for the paste to dry, we sorted out the stickers. For most of my classmates I selected "Be My Valentine". "I'm thinking of you, Valentine" was for special friends. On Donald's I put "I Love You".

I thought about Donald a lot. I could watch him all day long because, luckily, Mrs. Ergenbright had put me in the second-to-last row of seats across from him, or rather, he was put beside me when he first came to our class. I couldn't figure out what made me feel good when I looked at him because we never played together, so I didn't know him very well. But I liked the way he looked—calmly sitting up so straight, neat in a well-pressed clean shirt, straight blondish hair, carefully combed; and he had muscular arms. I didn't even know where he lived. At school we were always in class or on separate playgrounds. We did trade pencils, though, and I gave him paper if he ran out. As I wrote his name on his special, neat valentine, I wondered if he'd give me one. I longed for a frilly heart-shaped valentine with an "I love you" sticker on it. I put his in the first of the twenty-eight envelopes. In my head I went over the rows of desks in Mrs. Ergenbright's room and wrote a classmate's name on each.

At noon I ran all the way home. Usually it took an hour to get there, have lunch, and return to school. This day Mom had my favorite creamed chipped beef on toast waiting for me. I gobbled it up, rushed out the door, and got back fifteen minutes early. Almost everyone came early from lunch to see the Valentine Box.

I ran up the stairs, which was forbidden, and walked to our room. There, as Mrs. Ergenbright had promised, was the Valentine Box. It sat on a small table near her desk—pristine white with brilliant red trim. A train of flying red cupids armed with bows and arrows chased each other around the top edge. Big red hearts crowded the bottom corners. The box top was a huge valentine with red candy hearts saying "I Love You" glued to the box-top edges and the large slot into which we were to drop our valentines.

"Oh, Mrs. Ergenbright, your Valentine Box is beautiful!" I told her. My classmates, Armelda Welch, with pursed lips, and Lucille Getz, her curly, mahogany hair bouncing with excitement were standing beside me.

"Should we put our valentines in now?" I asked.

She smiled at me, and said, "Yes, Virginia. All you girls, Armelda, Lucille, and everyone else," she announced to the room, "may bring your valentines to the box now."

As we walked to our desks, Armelda, now smiling, but wistful, shaking her blonde, frizzy hair and I, as usual, noticing her perpetually scaly skin, wondering why mine wasn't like hers, put her hand on my arm and said, "Oh, Virginia, I hope Bobby remembers me."

"Oh, who cares what boys do," I answered and flounced to the back of the room.

But I did care. I was longing for Donald to give me a pretty valentine. Thinking of him always quieted me. When he looked at me with his brown eyes and his engaging smile, he pierced my heart. I'd forget where I was, and I often got called down by Mrs. Ergenbright for staring at his lovely hands. Of course she didn't know what I was staring at. She never separated us from our close-together seats.

Would Donald give me what I longed for: a valentine, saying, "I Love You?"

As we were wiping our hands and mouths after being served frosted heart shaped cookies using valentine napkins for plates, Mrs. Ergenbright said,

"Marjorie, come here please. You will remove the valentines one at a time, and all of you sitting in the first seat of each row—Bobby, Jeannie, Mary, Frances, and Charles—if the name Marjorie calls out is a person sitting in your row, come get the valentine and deliver it."

I grumbled to myself about never being the one chosen to do the fun things. I was never rewarded for good behavior by being seated in the first row. But I really didn't mind sitting second from the last seat in the middle row. I could twist my legs around my desk's legs, and Mrs. Ergenbright couldn't see. This was a much more comfortable position than the requested legs-together-shoes-on-the-floor. I didn't mind sitting with clasped hands resting on my desk, as required between activities, if I could remember to do so. Besides, with Donald sitting across the aisle from me, I had a true unknown-to-teacher reward.

The distribution began; names were called; valentines were delivered. I gave a sideways glance at Donald wondering if I could hope. He wasn't looking at me.

Marjorie hurried along calling out, "Arnold, Phyllis, Dagny...."

Paper crackled as envelopes were opened and dropped to the floor. Girls smiled at their friends. A few had enormous piles, some small. The litter on the floor grew.

For me there was one from Armelda, Lucille, Peggy, Dorothy, Bobby, Billy and others. That was very nice. But wasn't there one from Donald? Marjorie called out the last three names. My name was one of them! Would this valentine be from Donald?

Bobby brought it to me. The envelope was big and tan, not white like all the rest. It didn't look like a valentine. I hesitated, wondering. Then I tore open the envelope and pulled out—a piece of folded, yellow paper. I peeked, lifting an edge, and could see it was a picture. Unfolding it, I pressed it flat on my desk. Yes, a picture—of a redheaded, buxom lady with few clothes on, and she was riding side saddle on a runaway, snarling tiger, her arms thrown high, her yellow scarf trailing in the air behind her.

The words said, "Be My Lady Tiger Valentine." It wasn't signed.

Immediately I turned and looked at Donald. He was talking to the boy who sat on the other side of him. I knew it had to be from Donald. A quiet fury boiled in me. I made up my mind never to mention it.

"Boys are awful," I decided.

I looked through my valentines that to me signified being loved, and tried to forget my disappointment in not getting a romantic one from Donald. The messengers collected the debris in wastebaskets. Order reigned once more. Everyone was reexamining valentines.

Again I looked at Donald. Now he was looking at me—smiling his radiant smile, his brown eyes gleaming: he put out his handsomely formed hand.

I happily put mine in his, and together, eyes locked, we both smiled as our arms began to swing and swing in a lengthening arc between us—higher, higher, and higher until our arms drew a long half-circle between us. We didn't notice when Mrs. Ergenbright asked the class to get out our grammar books.

Our pendulum strokes cleaved the air. Both of us were oblivious to the snickers of our friends and the stare of Mrs. Ergenbright.

Finally she called to us saying, "Are you with us, Virginia, Donald?"

10

Each summer, until I was ten, on the first day of August Dad drove Mom, Cornie, me and sometimes Harold for six or so hours straight from Atlantic to Iowa City, left us with Grandpa Prentiss, then turned around and drove straight home again. At month's end he came back to pick us up.

For our trip there, Mom prepared a huge lunch to be eaten during the drive. While she finished cleaning up the breakfast dishes, we kids toted out the luggage, and Dad packed it into the car.

When we saw the first farm, Harold, Cornie, and I began our repertory of car games. A favorite was counting anything white: chickens got one point; a cow, five; a horse, ten. But spotting a man with a white beard—that was a winner—he counted twenty points. Whoever scored a hundred points first won the game. Sometimes, simultaneously we played "Alphabet". We searched all the signs along the roads and in the towns looking for letters to string them together in alphabetical order. X and Z were the test.

All games were interrupted to sing out the Burma Shave signs posted along the road; signs like, "Don't pass a car/On top of a hill/If the cops don't catch you/The undertaker will/Burma Shave." Hope was high that we'd find a new one.

By ten o'clock Dad would say, "I'm hungry. I think I'd like a sandwich."

Whenever there was food about, Dad couldn't resist eating; so none of us resisted either. Mom gave him his choice, and then we all dug in. In a blink, the lunch basket was empty.

When we were coming up on Waukee we were sure Dad would buy us Coney Islands, but no one dared to ask or even mention the possibility. Coney Islands were extra long hot dogs covered with a spicy hot sauce. At home we never used hot sauce. Dad told us, "It spoils the taste of good meat." So Coney Islands were a treat, especially when tempered with Hires Root Beer.

Of course he stopped at the wooden stand with its wide CONEY ISLANDS sign spread across the roof. I suspected the real reason Dad began lunch at ten o'clock was that he loved Coney Islands too. He wanted to be sure he was hungry enough to enjoy one by the time we got to Waukee.

We had several other stops along the roadside to "relieve ourselves," Mom's words for urinating. Often it *was* a real relief because Dad wanted to be sure we weren't just bored; so we had to be persistent in requesting a stop. The gas stations provided hideous, smelly toilet rooms in those days, so our meticulous Dad avoided them. Constant outdoor picnic training proved worthy: we girls squatted, sheltered beside the car's open door, while Harold turned his back to us and aimed toward the corn fields. We didn't flinch when a car passed by.

The wailing whistle of a train stopped all our games and arguments. When we spotted one coming from behind us, we kids immediately filled the window with our waving hands. As the engine gained on us, the engineer and fireman would wave back and sometimes tooahooooo—tooahoooo their whistle for us. This competition with the train caused Dad to speed faster as a great race driver should.

Eventually, in late afternoon, we arrived in Iowa City where Grandpa's housekeeper, Googie, had dinner ready for us. Dad turned the car around and drove back home.

I loved this punctuation of my summer, this peaceful month of swimming, of reading, and being with relatives. It was the only vacation trip we kids ever had.

During the hottest August days, or on the days when pouring rain interfered with our outdoor games, all of us would to Papa would cluster around the long mahogany refectory table in the upstairs parlor.

The table had fat carved legs and stretchers that ran the length of the table near the floor. They were exactly the right height to put your feet on. I loved this table. It sat at the end of the room, far from the windows that looked over the long front lawn running down to the Iowa River. This was where we drew crayon or pencil pictures during these stay-inside days while waiting for the grownups to join us for to-the-death competition in card games. This was a serious gambling enterprise—the prize being wooden matches.

Lining up on either side of the table, competing relentlessly, we played all kinds of games; our favorites were Hearts, Rummy, or Black Jack. Eight of us could sit there comfortably. The table was wide enough to easily hold all the cards, and narrow enough so that, with luck, one might peek into an opponent's hand. This was frowned upon.

In the summer of 1928, Aunt Lil came from New York bringing her newborn daughter, Cornelia Mary (another Cornelia), and Aunt Biddy arrived from St. Louis bringing her fourteen-month-old son, Prentiss, so that each could meet their Grandfather. Altogether, seven of us were at the table this special summer: Mom and her sisters, Biddy and Lil; my brother Harold, sister Cornie, and I; and Elsie Earle, Grandpa's cousin who lived in New York City.

For the three sisters it was a reunion; they hadn't been together since Lil and Biddy's weddings. The babies were new to everyone. Grandpa Prentiss was delighted; often he hurried home early from work. That August he smiled more than in all the summers I could remember.

On one blistering hot afternoon as we gathered around the refectory table, I was sent to the kitchen to get the matchbox. In Atlantic, we kids used Dad's chips for our gambling. He loved to play poker, and played often. But the lack of poker chips in Grandpa's house didn't reduce our enthusiasm for winning. I played with avarice and tried my best to win: but seldom did. Usually the last game played was Old Maid "so the younger children will have a chance to win," Aunt Biddy said. Much to my disgust, after never winning at the more important games, I ended up with that Old Maid in my hand.

In the cooler mornings we had swimming lessons, then ran errands for Googie and ourselves. Once on the way to the grocery store, I saw an unfamiliar word on a truck. UNIQUE CLEANERS was in big printed letters. Having been taught to read phonetically and loving new words, I immediately sang out "ee-yoo nih kee-oo." Cornie, in her infinite wisdom of being two years ahead of me in school, laughed, and corrected me. I didn't care—much. I learned from that incident that 'fooler' words existed.

One terribly hot afternoon, one so humid we could hardly breathe, Aunt Biddy told me that Iowa's humidity was necessary for the corn to grow properly; and since corn was the basis of our economy, we had to put up with it. On this boiling too-hot-for-cards day, Cornie and I were sitting in our underpants in the upstairs parlor with Mom, Biddy and Lil. Three rotating fans were trained on the sisters, and Cornie and I sat on the floor in the breeze. They were puffing away, filling the room with smoke from their Camel cigarettes. Grandpa didn't know they smoked, they thought. He was a bad example. He chain-smoked. His nicotine stains ran from his nasty yellow fingers up to his elbow. I often watched him smoking, watched to see if he'd light the cigarette he had ready in his free hand before burning his fingers on the butt smoldering in the other.

My aunts and Mom were sitting around undressed too. We were just there, doing nothing. I was listening to the adult talk. I found out a lot about the family that way.

Aunt Lil was poorer than we were. Here she was, sitting in the old Boston rocker with her first born, naked except for underpants, nursing Cornelia Mary while balancing her on her right arm and propped up by ample thighs. Lil's crown of curly red hair, fuzzed by the humidity, stood out like a halo. The talk was slow. Biddy reclined on the day bed, similarly naked, her dark hair in a chic bob, her blue eyes glowing. Mom, sitting in another chair, also undressed except for underpants, had her long, wavy red hair tied in a knot pinned high at the back of her head. Smoking seemed to be the only thing to do.

Aunt Biddy said, "Renoir would have loved to have us for models," making light of their heavy thighs and ample breasts which were not in style.

Sweat was running down between the women's breasts, pendulous from wearing tight bands, hoping to create for themselves a masculine figure in the fashion of the twenties. Biddy's baby, was napping.

Mostly Cornie and I watched Lil nurse the baby. Infant Cornelia Mary seemed content, sucking away. Lil's cigarette dangled from her lips; and she occasionally puffed on it, not removing it from her mouth, squinting as the smoke drifted into her close-set green eyes, eyes just like Grandma Lue's, Mom told me.

The fans rotated back and forth, back and forth, back and forth. Lil's ash grew ominously long, extending over her breast and the babe's face. She rocked casually, her eyes on Cornelia Mary, all other eyes in the room on Lil's cigarette; the ash grew longer, longer—while Lil, languidly puffing, let smoke drift out through her nostrils, while she rolled the shortening cigarette somewhat in her mouth. The ash seemed as long as the cigarette had been. The three fans turned right, then left, right-left, right-left. Silence reigned except for the baby's sucking.

Just when I was sure the ash would fall on baby's cheek, Aunt Lil removed the cigarette from her mouth and tapped the ash into a tray. A quiet sigh went through the room.

"Hello, are you in the parlor?" Papa called up the stairwell, surprising us. It was mid-afternoon; he was home very early.

"Yes, we are, Papa," answered Biddy.

Hearing his first slow step on the stairs, up the sisters sprang, tamping out the cigarettes, grabbing their robes, struggling into armholes—then buttoning buttons or tying ties. During this scramble, except for Lil who was tussling with her robe and the baby, we frantically swished the smoky air around, for whatever good that would do.

"Here! Dump the ash trays—here!" Biddy ordered. "Here" was a red metal wastebasket. Quickly she unlatched the window screen and put the basket out of sight on the flat porch roof.

Papa entered. "It was too hot in the laboratory to work there any longer, so I decided to come home and putter around in the yard until dinner."

They all nodded and smiled, by some miracle looking casual and relaxed. The moment he left, Biddy reached outside for the basket. It was on fire! It was scorching the newly painted roof! She wadded up a newspaper, and by scrubbing it around in the basket, she managed to smother the flames.

The next day, while Papa was at work, the sisters arranged for the painter, sworn to secrecy, to repair the scorched roof. To pay for the repair, they all chipped in.

It was a vacation as well as a reunion for the three sisters. My Mom, Cornelia, had a household of five to care for. My Aunts, Lil and Biddy, both worked as teachers and kept house. Lil's husband, Frank, contributed what he could with his painting while Lil taught Art. Biddy's mother-in-law, Lil Childs, lived with Mark and Biddy and tended little Prentiss while his mother and father worked. Biddy taught French in a private girls' school. Mark was a reporter for the *St. Louis Post Dispatch.* In those days money was scarce for these three families; but if they talked about it, I must have been asleep. It was only through Mom's primal urge to share everything that went on in her head that I eventually learned about Lil's life.

Her husband, Frank Schwarz, was an excellent portraitist, but his unusual personality got in his way. He often offended his clients before a commissioned portrait was finished. The client walked away without paying. Lil taught at the College of Industrial Arts for Women in Denton, Texas, before her marriage, and later at Hunter College, the Horace Mann School in New York, and in Tarrytown, New York. Her artistic talent enabled her to secure good commissions along the way, one of which was a screen for Mr. Philip Roosevelt of Oyster Bay, Long Island, New York. Later, both Lil and Frank received commissions from the Public Works Administration during the Great Depression. Frank's murals in Oregon's State Capitol are still there.

It was Aunt Nettie who generally looked out for them and everyone else in the family who needed a little money from time to time. She was secure in her teaching position at Hunter College. This month, however, the sisters were safe in their father's home, and enjoying a good time together.

Bob, now nineteen years old, on vacation from Hamilton College, worked for the university shoveling sand and making bricks for the new hospital being built not too far from Grandpa's home. I watched his small body, naked from the waist up, sweating in the hot sun, helping to construct buildings in which he soon began studying medicine.

Now seven, I'd been visiting Grandpa since I was two years old; Grandpa's face was etched in my mind. He had what I thought of as a rosebud mouth, small and bowed. I noticed Uncle Bob had one just like it, along with the same cleft chin. Both were small. Uncle Bob's resemblance to his Papa was uncanny.

Grandpa's face differed only in the mustache he wore. Mom told me that when the family moved to Iowa, one morning Papa came to breakfast—with NO mustache!

"Where is your mustache?" asked Lue'.

"I shaved it off," Papa answered.

"Grow it back immediately. Your mouth is too weak without it."

He did.

Mom told me that Grandpa had helped convince the Rockefeller Foundation to give Iowa part of the money needed to build the new State University of Iowa hospital. The new laboratories and Medical Building, built on the same side of the river as his home, had opened the summer before; now Grandpa didn't have to walk so far to his work. The new Medical Building was dedicated that summer, in 1928, before we arrived in August.

When I went down the driveway past the line of apple trees on my way to watch Uncle Bob work, I would pick a shiny green apple. Eating green apples, I had been told, would make you sick. So I experimented by eating one, and relished the sour taste. I didn't get sick. It was here in the yard by the apple trees that Uncle Bob would challenge us to a game of croquet after our Sunday dinners. I thought he was mean, for he'd bang my ball as far away from the course as he could whenever his ball hit mine. But he did this to everyone. He almost always won. Sometimes Grandpa did.

On the other side of the croquet yard, separated by mature shrubs were the cutting and vegetable gardens Grandma Lue' had developed. Now Grandpa kept them up, sternly forbidding us children to enter there. I peeked once: the vegetable part was orderly; but the flowers were rank, loose and lovely—a surprising way to be, rather like the idea I had of Grandma Lue'. We didn't trespass.

But we did have full use of the rest of Grandpa's yard. Since he was at work all week and sometimes parts of Saturday, we children roared around as freely as if we were at home. Once, while tearing around the house, I stumbled over a hose, and my left elbow hit Papa's metal sprinkler. In a twinkling my arm swelled so much that by the time I was in the x-ray room at the Children's Hospital, a nurse—to remove my beloved new blue shirt—had to cut off the shirt's arm.

I was shepherded there by Grandpa and taken care of by his good friend and neighbor, Dr. Arthur Steindler, the orthopedic surgeon from Vienna, Austria. I cried more over the ruin of that shirt than from the pain, for I loved it, and new clothes were a rarity. But Dr. Steindler soothed me. Talking in his strong accent, he showed me the X—ray of my elbow.

"There, see, Vah-gin-yah? Here—a chip popped right off the end of the bone. Nothing serious."

I saw, and can still see it. He put my arm in a cast, and that was the end of swimming lessons for the summer.

Grandpa insisted that all of his grandchildren learn to swim since his home was on the Iowa River. All of Mom's brothers and sisters had been given lessons in Iowa City. Aunt Lil was an especially strong swimmer. Mom had learned while living in New York City. She told me Papa hired a man to teach her. Off he took her to a dock on the Hudson River, tied a rope under her arms and threw her in.

"I floundered around, kicking and splashing, not knowing what I was supposed to be doing. In the midst of my sputtering, I came eye to eye with a dead and swollen bulldog floating into me. I began swimming soon enough! I raced arm over arm to the dock steps. Eventually I became a strong swimmer."

Harold had learned in the Iowa River with a little instruction from Uncle Bob who took him out in his rowboat. This went well until one day a dead fish floated into his face. But Cornie and I were taken to the Big Dipper, the pretty egg-shaped pool at the Iowa City Park. Here handsome, tanned university boys taught us to float on our back and stomach, to swim the beginner's backstroke and crawl, and how to force air out of our noses under water.

I watched Aunt Lil dive off the low board one day, and she didn't come up until she was under the rope separating the shallow from the deep end. How could she hold her breath so long? I visited that pool many years later when I was a student at the University and discovered that from the diving board to the rope was only about fifteen feet. In my memory the pool was huge; but it was just a tiny dipping pool—not a Big Dipper—a misnomer.

Although I was well taught, I never really tried to swim until I was in my home pool in Atlantic. It was unusual for a town the size of Atlantic to build a pool in the early twenties. But my Grampa Shrauger and his friend, Ross Camblin, were the Water Commissioners, and they saw to it that the pool was built, feeling it was a necessity for children to have a pool for recreation during the hot Iowa summers.

During our 1928 August visit, Papa once more, after repeated annual requests, said to Mom, Lil, and Biddy, "Children, now I want you to get together, and divide the family antiques according to value."

"All of us," Mom told me, "had ignored this request in previous summers for we thought it a ghastly thing to do while Papa was living. But this time he added, 'If you do not do as I ask you, I'll add a note in my will for Alec (who was the man Papa brought from New York to embalm the medical school cadavers) to take an ax and smash everything.'

"This brought action," said Mom. "Threats from Papa were not idle. Cousin Elsie helped, and it was done. Biddy, our organizer, saw to the evaluation of everything, and we drew slips of paper from a hat to see who got what. We did a lot of trading to get what we really wanted. Papa never understood why we didn't want to get this job done. Now I see the wisdom of it; I have allocated everything through my will."

The next year, in 1929, when I was eight years old, Grandpa Prentiss had a stroke. He recovered and returned to his teaching aided by Bennett, one of his medical students, who lived in Grandpa's house, assisting him in bathing, shaving, and dressing. As Grandpa was now paralyzed on his left side, Bennett also drove him to and from the hospital, and pushed him to his classes in his wheelchair. I don't remember Bennett, but Mom told me she and her sisters were very fond of him. I think his first name was Andrew; they called him Benny.

After breakfast on the porch, I would watch Grandpa as he finished eating. His left arm was in a sling. He'd pour a white powder into a glass of water and then stir and stir, for the powder didn't dissolve easily. This medicine was for his stomach ulcer. Finally he'd put the spoon on his plate, then drink the mix down, tipping his head back to get every drop from the glass, always leaving a milky mustache clinging to his nicotine-stained mustache. I didn't feel so afraid of him after he had his stroke.

Grandpa found no trouble having only one hand to draw the anatomical structures for his students.

"In earlier days," Mom explained, "standing at his blackboard he simultaneously used his right and left hands in drawing pictures to illustrate points of anatomy. His students marveled at this ability. Luckily, being fully ambidextrous, his drawing ability was unimpaired."

Uncle Bob worked hard during the summers, and in his free time, Mom said, he had a wild time, learning the pleasures of whiskey and of women. Once he infuriated Papa by bringing home a friend who infected everyone in the house with crabs. During the winters he attended Hamilton College in Clinton, New York. He was the only Prentiss child who did not earn a bachelor's degree at the State University of Iowa.

Two of Dr. Henry James Prentiss's children married secretly, Cornelia, and Bob. Bob had returned to Iowa City after graduating from Hamilton and was in his first year in Iowa University's medical school. He told Mom he'd impregnated, then secretly married a beautiful young girl, Alice Pogemiller, and was terrified that Papa, if he found out, would withdraw his financial support. He then arranged with Papa's assistant to have the fetus—a boy—aborted.

Papa found out about the marriage, and always disapproving of any wedding not performed in church, they were 'properly' married again in a church in Anita, Iowa. They made their home in Bob's attic rooms.

In 1931, Bob and Alice were at home when Grandpa's fatal stroke took place, two years after his first. Dad drove us Shraugers to Iowa City for Grandpa Prentiss's funeral.

We arrived early for the service. Dad was directed to park in front of the church. He would be notified when it was time for us to go inside. I hung out the window staring at the dressed up people crowding into the neat, gabled, board and batten, green-painted Victorian-style Episcopalian church.

A young woman in black came rushing past the church; she turned down the walk leading to a back door. Then she disappeared. Being wise in the way of church services, I knew immediately that she was late, was a member of the choir, and had to hurry to put on her robe to be ready for the introit.

I thought, "Good thing Grandpa isn't here to direct the choir. He'd bawl her out for not being on time. But she can get away with it today because it's his funeral."

We were escorted to the front pew. I saw that over Grandpa's casket was spread a many-colored mountain of flowers. To me it looked like a blanket colored with all the bright crayons in my crayon box. I wondered if there really was a casket under all the blossoms. Tall baskets of lilies, irises and gladioli crowded across the sanctuary hiding every inch of the paneling I knew was there. The sodden, heavy perfume in the air meant someone was dead, and I found it hard to breathe. It was my first and last attending of a grandparent's funeral.

Afterwards we didn't go to Iowa City any more. Grandpa's ashes were buried in Tarrytown's Sleepy Hollow Cemetery in the Bradley plot beside Grandmother Lue' and their two sons, the infant David and Hank, and near Lue's mother and father, Cornelia Fitch and David Ogden Bradley.

Of course Mom helped with the closing of the house and the splitting up of the family furnishings. Among some of Lue's treasures in an old trunk, she found a book of poems in a handmade birch-bark cover.

She told me, "Your Grandfather Prentiss long ago had illustrated the poems and given the book as a gift to Lue', your Grandmother." She added, "This romantic side of my Papa toward my Mama I never saw."

PART II

11

Back in 1909, when Dad was fifteen and of high school age, Grampa Shrauger moved his family to Atlantic, Iowa. He built a fine house at 1112 Chestnut Street. In later years, Graham Wallace, his nephew, told me Grampa checked every oak plank built into the house, rejecting any which weren't perfect. His house cost him $14,000, a large amount in those days. Gramma Sadie busied herself with her new home set on top of a steep hill. Dad began his sixty-five years of living in this town.

It was business which prompted the move to Atlantic. Grampa and Mr. William Johnson became partners; Mr. N. B. Nelson, a banker, joined them as book-keeper. I think Grampa and his partners chose Atlantic for their headquarters and factory because the Rock Island Railroad came through there in 1909, and they had big plans. Mr. Nelson soon went back to banking.

"Lightening rods were what they manufactured at that time. They sold millions," Mom told me.

By 1913, Mr. H. S. Rattenberg had constructed the building I came to know, at fourth and Walnut Street, where they made all kinds of sheet metal products. Among them were advertising signs, ornamental flower brackets, and, when roads became paved, they made highway signs.

World War I brought them a contract with the United States Government, "an enterprise that almost threw them into bankruptcy," Mom said. "Payment for the army camp stoves arrived so late, SHRAUGER & JOHNSON almost went broke."

But eventually there were four large buildings in town carrying the name of SHRAUGER & JOHNSON. Window sash, and washing machines were manufactured in one of them.

A terrible fire broke out in the middle of the night on February 28, 1922, a year after I was born, and burned down the plant at fourth and Walnut Street, destroying all the records. But Grampa and his partner rebuilt and soon were manufacturing farm equipment. Among other items were seed sprouters ordered by the Chinese for sprouting alfalfa and bean seeds.

Only when Harold, Cornie, and I went to the State University of Iowa did we return to Iowa City. Now we settled into life in Atlantic, Dad working at Grampa Shrauger's factory.

Mom established a pattern that became hers for life. Using her enormous energy and inborn qualities, she wrote papers and book reviews to present to various organizations; read many books for herself; had parties for visitors and friends; cared for us kids and Dad while doing the ironing, cooking, and most of the cleaning. She played bridge and golf; served the church as organist and the Carnegie Library as a board member; called on the old and the sick; welcomed new people to Atlantic; participated in DAR and Browning Club activities; and often provided music for the town's two funeral homes.

On Monday nights, once a month, wives of Elks club members attended a dinner prepared by the men. On Thursday nights she led choir practice. Often a friend would call and "stir up a game" of evening bridge or pinochle. Saturday nights brought the card playing couples together for a covered-dish affair, the host couple furnishing the meat. Dinnertime was six o'clock. The men who were in retail businesses arrived, ate, and returned to their stores to work until closing; then they came back for bridge and poker games.

Of course I was too young to know about this, but as I hung around Mom all the time, and these dinners went on for years, I soon learned the routine of the grownups.

But I had my own routine. By the time I was three, sometimes an angel cared for me in these early years. He was more important to me than Mom and Dad's activities. The angel's name was Grampa. That was the way I said it. That's the way I spelled it. He was my Dad's father, Darius Edgar Shrauger, my Grandfather. He had no visible wings, just a shock of soft, white hair, kind blue eyes, and a flaccid belly. Not at all tall, at least not as an old man. That's how I see him in my inner eye. By the time I was fifteen, he was diabetic, in pain with sciatica, and used a cane.

However, in my early years, sometimes we were alone in his pleasant living room of the house he had built, sitting in his big leather chair in front of the solid oak mantel, flames leaping above the burning wood in the brick fireplace, I, on his knee, squashed into his big belly and looking through his white chin-hairs up into his blue eyes. He'd tell me about the house he grew up in.

"It was a log cabin with a dirt floor."

"No rugs?"

"No rugs. We had a wood stove. I was the official wood-chopper. And we didn't have any sugar either. Maybe that's why I like to eat lots of pie and cake now."

"What did you put on your pancakes, Grampa?"

"A barrel of molasses sat in a corner near the stove. Molasses is what we put on our pancakes."

"I don't know what molasses is. But I think Mom has some in a bottle. Did your Daddy give you pennies?'

"No pennies either. No white sugar, no pennies."

Since pennies were the only coins I had, that was hard for me to believe.

"But if your Daddy didn't have pennies, how did he buy things?"

"We didn't use coins at all, Virginia. Everything brought into our cabin came from trading. We'd trade chickens for dried beans or eggs for a new mop. We grew most of our grub—that's the word we used for food—all our vegetables and fruit.

"My mother, your Great Gramma Shrauger, made our clothes. We grew broomcorn, and she made our brooms. When we'd have a good harvest, my Daddy, your Great Grampa Shrauger, would bring a little bag of white sugar home for a surprise. If we needed new tools for the farm, or cloth to make clothes, we'd trade a calf or a hog, or sometimes baby chicks or baby pigs for those things."

"Did you buy your bread at the store?

"No, dear, we grew corn and wheat in our fields, just like you see in the fields when we go for rides. This is how we got our bread. At harvest time we'd take our wheat and corn to the mill, and the miller would grind the grain into flour. We traded him some of the flour for milling grain. We called that barter and trade, and my Daddy would bargain to be sure we got an even trade. My Mama turned that load of flour into biscuits and bread, pancakes and cornbread and piecrust until the next year's harvest was ready."

Grampa was a hard worker. Mom told me he was out on his own by the time he was seventeen, selling hand plows to farmers. I learned that later he began to invent and design metal things used on farms, then manufacture and sell them.

Born in Parkville, Michigan, March 2, 1869, the son of Francis and Anna Shrauger, he was named Darius Edgar, but he was never called by either name. Everyone called him Dice. Our big dictionary told me the Darius mentioned in the Bible was a king. That made me proud because Grampa was a king in my eyes. When he was six he traveled with his family in a covered wagon, first to Brayton, Iowa, then to Exira, Iowa, where his father farmed and later started a factory. His father died early, and Grampa, in his twenties, took over the family business. I never heard what was made in that first factory.

But I know he owned a furniture store, and out of it he ran a funeral parlor. Why those two businesses were bonded in those days, I never learned. Grampa gave up funerals when a typhoid epidemic struck killing over a third of those who caught the disease. He had to bury many infants: "helpless tykes," he called them. Mom told me Grampa was too tender hearted to be in that business. I later learned that it was during this time he courted Sarah Nancy Hunter.

My Gramma, Sarah Nancy Hunter, was born on March 26, 1864, in Woodsfield, Ohio. She was the oldest of twelve children, but I knew only four of them. Gramma traveled to Iowa in a covered wagon with her parents and brothers and sisters. Her mother, tired from having babies Mom thought, died along the way. After spending time in several Iowa towns, Mr. Hunter and his children found their way to Audubon, Iowa, to stay with relatives named Graham until they got settled. But Gramma's father moved on to Oklahoma taking with him a new wife and a mule to the forty acres the government gave him because he was a Civil War Veteran. Who took care of his children I never learned, unless it was my Gramma.

She was always known as "Sadie". When Grampa got to know her, she was earning her living as a milliner. I don't know how he met her, but the little Iowa towns were not too far apart: maybe it was at a fair, or at church. Unfortunately, after they became engaged, Grampa fell ill with scarlet fever.

Sadie wasn't about to lose her husband-to-be. She moved in with his twice-married and twice-widowed mother whose last name now was Statzl. She and Mrs. Statzl were quarantined with Dice, as was the law in those days, to stop the spread of diseases for which there was no known prevention and no cure. The two women did everything his doctor could think of to reduce Dice's raging fever and bring him back to consciousness.

Finally the doctor said, "Pack him in ice, Mrs. Statzl. If anything will reduce the fever, that will."

With the doctor's help, they got Grampa into the bathtub and packed him in ice.

As Uncle Harlan, my Dad's brother—younger by ten years—told the story, "Mrs. Statzl called in another doctor. The two physicians stood over Dice arguing about how to treat the patient. Dice, unperceived by the two, was floating back to consciousness and heard them arguing.

"I think you'd better get him out of that ice and put him in hot packs," said doctor number two.

"Hell, no! That'd kill him"

"Well, you said he was going to die anyway, so what difference would it make?'"

But Grampa was already on his road to recovery. The disease cost him his hair, which grew back a beautiful snowy white. Sadie had risked infection to help bring him back to health. But what attraction she had for him, I could never understand. She was preachy, nosey, and not nice to my Mom, for which I never forgave her. But she was always kind to me.

Grampa and Gramma married in 1892, and my Dad was born December 6, 1894. Sadie adored her first-born son, Harold Frances, born December 6, 1894, who was named after his Grandfather Shrauger. There is a picture of my one-year-old Dad, sitting ramrod straight in his long white dress, staring boldly at the camera.

On the back of the picture Gramma had written, "Here is my darling baby boy. Don't you think his hands and feet are the cutest you most ever saw? Isn't he perfect? Isn't he darling? See his cunning tiny toes. There has never been a sweeter baby."

Having helped rear some of her eleven siblings, she being the oldest, she recognized and was pleased with baby Harold's easy disposition.

Little Harold was a rambunctious toddler often undoing the gate latch, thus escaping their fenced yard. In this way he showed his considerable mechanical abilities early.

Neighbors would see Sadie rushing down the streets calling, "Has anyone seen my boy?"

Not until Gramma died did Grampa know how old Sadie was. She kept it a secret. She didn't let him know she was five years older than he. But after her death, her papers revealed the facts. She was twenty-eight, and Grampa was twenty-three when they married.

Mom told me that an unmarried woman of that age in those days was considered an old maid. No wonder she kept it a secret. She must have thought marrying my Grampa was her last chance. I always thought of her as crusty, taciturn, and unsmiling, but I came to believe that Grampa saw her as loyal, industrious, and strong.

When Mom first moved to Atlantic as a bride, she played the organ at the Congregational Church. That meant we kids went to Sunday School there. Later Mom was hired by the First Presbyterian Church at Sixth and Chestnut; we kids moved with her.

"I love the ritual of the Episcopalian Church. The Presbyterian service, I think, is but a dilution of the Epicopalian. But since the Presbyterians broke off from the Episcopalians, it was the next the best thing as there's no Episcopalian church here in Atlantic. I'm happy with it," she told me.

I think she was glad to become a Presbyterian because the Congregational church was Grandma's church. By then it was unmistakably evident that Mom would never be forgiven by Sadie for marrying Dad; I learned that she criticized whatever Mom wore, wherever she went, and she didn't like any of Mom's friends. To detach herself from all this, Mom made every day as pleasant for herself as possible.

As a little girl I watched while Mom practiced the pieces she had selected for the morning service.

She played as much Bach as "I think wise—to bring the congregation along—but generally I play the old war horses. The varied diet keeps both me and the parishioners happy," she said.

When it was time for Sunday School to begin, off I'd scoot doing little but fooling around with sand in an elevated sandbox. When it was over, I dashed out to Grampa where he waited for me in his blue Buick. He had a special function in my life; he was my after-Sunday School baby sitter.

As I crawled up onto the seat beside him, I could see his big belly filling the space between the back of his seat and the steering wheel. I'd look up at him, and see him kissing me with his dear, blue eyes. I'd struggle to shut the door, then settle back, and off we'd go to survey the Sunday morning downtown emptiness.

Grandpa never was in a hurry like Dad. He leisurely pulled out into Chestnut Street beginning the six-block drive down to the railroad station. After we passed the Park Hotel on the corner of Sixth Street, I'd review all the signs on the stores familiar to me as we poked along between the row of businesses and the few cars parked slantwise into the center of the street or curbs. Not often was anyone out walking. I decided the people living in the apartments above the stores must still be in bed.

Grampa always parked in front of the red brick railway station which faced Chestnut Street. He explained the funny looking pipes and tubes we saw off to the right along the main tracks through which water was squirted into the water boxes of the steam engines; further away was a black chute which dumped coal into a train's hopper.

Grampa knew a lot of the people who used the trains for business: all his salesmen traveled that way. On summer evenings, we'd sometimes drive down to watch the passenger trains unloading. But Sunday mornings were quiet. We sat, and I counted red bricks on the Station wall until he decided to drive back up Chestnut Street to La Vista Place.

This was my cue to think hard and get him to stop at the dairy store. Mom said not to ask for goodies, but hinting wasn't forbidden. I always longed for 'white' ice cream. The dairy store was a block from the station. Hurrying, I'd rack my brains for hints.

"It's so hot today, Grampa, wouldn't ice cream make me cooler?"

He'd pretend not to hear me, so I'd turn to face him asking, "Grampa, what's something cool that would make us feel better on this hot day?"

He sometimes ignored me so completely, I worried. But he'd have his sweet smile on his wrinkled face as he rhythmically chewed his tobacco. Gently he'd coast to a stop at the dairy.

"I think I have a nickel. Do you think they'd take a nickel for an ice cream cone, Virginia? If I have a nickel you can see if they have ice cream for sale today."

I'd shoot my hand out, and wait. With great effort, scrunching up his hips, he struggled to get into his pants pocket hiding under his belly. I'd breathe a little faster in anticipation and witness his difficulty, but he never failed to find the nickel.

Out of the car I'd dash, get my white ice-cream cone, and happily consume it sitting back in the seat, licking around the edges as the ice cream melted, pushing the cold stuff down into the cone as the lump got smaller. Grampa seemed to enjoy this little game as much as I did. He always understood my hints. I'd glance at him between licks and see a big shut-mouth smile on his face, with brown rivulets of tobacco juice running down and staining the wrinkles in his chin.

We'd roll by the City Park, and Grampa would slowly come to a stop at the sign on Seventh Street, U.S. Highway Number Six. Seeing no travelers, he'd shift gears and go past eighth, ninth, and on past his and Gramma's yellow-painted house. At the intersection with La Vista Place was the first triangular flowerbed. We turned left there.

Grampa drove past my house on no-name Street lined with huge elm trees stretching up, up, and out—like overlapping green umbrellas. At the second flowerbed, at Jeck's house, he turned right, passing my friend's homes.

If Grampa wanted to, he could turn right at Pellet's and go down the narrow cinder and gravel road and rejoin Chestnut. But he never did. He always preferred to turn left, to pass Jane and Percy Chase's yellow house, and continue around the loop. Down a long slope off to our right, we could see huge fields—square and oblong plantings of long-leaved corn next to green meadows—stretching far out into the country. Finishing the loop we'd pull into the double driveway between the Allen's and my house. Then he'd entertain me as we sat and waited for Mom to come home.

Once he told me that when he was a boy, not much older than I, he shot a bear that came poking around his father's barn. He took me to my first movie. The scene I recall was of an old man and a small girl following a flock of geese. Now I wonder if Grampa thought of the actors as if they were us. And now I wonder if I would have seen so much of Grampa if Gramma had been nice to Mom. He filled a giant empty space in my life. I never refused his request for company.

My being the youngest child in our family meant that Mom dragged me around town when she went to "pay calls," as she said. In this way I went into many different houses. One Christmas we went to see Sadie Steffen's Christmas tree. As we walked into her living room, I saw the shape of a tree, but no green. The tree was entirely covered, every square inch of it, with round glass bulbs of different sizes and colors, gold and silver foil stars, tiny dolls, small squares, triangles, and boxes made of straw, miniature wooden animals, pretend houses, Christmas cards, red and green paper circles and chains, tinsel, necklaces, rings, trinkets—a solid mass of things. Myriad tiny light bulbs twinkled among them.

This was a new idea to me. I loved the look of the stabbing pine needles of our tree and of the sweet scent filling our living room. But I had to admit, Sadie's tree was a triumph of a different kind. My imagination learned to stretch a bit.

Sadie was the lady who, when church members were asked to bring potluck for a supper, always came with her special baked beans. Raves were heaped upon her, and she accepted them graciously. Everyone looked forward to Sadie's beans. After she was dead and buried (Mom's way of referring to the departed), her daughter, Jo, told me a secret about those beans. Sadie's husband, Joe, did all their cooking. Maybe Mom thought Joe made the beans. NO! Devious Sadie always commissioned an unidentified woman in Atlantic to prepare the pot of beans each time the need came up. She never told a soul, not even Mom, or maybe, especially not my Mom. Jo told me she and her mother had a lot of laughs over the years about that deception.

From Sadie's we went next door to visit a good Presbyterian member, who, Mom said, had poor bladder control, and needed to be called on.

"Virginia, you may smell urine; simply don't notice it. This is something our hostess has no control over. It is always wise to overlook disabilities." A lesson learned.

Mom, being trained to pay attention to all members of one's family, took me one day to call on Gramma Shrauger's sister, Lucinda Amelia Wallace. Such a pretty name I thought, as was Gramma's Sarah Nancy Shrauger. But unfortunately to my ear, Lucinda became Aunt Cinny, and Sarah became Sadie.

Aunt Cinny had married a veteran of the Civil War, a man seventeen years older than she. When we went into their little frame house, there sat old Mr. Wallace. His grandfather was born in 1797; his father was born in 1849; his son, Graham, my Dad's cousin, was born in 1908. Mom told me there weren't many men in Atlantic who could say, like Graham could, that he had a grandfather born in the eighteenth century.

Aunt Cinny lost all her hair, like Grampa, to a high fever, but hers grew back wispy so she wore an "unfortunate" wig, as Mom called it. I thought it looked like an old bird's nest falling apart. I supposed all wigs looked like this. She was very kind and very wrinkled and served us with some wonderful gooseberry pie.

One day Mom and I visited Mrs. Jess Jones, the "forbidden" doctor's wife, forbidden by Grandpa Prentiss because Dr. Jones wasn't a member of the American Medical Association for some mysterious reason. I wasn't told why, and I don't think Mom knew either.

Mrs. Jones was bedridden with rheumatoid arthritis. Her house was the biggest one I'd ever been in. To me it appeared to be big square rooms joined together. The outside was painted white, a huge frame house sheltered by many porches. Her bedroom was downstairs in a room off the large living room.

The maid brought chairs, and we sat down by Mrs. Jones's bed. She sat leaning back on a white satin pillow, the matching coverlet pulled up to her waist. A pearl necklace rested on her wrinkly neck, and several diamond rings decorated the unmoving fingers of both hands. Covering her arms and her nightie was an elegant pale pink silk bed jacket trimmed in lace.

Mom was very fond of Jess. She was a smart woman who read a lot, so they discussed books. One of Atlantic's beauty operators, Carmelita Quinn, whose shop was located on the first floor of Dr. Jones's hospital, and who would give me haircuts and permanent waves when I was older, came regularly. She kept Jess's hair in perfect order, and made up her face with mascara, rouge, lipstick and powder—as if she were going to a party. I had expected to see a pale invalid: but no, Carmelita's subtle rosy makeup for Mrs. Jones was perfect.

Her face was made almost immobile by her disease, and to me she looked like a pretty puppet that would move only if her strings were pulled. I was sure the real Jess was disembodied, out in space somewhere, talking through this puppet. I had never before thought we might be made of two separate parts.

To change position, she carefully lifted her almost immobile arms. Her hands hovered over the coverlet, stiff, rigid hands. They came to rest near her chest—then moved to her waist. The fingers somehow interlaced themselves a little, those long and crooked fingers tipped with the bright red polish Carmelita had painted on Jess's fingernails, matching her lipstick. Her hands didn't move again, but lay still on the silk coverlet while Mom talked with her. I felt sad that she had to be in bed all the time. I couldn't imagine how that would be. This was the first and last time I ever saw Mrs. Jones.

One hot summer day, when I was old enough to walk to town by myself, I went to Fourth and Walnut Streets to Grampa's sheet metal factory. Being the banker for my gang, I wanted to get some round metal punch-outs which my friends and I used for play-coins. As I passed the Clithero Laundry before I got to the factory, through the large, tilted glass windows I could see women ironing other people's laundry. Clithero's washed our clothes and returned them as 'Wet Wash,' damp and ready for Mom to iron. Mom let me iron the handkerchiefs when I was tall enough; we all owned a drawer full. We knew we'd get new ones in our Christmas stocking.

From the open windows, clouds of moisture flowed. As I passed by I felt the moist heat on my skin. It made the hot day seem hotter. I wondered how the women could iron all day in that steamy room. I'd left Mom ironing Dad's and Harold's shirts. She stood in her underwear, sweat pouring down between her breasts, her whole skin shiny with moisture. But these women couldn't undress like that. If I said anything about Mom's perspiring, she'd joke saying, "Horses sweat, men perspire, and women glow."

Dad, who was the factory foreman at the time, kept the large overhead entrance doors open to catch any passing breeze. I hurried into the noise flooding out of the factory door. Although my ears hurt, I went right to where Dad was, past men tending other machines. A long black belt wiggled around a flywheel attached to the ceiling, making the punch-out work. As soon as Dad saw me, he switched it off. Then the belt wriggled worse than ever, looking like a huge black snake. Would it fall on me?

When all motion stopped he asked, "What do you want, Virginia?" although he knew, and I knew he knew.

"Can I fill up my sack with punch-outs?"

He said yes. I scooped them up gingerly, for there were sharp points and edges.

My mission accomplished, I thanked him and went into the business office through the nearby heavy half-glass oak door. Ruth Marker, Grampa's book-keeper, sat on a stool at her high desk in the long, narrow room. She welcomed me with a smile. I could see Grampa and his partner, Mr. Johnson. They sat behind their desks looking out the wide plate glass window which separated their office from Ruth and the row of desks for salesmen lined up against the inside wall stretching to the front door. I learned along the way that the men were on the road selling the sprouters or barn bats that covered the cracks made by the drying, green-wood barn boards as they shrank. They also sold Grampa's Chief Cupolas and door latches for barns, and screens and storm sash that were installed from the inside of houses, so people wouldn't have to teeter around on ladders on the outside. Grampa held the original patents for the E—Z—UP windows and screens. Dad put them in our house. Later Mom told me that for some unknown reason, the patents weren't renewed when the due date came up; so other people profited from his invention instead of Grampa.

My brother Harold explained to me how Grampa made rotary, electric-powered Chicken-pickers for George Jeck, our neighbor, the manager of the Atlantic branch of Swift and Company. These pickers held the dead chickens by their legs as they went round and round in hot water while waiting their turn for a rubber banger to rotate them and remove their feathers. I wished I'd been taken to see that. I never saw any of the factories where Grampa's inventions were made. I visited only the building where Grampa and Dad worked. Harold knew about everything.

Grampa, melting into a smile, beckoned me to come in. After a struggle with the oak door, I went right up to him and curled up against his squishy belly as he hugged me to his side. He was so soft, and being with him always made me feel wonderful. I thought his big belly was friendly, but Mr. Johnson's wasn't.

Noticing my sack Grampa said, "I see you've been to the bank."

"Yup, and now I'd better go home. Mom said to come right back."

"I think you need an ice-cream cone to keep you cool on the long walk up Chestnut. What do you think?"

I never said no. He reared back in his springy office chair, got his hand down into his pocket under his belly, and after a tussle, brought out some coins.

"Here's your nickel."

I thanked him. He smiled at me and patted my head. I left through the front door glancing in the big glass window at samples of what Shrauger and Johnson sold. After I bought my ice-cream cone at Dick and Janie's, I walked up Chestnut Street, happy with my trip downtown.

12

My sister and I had the biggest of all our bedrooms. The ceiling was flat under the roof's peak, then followed the slanted rooflines to five-foot upright walls painted white. When the lamp was on at bedtime, dark and light shadows ran across the ceiling interrupted by all the angles which made oblongs, squares, and triangles in shades of gray. I'd stare at these shadows, amusing myself until Cornie got into her bed and turned off the lamp.

Each morning at eye level, while still in bed, we were treated to the cheery smiles on the larger-than-life-size faces of Ginger Rogers, Fred Astaire, Buddy Rogers, Nelson Eddy, and Jeannette McDonald. This room decoration happened as a result of our love for movies. We attended the Atlantic Theatre every Sunday afternoon. Cornie and I asked the manager if we could have the advertising posters of movie stars when he replaced them with others. To our delight, he said yes. We fastened our posters to the top of the five-foot upright wall. That was our solitary attempt at room decoration. Maybe it was lack of money, but Mom didn't seem interested in house decorating. I was content with the way things were.

Cornie and I slept in matching twin beds which came from the Grandpa Prentiss's house. Their mahogany bedposts were topped with carved pineapples, just like the big bed I admired in Grandpa's bedroom.

During the killing heat of the early nineteen thirties, day after day the thermometer read a hundred and ten or more. Our bedroom was so hot Cornie and I were allowed to drag our mattresses into the back yard for the night. On those roasting and humid nights, a sheet would do for a cover. Lost in the mass of stars covering the dark and cloudless sky, I'd drift off to sleep, comforted by the music of crickets, and eventually pulled the sheet over my head to defeat mosquitoes.

We never saw a dawn: about two in the morning, heavy dew would sink through the sheets waking us. Half asleep, we then dragged the mattresses back to the house and finished our sleep on the living room floor.

Balancing the heat of the summers, winters were frigid and presented us with a different problem. During the extreme and constant cold, news of our below-freezing temperatures reached our Great Aunt Nettie Prentiss through the *New York Times*. But she didn't know that frost seeped through our uninsulated walls and tried to get through our blankets. Hot air was supposed to come up to our room through a large grill, the end of a heat run: it never did. Dad said the run was too far from the furnace for the gravity heating system to warm our room.

But Cornie and I defeated the chill and got used to the cold. We made up a game of Bed First. It was a question of who had to turn out the light. For warmth, we first put on our nightclothes (mine a nightie, Cornie pajamas) and wool socks. Then we wrapped ourselves tight like mummies in a light cotton blanket, stumbled into bed between icy sheets, and ended the exercise by pulling up two, folded-over, double-length wool blankets under our chins—or in my case, up and around my head. We then jacked our feet up to our chests, shivering mightily until our body heat warmed our beds. Whoever lost the game by being the last into bed had to untangle an arm from the mummy wrap, and turn out the light.

I always laid out my next day's clothes before undressing. As soon as my alarm clock went off, out of bed I scrambled, grabbed my long underwear, lisle hose, undershirt, cotton dress, sweater, my brown lace-up shoes, and rushed around the L-shaped hall to the always-warm bathroom. Opening the door, I'd be greeted by heat bursting up from Dad's well-banked coal bed. There I dressed in complete comfort. I had my own alarm clock as Cornie did because on some days she got up long before me. I don't know how she coped with those ordinary icy mornings. My way of ignoring her was already developing. I wonder what it would have been like if we had been more congenial.

On either side of our bedroom, were low-ceilinged storage closets under the slanting roof. Cornie and I never played in them in winter because they were as cold as our bedroom, as cold as outdoors. But after the weather warmed in spring, and on rainy days in summer and fall, these small areas were fine play places. We never shared these private rooms with anyone.

In one closet Mom stored mementos of her school days in a great steamer trunk bound with steel straps. The lock was shaped like a keyhole; and it was a keyhole, but the key had been lost. Mom told me the trunk belonged to Great Grandmother Cornelia Fitch Bradley. She had taken it packed with the voluminous clothes worn before the turn of the century on her trip to Europe—just before she died.

The trunk was so large Cornie and I could have gotten into it. But we never did. Here were Mom's high school and college scrapbooks into which she had pasted party programs filled with the names of every dance partner. I learned that going dancing was a weekend activity of hers.

As I grew older, Cornie's and my forays into the steamer trunk taught me to see Mom as someone who had a previous life completely different from her life in

Atlantic. Shaping a vision of what she was like before marriage, I saw a person with a past that was romantic, charming, full of friends and fun. I wondered if, when I grew up, I might have such a life.

Grandmother Lue's exquisite wedding gown was stored in the trunk's bottom drawer. Both Lil and Biddy, Mom's sisters, were married in the dress; because Mom eloped, she missed that privilege. Since Cornie and I were the oldest cousins, it had been deposited in our attic waiting for our weddings. It was made of lined, heavy cream satin, the floor-length skirt hanging straight down in the front while the back of it flared in a graceful, short train; the bodice was of fine lace encrusted with seed pearls sewn over the satin. I thought the way the bodice came down to a point over the skirt was a special touch.

Downstairs in the guestroom Mom hung a picture of Grandma Prentiss wearing this wedding dress. Huge balloon sleeves, fashionable at the turn of the century, made her shoulders look enormous. She looked regal and happy. When they married, Lil and Biddy cut down the sleeves. The styles of the twenties had little to do with huge sleeves.

Cornie and I never took the dress out of the trunk, tried it on, or disturbed it in any way. We just looked at it as it lay in the bottom of the huge trunk. It was too precious. Knowing we were to wear it someday made me certain we were expected to marry. Cornie and I never talked about this.

In the storage space on the opposite side of the bedroom, under the slanting roof a few inches above our heads, Cornie and I set up our collections. The only light in the place was a bare light bulb beside the door. There we sat and cut hundreds of pictures of animals from Mom's many magazines and stacked them in piles, never doing anything with them. Our heads were so close to the roof, we frequently had rain-music accompaniment as we cut and chatted.

Some days we lit candle ends and turned them into a collection of wax hands. Mom always used candles on her table when she had company, so we had boxes full of stubs. We dripped the warm candle wax over our hands: first palms, backs, then thumb, and one finger at a time. We were patient and careful to cover all the skin in a thickness that held. We found that if we let the wax cool on our hand, the shell would loosen in as it cooled to lukewarm. Then we gently slid our hand free from the casing. We had a fine collection of them.

Later, when Cornie and I were in college, Mom hid her gold wedding ring in a dark corner of our private playroom. It was during a time when there was a rash of burglaries in Atlantic. We always left our front door unlocked until the last person came in for the night. I think her wedding ring was the most precious thing she owned. Her gold and diamond Starburst, designed by Great Grandmother Bradley and made by Cartier, was in the vault in the bank. But why didn't she hide her baroque pearl little-finger ring, or the green jade parrot ear-rings, or the gold bracelet with the large topaz surrounded with seed pearls—all of which also came to her through her mother, Lue' Prentiss, and her Grand-mother Bradley. It was the plain gold wedding ring she hid, and then forgot where she'd hidden it.

She later told me that when it came time to move, (Cornie and I were in col-lege) she searched and searched and finally thought to look in Cornie's and my old play place. Miraculously she found it where she had placed it—hung on an old nail in a dark corner. Eventually the ring became thin after many years of marriage. So when Dad finally had some money after World War II, he replaced it with a handsome gold ring set with five different gemstones.

Besides the beds, in Cornie's and my room there was one other elegant piece of furniture, a charming mahogany dressing table that had come to Mom from the Prentiss estate. Observing Lue's ordeal drying her long hair after the weekly washing of it, Grandpa Prentiss had given it to her so she could sit down to brush her hair dry, not stand by the fire. Because Cornie wasn't interested in the piece, it became a beloved prize for me.

In one large drawer, I kept my collection of perfume bottles: beautiful blue ones with the name Evening in Paris on them and less flashy ones named Chan-nel Number Five. They came from Mom as she used up the perfume Dad gave her every Christmas. I kept my collection of letters from Great Aunt Nettie and Aunt Biddy in the smaller drawer below; and in the two matching drawers were the flowers from my wedding dress which Mrs. Smoller made, and my junk jew-elry.

One Christmas, before the days of perfume presents, Dad gave Mom a hand-some knit suit. The next spring she wore it on a shopping trip downtown. As she walked along she saw a heavy woman reflected in the window of Bullock's Dry Goods Store; her outfit for the day was a purple knit suit.

"It was I," Mom told me. "I had seen myself in the slanted store window which was like a full length mirror. Having caught this glimpse of myself, I decided then and there to give the suit to our hired girl. I couldn't bear seeing myself looking so fat."

Mom often repeated this story, and always mourned the fact that in giving the suit away she had "mortally offended" Dad. From then on she learned her Christ-mas present from him would always be a small bottle of Channel Number 5 per-fume and a pretty nightie. No more surprises.

Our upstairs bathroom was at the top of the stairs. I never bothered Dad's medicine cabinet, but I saw into it now and then when he was treating one of my medical emergencies. It was stuffed full of his neatly arranged paraphernalia: razor and styptic pencil, creams and cologne, tooth brush and paste, brush and comb, Listerine, and various medicines including iodine. A razor strop hung on a hook beside the sink. This was his bathroom, but we kids used it too. Mom's toilet articles were in the downstairs bathroom. Except for the toilet articles, there was no clear assignment about the use of the two bathrooms.

A short door opposite the bathroom led into a small space with little headroom. It contained our Christmas decorations and a huge box of toilet paper. One summer day when I was quite little, my girl friends and I opened the door and entered this confined space. The big box of toilet paper rolls was on its side, almost empty. We crowded into the box and somehow got to sniffing each other's genitalia. Maybe it was suggested by the presence of toilet paper and the fact that we had all just used the bathroom. Perhaps we had run out of toilet paper, and I had gone to get another roll. However it came about, there we were rubbing our noses in other people's business and doing a little licking too. I pressed the face of one of my friends tight against my crotch and that felt good; but I didn't like the acrid taste when it was my turn. This was a one time thing.

Opposite this little door, was a bookcase. On its top Grandpa Prentiss's plaster of Paris bust kept company with Dad's dusty stuffed pheasant—an odd coupling.

From there on was—lining the hall—a row of storage cabinets which sat on the floor; they were topped by set-back bookcases. So here was a flat place to sit and read; Mom kept all the kid's books in the bookshelf above the first cabinet. Breezing by Grandpa's bust, I'd scramble up and settle down cross-legged for a long read.

First I'd choose my favorite book, Robert Louis Stevenson's *Garden of Verses*. I relished Christopher Robin, his boots, and his riding up in a swing so high. Then I'd puzzle over the Indian boy, *Little Black Sambo*, and how the tigers twirled and twirled until they melted into butter. I was intrigued by the uncut pages in Beatrix Potter's *Peter Rabbit*. As for Peter, I thought that if his buttons hadn't been so large, he certainly couldn't have been caught in Mr. McGregor's net. I cried over *Bambi*. And my favourite fairy story was about the *Princess and the Pea*, which made me decide I, too, was a Princess who accidentally got into this house in La Vista Place. I knew my Prince would come some day, and take me to my true home, my Castle.

But it was the nobility of the Dutch boy who saved the fields from being flooded by holding his finger in the dike's leak that gave me a goal to aim for in my behaviour. That remained a dream. And I felt sympathy for the hungry boy who spread his molasses around his plate by tipping it back and forth, fooling himself into thinking that by spreading it he had more. I'd never been that hungry and always knew dinner would be served soon.

Mom had placed on my reading counter the Mother's Day gift I gave her when I was in second grade, the construction-paper lilac. It welcomed me every time I climbed up there. I knew Mom loved me, because she never threw it away.

Mom and Dad's bedroom was off this hall. Once I went in to see the pigeons that roosted all summer in the eaves outside their window. I rattled the window and clapped my hands, but they ignored me.

After that total failure, I stood on tiptoe to see if Dad had left coins on his dresser, as was his habit. I shuffled the nickels and pennies around and was sorely tempted to take one or two. But so strong was my training to leave other people's belongings alone, I honoured the teaching. Or perhaps it was because I had proper respect for my Dad that I didn't follow where temptation led.

Being in their room, the idea came to me to ask if I could sleep in their bed. I imagined how warm it would be under their covers. Mom and Dad were going to Lake Okoboji with the Hopley's for the weekend, so I asked Mom for permission.

"Of course you may, Virginia. I'll tell Mabel to see that you get settled there for the night." Mabel was our live-in helper at the time.

At first I enjoyed a big stretch out, not being able to feel the sides of the bed with either foot. Then I began missing the cosiness of my smaller bed. So much space was too much space. Since my eyes wouldn't stay closed, I noticed ghost shadows lurking in Dad's closet. I'd left the closet light on and the door open a little; but these precautions didn't make me at all comfortable. I had terrible trouble getting to sleep—a first time happening. Pulling the sheet up over my face didn't dispel my fear. Finally, getting tired of twisting and turning, I burst out of bed, yanked the closet door wide open, and stared at the ghosts. Nothing greeted me but shadows of Dad's shirts hung between the night-light and the wall. I scrambled back to bed, proud of my bravery.

The glorious lulling of our pigeons awakened me at dawn with their muted soothing sounds. Every spring they returned to their summer home. I decided the pigeons' favoured the place because the sun's first rays rested there, waking and warming them. Dad got furious with their disturbing his sleep early each morning. So one day he brought his shotgun from the basement and would have blasted them if he could have figured a way to do so without breaking the windows or damaging the siding. So the pigeons won the battle. I never asked to sleep in my parents' bed again.

Harold's room was only as deep as the length of his bed. Because of the solid bank of southward facing windows it was always bright and cheerful. A bed, bookcase, small desk, and a chest made up the room's furnishings. One spring night when he was away, Mom allowed me to sleep in his bed. It was more of a cot, narrow and not as soft as mine. A dark fringed plaid wool blanket served as a bedspread. I enjoyed running the fringe through my teeth. It grated a bit, but felt rather nice. I think I loved this room so much because I loved my brother.

When the early light filtered in, announcing morning, I got up to see the world from Harold's windows. Was this Dad's vista? I saw no more in the distance than what I could see from our backyard. The yard was looking green and lovely. Heavy buds now made the stems of the peony border droop; Dad held them up with chicken wire circles. They'd bloom by the end of May. Overnight the Spirea bush had turned pure white, as if a sneaky snow had landed on it. And I could see spears of asparagus popping up, turning up tiny clods in their bed at the edge of the lawn.

I couldn't make out the gravel road which rimmed the meadow, but I could see a stretch of the road which led up and over the hills to the Atlantic Golf and Country Club.

By now the sun was filling the room with yellowish light, so I thought this would be a good time to look at Harold's chemistry set, a Christmas gift from Great Aunt Nettie. I lifted the heavy box from his toy shelf, quietly put it on the floor, and opened it. He had allowed me to watch him do experiments, so I decided it was safest to repeat what he had shown me.

I got out a long, slim, silver piece of phosphorus and matches. I lit the phosphorus. It burst into brilliant light which blinded me for a moment. That done, I experimented with a small piece of litmus paper. Colors changed! Hearing sounds of someone awakening, I put everything away as I had found it.

One winter night I had just gotten into bed when I heard the fire sirens coming closer and closer up Chestnut Street. Everyone else was downstairs listening to the radio.

Then I heard their excited voices in the living room saying, "It's the McDermott house!"

I sat up in bed. Then the front door slammed.

I rushed to Harold's room and threw up a window. Looking across the rear end of Mr. Smoller's garden, across Chestnut Street to the top of the hill, I could see flames and black smoke flying from Randy's roof straight up to the stars, twisting down and about, outlining the little house which was still whole. Weird sounds came all the way to the window, crackles and sighs, then crashes and explosions. Screaming sirens rushed ahead of the fire truck announcing to anyone in the neighborhood who didn't yet know of the fire that something was up. I saw the silhouettes of the firemen as they attached their hoses to the water hydrant, then saw steam billow above the flames piercing the night sky; our champion firemen quickly got the fire under control. I watched until the flames disappeared, and the smoke hunkered down. Little did I know that one day Mom and Dad would live in that house after it had been rebuilt.

One bitter cold and snowy New Year's Eve, I was alone in Harold's room. If anyone else was home, they didn't make their presence known. The full moon was brilliant in an empty sky, the stars invisible. Opening a window, I leaned out on the roof and saw it was lumpy with ice and frozen snow. Shingle patterns were thrown into relief by the intense light and looked like narrow white bricks. Plainly visible, our neighbors' roofs and the distant fields were crystalline with frost-covered snow. Our poplar trees were shrunken by the cold, and the bare boned boles and branches sparkled, were rigid, and looked like mantel decorations. The silence of the night was punctured by timid creaks and sharp cracks from tree branches.

In my hands I had a tin drum and drum sticks that I hope were mine. If not, too bad. For when Harold's clock said midnight, I rested the drum on the window sill and began to beat the drum, slowly—then accelerating—then beating fast, and faster—beating and beating, harder, and harder—sending crashing sounds forever and forever out into the frigid night—beating until the rims of the drum broke away, the sides fell apart, and it wasn't a drum anymore. I was enthralled by my exertion and the sound of the metal clashing against the quiet of the night.

On and on the sound of the wood on the tin rang in my ears, and I stayed there, bathing in the silken moonlight, drinking in the cold air—until my heart and my ears quieted—until I became aware of the metal of the broken drum chilling my hands—until the icy cold moved up under my nightshirt sleeves. Then I put the window down and went to my bed.

After Dad stopped the family holiday meals, the former dining room became the music room and home to Mom's long awaited, new, Voss mid-size piano. Now she could prepare for Sunday Service by practicing her music at home.

The piano filled the whole room along the windows on the front porch side. Mom draped its top with a thick orange and black woolen Navaho Indian blanket, a wedding gift. On this she placed her metronome and stacks of music. Always in the autumn, a bulky, rotund, brown ceramic Indian pot appeared filled with papery orange Japanese Lanterns woven through with bright red and orange bittersweet berries. Helen Hopley, Mom's longtime friend, brought her a bunch of each from her farm when they were ripe, signaling the arrival of fall.

One Saturday I learned that Al Jolson was playing at the Strand Theatre in *The Singing Fool,* with music I could hear! When I asked to go to see it, Mom didn't hesitate.

"Yes, Virginia, you may go to the two o'clock show," she said. "That will allow you to be at Mrs. Taylor's for your four o'clock piano lesson."

I ran all the way to the theatre and, for once, behaved myself, not sitting in the balcony throwing popcorn as I did during cowboy movies.

Empathy engulfed me. I was devastated by the depth of love Daddy felt for his Sonny Boy. He was three years old, and Mr. Jolson didn't think baby would know how much he was loved. This set me off burbling and crying, almost wailing. I couldn't stop when the movie was over. Distraught, I ran up the hill from the Court House onto Walnut Street while wiping the snot off my nose and the tears from my eyes onto my hands, and my hands onto my skirt. I finally got myself together as I walked the last few blocks to Mrs. Taylor's house.

In my usual way, I sat at the piano, twisting and squirming. This day bulky Mrs. Taylor, sitting in a chair to my side and a little behind the piano bench, said,

"Would you like to use the bathroom, Virginia?"

"No, why?"

"You're hardly able to sit still, my dear."

I turned, looked at her, and saw her serious, jowly, pale, course-skinned face topped with fly-away pure white hair. I watched another second while she, staring straight ahead at the wall, forgetting me completely, pushed a little ivory hand attached to a long, thin ivory stick down under the collar at the back of her dress. The hand-stick had a permanent place on the piano top next to her shiny black metronome. She gave her back a good scratch midway between her shoulders, resettled her hulk of a body, and then said,

"Continue playing."

Why didn't I work hard at my music lessons? I loved music, but I practiced little and was always ill prepared. Although Mom seemed not overly concerned that I should work hard at school, or at the piano, I believe she understood that I worked hard at doing what truly interested me.

Unfortunately, much later, and by the time I finally became interested in classical music, my sister had taken Mom's collection of records to school so the music teacher could use them for a while. However, a short time later, he left town along with Mom's records. But Cornie had overlooked the overture to *La Giaconda* which was on the turntable. I played it over and over, so that whenever I think of it, I hear the first few bars which to me sound like galloping frenzied horses.

Earl Montgomery was usually available to play when no one else was. He was the only child of a brilliant doctor, Atlantic's Eye, Ear, Nose, and Throat specialist; perhaps that was Earl's problem. He was nothing like his father even though he shared his name. He didn't have his brains, or if he did, he kept it a secret. But he was nice looking with dark, smooth skin, regular features, and noticeable light blue eyes under straight blond hair. He always had the newest bat or ball, and the gang always saw to it that he was in our games even though he was not good at baseball and avoided football. Once he managed to put me in my place during a child-size argument when I lost my temper, and socked him. He returned the sock registering a bull's eye. With blood from my nose pouring over my dress, I decided that getting into physical arguments with boys wasn't a good idea.

Somehow our collective group felt that Earl was deficient in some necessary quality. He had gotten too punky to be bearable. He sniveled and cried the day the gang was building a tiny town among young trees boles growing on the steep hill back of Marshall's vacant lot. He had come late, as usual. The hill was already full of winding roads for our toy cars, and lined with miniature gas stations, stores, and houses. He stubbornly refused to set up his road a little downhill from us, so we felt no guilt when he went home bawling.

When we played marbles we envied his beautiful collection of aggies, glassies, his steelee, and the fringed leather bag he kept them in. But we caught him cheating by nudging the marbles around, and he exhausted our patience once too often when he took his new baseball and bat and went home in the middle of a game.

To express these feelings, one fall several of us decided to stuff garbage into small pumpkins and throw these pumpkin bombs on Earl's porch Halloween night. I put my garbage stuffed pumpkin beside the walk to our back door. It sort of cooked, rotting away in the bright October sun.

On Halloween Eve we culprits crept in the dark and the cool of the night and threw our four sagging bombs onto the Montgomery porch. They disintegrated to produce a wonderful, awful smell that followed us as we ran.

This action caused me severe guilt feelings, for I soon realized we were not penalizing Earl. It was Mrs. Montgomery who would clean up the mess. I guess that taught me to be more careful, surer of the target when planning revenge.

I knew all was forgiven for the porch pumpkin bombing when Earl invited me to his huge attic playroom that filled the entire attic of the big Montgomery house.

I felt awe as I reached the top step of the attic. This huge room was almost as big as the whole downstairs of my house, or so it seemed. It had a solid oak floor, overhead lights, and fine storage shelves for Earl's large collection of expensive toys. He wanted to show off his new Lionel electric train layout. Harold owned a train too, but it was a midget compared to this one.

The cars must have been a foot long and six or seven inches high. The engine was spectacular, for it emitted steam. The track took up the whole center of the room running in a huge oval, with inner tracks circling and crossing in the middle. At the main station Earl, as engineer, could switch the train onto a different track, blow the whistle, and start and stop the engine. Little shelters sat at each track crossing guarded by tiny tin men; and near the station were metal houses and stores. He let me work a knob once or twice, and as I persistently nagged him to give me a turn being engineer, he finally agreed. I kept on being engineer, and kept on being engineer until Earl raised his voice in protest and wouldn't shut up.

Mrs. Montgomery must have heard his shouting for she sweetly called up the stairway, "Virginia, I think it's time for you to go home now."

I had run out of steam myself and was glad she gave me an excuse to quit. Earl didn't graciously take turns like my other friends did, so being piggy was my retribution.

13

Mom's enormous *Webster's Dictionary* sat on the bench near the fireplace. I loved reading this book, going from reference to reference, one word leading to another—looking at derivations and synonyms. Since it was too big and too heavy to hold on my lap, I kneeled on the floor in front of it.

One hot summer day as I was ambling home from a walk around the loop with nothing on my mind, I noticed four printed letters on the sidewalk, one letter to a cement block, written large with white chalk. It was a new word for me. I found Mom ironing in the kitchen, dressed in her bra and silky underpants, sweat dripping onto the flattened shirt.

"Mom," I said, "I saw a word on the sidewalk I don't know."

"What is it?"

I spelled, "F-U-C-K."

"That's a vulgar word for intercourse, having sex, or propagation."

"Oh, thanks." In this manner, Mom being graphic in her descriptions, I later learned among other interesting things, that a steer was 'an unsexed male bovine.' The kitchen became an ironing board schoolroom.

But propagation, yes. I heard the word again when our neighbor, Mrs. Herbert, called Mom on the phone one Saturday noon.

"Yeh-us," Mom said in her best baritone voice. "Yeh-us, Mrs. Herbert. I'll talk to Sunny about it, immediately."

She hung up the phone and called us three kids, who had gathered for lunch, "Come along, all of you."

We followed her and sat in a row on the bed in the guest room. I was on the end beside Cornie, and Harold sat on the other side of Mom. I couldn't see his face.

"Sunny," she began. "Mrs. Herbert said she found you and Lodema under the bushes by their porch and that you were having sexual relations with her. Is that true?"

"Yes, Mom."

"Didn't you read the book about sex that Aunt Nettie sent you?"

"Yes, Mom."

"Then why were you under the bushes with Lodema?"

"She wanted to go, and the book made me curious."

"For your information, children, the way we make babies is to introduce the male member, the penis, into the female member, the vagina. This is a process reserved for the time when you marry and wish to propagate children. Do you understand?"

"Yes, Mom," said Harold and Cornie. I mumbled, wishing he'd stayed out from under the Herbert's bushes, so I could eat lunch and not have to listen to this lecture. I escaped the issue by gazing at the big mirror hanging above Mom's dresser, seeing in it a trail of bright light careening over the window box. Beyond was her little cutting garden and I noted that some of the flowers were ready to bring into the house.

"I'm sorry this happened, Sunny. I shall talk further about it with Mrs. Herbert. I expect you not to repeat the experience."

With that, we all went into the dining room for our milk and sandwiches, and later, out to play. But this talk of propagation made me curious about Lodema. I'd never paid any attention to her before. She was too old to be interesting. I knew she had come from the orphanage, wherever that was, to help Mrs. Herbert with her housework, and that she would go to high school in the fall. I decided her wide bobbling bottom and her big breasts, which completely filled the top of her thin cotton dresses, made her more of a grownup than a child, so she should have known better than take Harold under the bushes. He hardly came up to her shoulders and had just a little hair growing on his legs. She was no kid. Harold was twelve. Lodema was sixteen.

Having watched the neighborhood dogs and robins, flies, butterflies and bees, I had a rudimentary knowledge of what Mom was talking about, and she had used the word "propagation" when she explained the word "fuck." I took advantage of Harold's absence one day and searched his room trying to find the book Aunt Nettie had sent him, but I couldn't further my education that way for it wasn't to be found. I didn't think to look for it again.

Early one morning the next frigid winter, Harold and Cornie were out delivering Collier publications, *The Saturday Evening Post* and *Country Gentleman,* on their separate routes. Harold was the district manager, and had over two hundred customers. Cornie worked as one of his employees; but she lost her job the next time the regional manager came to town. He called a meeting of everyone—all the local managers and carriers.

When he saw Cornie, he asked Harold, "Who is this?"

"My sister," Harold answered.

"She can't be a carrier, Harold. Girls aren't allowed."

This was my sister's first experience of not 'being allowed' because she was a girl. The second time was later when she wasn't allowed to take Shop in high school instead of Home Economics.

"Girls take Home Economics; boys take Shop," she was told by the principal.

But this day they were still out on their routes. The faint morning light of late February awakened me before they returned home. I quietly tiptoed back to my room after I had dressed in the bathroom. The house sounded creaky, and as I came to my parents' room, I paused. I didn't enjoy the magazine delivery mornings when I had to be alone downstairs before my brother and sister returned.

I stood in the open bedroom doorway, aimlessly staring into it, longing for company. The bed stood near the door, and by the slowly increasing gray light, I noticed that Dad was flat out on top of Mom, and was rocking back and forth. I realized the noise I'd heard was the squeaking of the bed springs. I rather liked the small noise: it was company.

I suppose Mom sensed my standing there, for turning her face toward me she said, "Sunny and Cornie will be home soon, dear. You go on downstairs, and start setting the table."

I went to the kitchen thinking about Mom and Dad's position. I knew that humping motion: I knew what was going on.

"That's what dogs do sometimes," I thought.

That latest propagation lecture had added to my knowledge, and seeing my parents cozy in bed clicked it all together with the word "fuck" and Harold's experience with Lodema. I decided to check out the word 'propagation' in the dictionary. Mom had given me something to do.

So I delayed setting the table, turned on the living room light, and knelt on the floor in front of the giant dictionary.

"PROPAGATION, PROPAGATE—GATED—GATING. To cause (an organism) to multiply by any process of natural reproduction from the parent stock" ("I sure know what parent means," I said to myself.) "... to transmit hereditary features." ("Oh! thought I—red hair—and that I certainly know about. Both my Great Grandmother Bradley and my Grandmother Prentiss had red hair, and so do Mom and I!")

So propagation transmits hereditary features, yeah, OK. I said the word over a few times. This was not a problem since I knew how to sound out words. Although I didn't know the word "genetics," this was my introduction to the subject.

I was deep into looking at synonyms and derivations, enlarging my horizons, and engaging in a game that gave me great satisfaction until, finally, Harold and

Cornie came in from the cold. Snow covered and red cheeked, they carried their now empty cloth bags labeled in blocky black letters COLLIER PUBLICA-TIONS. Harold looked like the Norman Rockwell boy on the covers of his *Saturday Evening Post* magazines with his brown curly hair, hazel eyes, corduroy knickers, wool socks, and boots. Cornie had on knickers too, with wool socks and boots, a too-big boy's hat on her head, and a heavy wool jacket. She looked like Harold's non-existent brother.

He said he'd make the cocoa, Cornie said she'd make the toast, and "You," she ordered, meaning me, "go get the butter from the icebox, and set the table." I did.

I didn't envy their having to get up in the dark and the cold of the mornings they delivered the magazines. They worked hard for their spending money—they worked like dogs. Cornie was always being nipped by neighborhood dogs, and as a result became afraid of them. But she wasn't allowed to be a carrier anymore, and Harold soon found a better job with Mr. Pellet, our dairy farm neighbor.

Our downstairs bathroom was small and cozy. Mom and I had many talk sessions here, me perched on the toilet lid, and she, already in the tub, having her late afternoon bath. I arrived from school about four-twenty, her favorite bath hour. I loved to watch her. Her long red hair, braided into a tail, was pinned high on her head. The hot water made her so pink, her skin so shiny. I thought her soft, fleshy body was perfect. After she scrubbed herself with a washcloth, she swished down on her back in the half-full tub to remove the soap. I watched the soap-sudsy water as it scooted through her red pubic hair.

Once, while standing in the tub to dry herself, she slipped and fell on her side. I let out a hoop of laughter thinking she looked like a cartoon character. Up she scrambled, in great anger, breathing fast, her face red.

She called me down saying, "Falling in the tub isn't funny, Virginia. I might have hurt myself."

"I'm sorry Mom. I laughed because you looked so funny."

She gave me a sideways glance and half-smile as she got out of the tub, and I knew we were still friends.

On Saturday mornings Mom would call me into the bathroom for my weekly head scrub, so I'd be immaculate for Sunday School. It took a lot of scrubbing. I wetted a washcloth, folded and placed it on the sink edge while she filled the bowl with water. On tiptoe I dunked my head in, Mom helping me. As she poured soap onto my hair, I buried my face in the wet cloth, and had no fear of stinging eyes. After a good scrub and a thorough rinse, she filled a glass half and half of vinegar and water, then poured it over my head, crooning, while giving my head another rinse, "lemon for blondes, vinegar for redheads and dark heads." Then she toweled my hair dry.

After combing my Dutch-bob into place, she gently brushed my hair and finished the ritual saying, "Now, Virginia, I want you to remember—your red hair is beautiful. Both your Grandmother Prentiss and your Great Grandmother Bradley had red hair. Your hair is your crowning glory."

"And you have red hair too, Mom." I'd stand, stretching tall to look at myself in the cabinet mirror, but managed to see only the top of my red head.

I think she often repeated this mantra because Bill Allender, an older neighboring boy who looked so handsome and behaved so abominably, constantly teased me about the color of my hair. He had red hair himself, but I guess he liked his shade of red better than mine.

He also called me "elephant ear" because my left ear stuck out through my bobbed hair. Grandpa Prentiss had one exactly like it and wouldn't let Mom have my ear surgically changed when I was a baby, saying, "You're insulting me, Cornelia. Haven't you ever noticed my left ear?"

Mom did everything she could to make me feel proud of "what the good Lord gave me." But I learned it was inheritance, not the good Lord, who gave me red hair and an ear that was a nuisance.

For all the activity in the bathroom, one would think it was larger. But it was a small room with the sink just inside the door causing you to step around it. The tub was beyond, an inch or two away from the sink. From where I sat on the toilet seat watching Mom bathe, there was about three feet to the tub that stretched the length of the room. Over the sink was a mirror on the door of the cabinet, and on the opposite wall was another mirrored cabinet. By adjusting these mirrors, you could see the back of your head, your profile, and, of course, your face. It was a wonderful place for arranging hair and seeing if you were well-groomed. I learned this by watching Mom. Later I tended to monopolize the mirrors.

Inside the wall cabinet, Mom kept all kinds of treasures: Pond's Cold Cream, pale pink rouge, powder and puffs; mascara, tweezers, squeezers; all kinds of grownup stuff. I wish I could say I respected her property, but no, it was too enticing.

A cosmetics saleswoman came to the house one day and sold Mom a few items. The one that intrigued me most was the white face masque. It looked like cold cream, but as you spread it on your face it began to sizzle, bubble, and sting; so I used it only once. Besides, I couldn't see that it made me look any different.

Later, when I was about eleven, one Saturday I experimented with her mascara. I kept laying it on and laying it on my eyelashes until I thought my eyes would pop out when I looked at myself. The front door opened. I heard Harold coming in with Skin Marshall, our neighbor from across the street. I entered the living room with my mascara-eyes just as Harold left for the kitchen.

"You've painted your eye lashes," said Skin.

"I didn't either," I denied, wanting him to believe it was my natural look.

"Oh, yes, you did. I can tell."

I didn't try mascara again until later when I was in high school, after I had read in Mom's *Ladies Home Journal* how to put it on for "that subtle look." I wonder if I mastered it. Whether I did or didn't, I used mascara from then on until an eye doctor told me to stop: I had become allergic to it.

Another thing that intrigued me in Mom's cabinet was one bottle that belonged to Dad. Concerned about the regularity of his bowels, he sometimes took a Hinkle pill. They were tiny and a bright orange-red, a lovely color I thought. One morning I decided if they were good for Dad, one would be good for me. By afternoon I was attached to the pot, my intestines heaving, and I, almost groaning. How could such a pretty pill produce such a terrible result?

Unfortunately, right then Dad came home and wanted to use the toilet. He knocked.

I called, "Just a minute."

But just a minute became several as I struggled to finish the proceedings and clean myself up. Dad kept pounding on the door. He was getting angry. I finally flushed the toilet, pulled up my underpants, and opened the door.

"My God, what a stink!" he said, but quickly came in as I went out. I never took a laxative again.

The guest room was next to the bathroom. I always thought of it as Mom's room for it smelled of her skin and perfume. I loved the wallpaper, the long neat rows of tiny-leaved lavender flowers going up and down darker lavender stripes, the small spaces between being pale blue.

One of two small windows in the room looked to the Allen's house, over our common driveway. Our half was nothing but two narrow strips of cement; the Allen's had a full drive. In the autumn a horse-drawn wagon full of corncobs would pull up in the Allen's half, and Mr. and Mrs. Allen met it bringing bushel baskets. They filled them from the wagon, and dumped the cobs into a chicken wire bin in their garage. Mom told me they used the corncobs to start fires in their cast-iron cook stove. The cobs came from a farm they still owned.

After the horses backed the wagon out to begin their return trip to the farm, flies and sparrows fed on debris in the horse droppings, and a few stray kernels of corn sparkled among the balls of dark brown manure. The Allen's chickens joined the sparrows. Dad said it was hard for our neighbors to give up their country ways; eventually the chickens disappeared—into a stew pot, I suppose.

Once, when Dad turned our car into the driveway, I noticed Mrs. Allen's long, sharp nose poking through her curtains, watching us pull in. From then on I always watched to see if she were watching us. If home, there she was.

Pointing, I'd say, "There's Mrs. Allen again, Mom, right there in that upstairs window."

I guess she didn't miss much of what went on with us.

Mom told me, since farmers lived so far apart in the country, it was their habit and recreation to watch passing cars or any event that happened. It was a lonely way to live for most farm wives. In those days few had cars of their own.

"Think nothing of it," she said.

Out the other window I could see Mom's little cutting garden. Under that window was a built-in box containing our board games. At Christmas time it was crammed with Christmas presents, the overflow filling the top shelf of Mom's adjacent clothes closet. There, on the floor under her hanging clothes jammed together on the rod, lay her shoes in a jumble. That haphazard arrangement wasn't much different from Cornie's and mine.

Mom's underclothes, nighties, and hose were stuffed into the two-drawer chest that matched the bedstead. Aside from the full bed, it was the only piece of furniture in the small room. When I was sick, I liked being in that comfortable bed. Here Mom napped when she had the time and felt the need of a rest. This usually happened shortly before dinner time.

If I were around, she sometimes asked, "Virginia, would you like to lie down with me?"

I often did, seldom slept, but would watch her drift off into deep breathing. She liked to lie flat on her belly on the edge of the bed with her hands under her hipbones, her legs straight out behind, and her head turned to one side. She looked like a soft nosed bullet. I think she slept that way to avoid falling out of bed, for in later days she mentioned that Dad was so big, he spraddled out taking most of the space. Becoming a bullet, she spent her nights balanced on the bed edge.

I never got tired of looking at my Mom. Often she asked me to call her at five o'clock so she could get supper. I felt like I was watching over her.

Other times she'd rest for a while, then say, "Would you like to brush my hair?"

I'd get the silver-backed brush engraved with HJP, her Papa's initials, and sit on my knees on the bed while she sat by the window with her legs in the narrow space between the bed and the wall. I'd brush her long hair from scalp down to the farthest ends. Her hair was a great mass, and it took muscle to do this. She'd let her head fall back, or to one side, pulling against the direction of the brush. I watched as she closed her eyes, obviously enjoying this brushing.

Her profile with its small, straight nose and firm chin was outlined against the white glass curtains; and the flowered lavender-blue wallpaper was behind her red hair. The white chenille bedspread with its little lavender tufts made dents in my knees and legs.

After a while she'd say, "That makes me feel wonderful, Virginia. Thank you. It's time now to 'stir my stumps' and get supper."

Up she'd get, pin up her hair, and straighten her housedress; I'd follow her through the dining room to the kitchen.

But often I'd stop in the dining room and bring from the small closet, where Mom kept her coats, the two huge picture books of Matthew Brady's Civil War photographs. They had purple covers. I'd get down on floor and study them.

I saw the campsites, how the canons were primed and fired, sometimes with women helping; and I examined the broken bodies and piles of corpses. I came to the conclusion that war wasn't for sissies and that it might be better for everyone if there were no such thing as war.

All went well until the stock market crashed in 1929. Then the farmers and all the businesses were in trouble. Everything changed.

I learned about this when Mom told us, "You kids have been so thrifty, and all for naught. Your savings accounts are gone."

Dad left Grampa's factory, because there wasn't enough money coming in to support three Shrauger families—Grampa's, Dad's, and Dad's brother, Harlan's—plus the workmen Grampa kept on. Later I saw a list of the men employed at Grampa's factory; I was surprised to see many names of my schoolmates' fathers. At the time, I only knew that Dad looked for work elsewhere. Years later Mom told me that Dad left the factory thinking he'd fare better than his brother in finding other employment.

Gramma added spice to my life. One of the little sayings she enjoyed repeating for me was, "Change the name but not the letter, marry for worse and not for better." She changed the letter, and she certainly married for better. Better to be a homemaker in a fine house than making hats forever, I thought.

When I was busy practicing whistling, Gramma would say "Whistling girl and crowing hen are sure to come to some bad end." The effect that saying had on me was that I stopped whistling in her house; at home I even practiced whistle-scales.

On one of the coldest days of winter, for some reason I was walking to school by myself. Why didn't Dad drive me and Cornie and Harold to school that day? By the time I was almost to Gramma's house I couldn't feel my hands or feet. My arms were cold up to my shoulders, and my thighs were bright red. I felt frozen and was in tears. Of course I went to her house and walked in.

"My child, my child, come in, come in! You're frozen!" She greeted me with open arms. She rescued me. Whatever she did to warm me, probably gave me a cup of cambric tea—green tea sweetened with lots of sugar and milk—she made me feel safe and in sympathetic hands.

Mom and Gramma may not have gotten along, but I never felt their problem spilled onto me. Occasionally I would visit my Grandmother on my way home from school or downtown. She was always glad to see me. Ceremoniously greeting me from her great height of five feet eight inches, she'd offer me a treat—a melty fat pillow mint or a brown aromatic horehound drop. I was allowed two mints, or one horehound drop.

Occasionally on a Saturday morning, I'd catch her with her long, absolutely straight hair done up in rags, preparing to look well coifed for Sunday church. Grampa put a barrel under a downspout off the back porch so Gramma could wash her hair in soft rain water.

She often asked me to come and nap with her if I arrived in the late afternoon, her naptime. Our school let out at four in those days. Usually I didn't stay, but I obliged her once. She fell asleep on her back. Her pure white hair was pulled back into a knot but wisps framed her wrinkled, rough textured face. I don't think she used face cream; there weren't any jars on her dressing table. I watched as her mouth opened slowly. She fell into deep snore. Now I understood why Grampa slept in the room with the tiny alcove.

I decided I'd been there long enough, swung off the bed, and fell flat on my face. I'd fainted. Up I got and walked on home. I never told Mom about this.

Some people of my Gramma's generation believed that a red haired woman automatically became a 'fallen woman' and any man interested in her also became fallen. But I decided that any bride Dad brought home would not have suited Sadie Shrauger. Maybe she was more than a little jealous of Mom. She was everything Gramma never had a chance to be. After all, Mom could play the piano and organ, had graduated from college, and came from an educated family. Too bad she couldn't rejoice and feel lucky her son had such a wife. Later I learned that Gramma was ambitious for sister Cornie and me.

Along the way, Cornie and I were brought into this continuing simmering underground—sometimes above ground—unpleasantness. Gramma, one summer, decided to make the two of us fall coats and hats. They were of an orange, loose-woven, wool material, which didn't keep its shape. Even I, who paid little attention to clothes at the time, knew something was wrong with these coats. The hats, which were a sort of tam and matched the coats, were frowsy: mine wouldn't stay put and continually fell over my eyes. Cornie and I protested to Mom. We hated them. We refused to wear them. Mom made us wear them.

"Your Grandmother went to a lot of effort for you two," Mom said, "and it's proper that you show respect by wearing them."

Mom always made us do the dutiful thing, as she would do. Gramma might have been a good milliner, but in our minds, she didn't make becoming hats for girls, and she wasn't a very good seamstress either.

But Gramma gained points in my estimation when she was a delegate to the Democratic National Convention which nominated Franklin D. Roosevelt as a presidential candidate. Grampa drove her to Dallas. I felt it was an honor for her.

When they returned Gramma said, "Texas is a hot box. Iowa isn't so bad after all."

The last time I saw my Gramma, I was going off to college for my freshman year. Dad was driving Cornie, her best friend, Jeanne Howorth, and me to Iowa City. We stopped briefly to say goodbye. As we drove away, she stood in the side yard on Eleventh Street, gaunt and thin in her neat cotton dress. She stood up very straight, as she often cautioned me to do, for I was now her height. She already had stomach cancer when she took me to Chicago five years before. Like many country people, Mom said, Gramma didn't trust doctors, and never consulted one.

But Gramma was unable to take care of Grampa and herself any longer, so she allowed him to put her in the Atlantic hospital. Mom, of course, visited her regularly.

"Cornelia," Gramma said to her one day, "I've never been happier in my whole life. All the nurses are so kind to me." And Gramma smiled on Mom. Mom couldn't believe it.

Seven weeks later, the local paper said, in this—her last home—well taken care of by strangers, Gramma died.

14

Our neighbor, Mrs. Herbert, was a big influence on my life. She asked my Mom if I'd like to take dancing lessons from her, for free. I'd never given dancing a thought. But, as it turned out, I loved to dance. I was strong and agile, responded to music, and even though I had a mediocre memory, I had no trouble remembering dance routines. I suppose Mrs. Herbert, observing my excessive energy, had decided I would be a good addition to her class. My sister eventually was in the tap dancing group. I became a balletomane and thought tap dancing was beneath me; however, I learned tapping anyway as all dancing became a challenge. We learned the rudiments of ballroom dancing too, so when party time came along in High School and college, I experienced no trauma.

Every Saturday morning at nine I appeared at the basement studio, a long room with a silky–smooth varnished oak floor. Huge mirrors lined the inside wall, a barre in front of them. Here we met for an hour, stretched on the barre, learned the five basic positions, how to stand, leap, and how not to get dizzy on turns. I found that hour a joyous time; but, in my usual way, I was content to have it be only a Saturday morning thing.

Of course there were the requisite recitals. For years our gang had gone to cowboy shows on Saturday afternoons at the Strand Theatre. Off we'd go, whooping and hollering down Chestnut Street, dimes clutched in our hands, and a nickel for peanuts or popcorn in our pockets. The front row of the balcony was our choice of seat: throwing peanut shells on the heads of those below us was our occupation; cheering for our heroes, Tom Mix, Gene Autry, or Hoot Gibson, and booing the villains was our pleasure. No one ever told us to pipe down. I was secretly in love with Hoot Gibson. The profile of Hoot on his rearing white horse, both certified heroes and always shown as his movies ended, was embedded in my mind forever.

Now, however, I was to be part of a performance on the Strand's stage. A dingy, dirty, tiny dressing room in the cold basement was where we changed into our costumes, Cornie's and mine having been made by Mrs. Smoller.

"Well," I thought. "If this is what dancers have to put up with, I'm not sure I want to dance for a living."

Mrs. Herbert made up our faces, laying on the rouge, mascara, eyeliner, lipstick and powder which made us look like red faced, expressionless dolls. All that stuff made my skin feel desert-dry.

In a white satin costume made with a long skirt trimmed with tinsel, I was one of a group that did little but fling fine net veils up and down and all around, twisting and turning. Unfortunately, I became hypnotically entranced by my veil, floated off from its edge and stared—mentally levitated above the heads of the audience—an ephemeral moment. I didn't realize I'd stopped dancing until Mrs. Herbert's voice brought me back to reality with a loud stage whisper, "Virginia, dance, dance!"

Instantly back from dreamland, the music told me where we were: I resumed the veil-wafting. I guess no one noticed my defection except my teacher.

Mrs. Herbert needed one more person for the tap dance to make an even number. She asked me if I would learn the routine and perform with the other girls. I would (as a favor to her, I said to myself). Mrs. Smoller also made this required costume. We wore the skimpiest of white satin shorts. At one point we were to turn our backsides to the audience, and in time to the music, wiggle our butts. I did this under silent protest thinking it very unladylike.

Mom must have kept Aunt Nettie informed about my progress in ballet, for at Christmas time, my present from her was a pair of beautiful, pale pink toe slippers. I was enchanted. Now I would be a true ballerina, rise on my toes to become a fairy, a leaf, whatever I wanted to be, or whatever was required.

Lessons had been canceled until after the holiday. With great anticipation I went to next Saturday's lesson, sat down, and, with Mrs. Herbert's help, laced on my slippers.

Was there cotton wool in the toes of the shoes? Whatever or no, those shoes hurt my toes unbearably. I tried using them for a while, and again the next Saturday. But the pain was beyond my endurance. I don't recall having any particular encouragement from Mrs. Herbert. At least I didn't disappoint her, for she said nothing when I left the toe shoes at home.

It was a good thing I always wrote my Christmas thank-you notes right away, for if I had written Aunt Nettie after I had tried the shoes for two Saturdays, I would have lied to her. Sadly I put the beautiful shoes and their false promise away in my dresser drawer, looking at them from time to time, realizing I preferred feet that didn't hurt to becoming a ballerina.

Mom always cautioned us never to make personal remarks unless they were complimentary. So Mrs. Herbert surprised me one morning by singling me out to the class as having the kind of thighs that dancers should have. She explained that the muscles of my thighs met when I stood with legs together: there was no space between.

Curious staring and subtle hostility from the class was the result of that unfortunate remark. I didn't like her doing that, especially when three sisters, "The Spies Sisters", as they were billed when performing, had joined us and proved to be in a class by themselves. They had perfected an extraordinary routine of acrobatic dancing. I envied their skill.

But God hadn't made their legs to suit Mrs. Herbert. To be put up as an example they could never attain, for reasons they or I had no control over, I didn't think was fair. I then realized what Mom meant, even though this occasion wasn't exactly what she had in mind. I appreciated Mom's constant little tutoring about how to get along in the world.

My right knee began to give me trouble when we kneeled in dance class, so Mom took me to Dr. Harvey Johnson.

The doctor put an Ace Bandage on my knee, but it didn't relieve the pain. Mom then took me to Iowa City to see Dr. Steindler, the orthopedic specialist and family friend. I was diagnosed as an Osgood-Schlatter patient.

"Why, Virginia, only athletes have this problem," he told me in his thick Austrian accent. "This is very unusual in a child of your age."

To cure it, he put my leg into a cast from thigh to ankle "to give the knee a good rest."

I endured that for six weeks, comforted by my new label, 'athlete.' The cast, however, was a sure cure, for my knee never bothered me again. When I thought about it later, I wondered if I hadn't caused that bone to begin to pop out when I foolishly took a flying leap into the eight-foot-deep hole dug for a new house basement.

The true heart of our gang's activities was the meadow which was behind our houses. Of course it wasn't ours. The owner came in June, and depending on rainfall, once again in August to mow and bale the grasses and clover. That was perfect with us. We could find our baseball faster in stubble.

In March our meadow season began. On the first windy day, Cornie and I would trek downtown to Woolworth's to buy a ten-cent kite and a twenty-nine cent roll of string. We'd race back home, put the wooden sticks into the corners of the diamond-shaped kites, attach the string, and later on, after learning about attaching a tail for balance, we did that too. By trial and error, we learned the art of kite maneuvering. The wind blew, the sun glinted off the kites, and we felt pleased having properly welcomed spring.

As the weather warmed, our gang began to think of baseball. Our season would last until the heat of summer arrived. Earl, who had everything, of course appeared with a new bat and ball. We regulars, as well as Earl, were Dorothy, Helen and Louise, Skin and Bob, Sister and Dixie, Cornie and me. Sometimes younger kids joined us.

First we paced out the bases, marked them with boards, or just scrubbed down the grass with our feet. We didn't bother with a pitcher's mound because the pitcher had to come forward or go backward according to the ability of the batter—or the pitcher's skill—a judgment call.

We chose sides in our usual way. The two of us who had browbeaten our way into being captains for the day tossed the bat, one to the other. Then it was hand above the other's hand up the bat until the one who had the last full handhold was the first to choose a player. With precise cruelty, each chose in turn a player thought best until only the uncoordinated and youngest were waiting. Chosen among the last was always Earl.

We knew how to play the game because we made up the rules. Actually, all the choosing of sides was just a gesture, for "Work Up" was our game. We never had enough kids to play real baseball.

But playing Work Up had to wait until we spent time showing the youngest kids how to hold and swing a bat, how to keep their eye on the ball, and how to pitch and catch. We spent a lot of time instructing until we tired of it. Then we'd begin a game knowing it would be slow going.

In Work Up, the two captains assigned their players to any positions they chose: that meant the best players began as pitcher, catcher, and batter. The rest filled the bases and the field positions. We didn't bother with a short stop. We were lucky if we had enough to get the bases covered. There wasn't any team competition. Scoring was not a problem. It wasn't an objective. We simply wanted to enjoy being part of a game; to breathe the spring air; to rejoice in a good hit—especially a hit made by one of the younger kids.

We followed these rules: when the player batted out, he became the catcher, the pitcher became the batter, the first baseman became the pitcher, the second baseman became the first baseman, and so forth. This way everyone had a turn at all the positions, and we had some kind of a game. It only looked disorganized; we felt we had method and order.

Cornie could hit a ball 'a country mile' when Skin pitched to her. Dixie and I hit well too. I never became a big league fan, but our sandlot baseball was the beginning of my understanding of what goes into making a good player of any game.

Sometimes when there was no one to play with, or because it was a nice day and I felt like being alone, I'd go to the meadow to examine the wild flowers, and watch the bees as they gathered pollen, weighing down the fat, lavender heads of the red clover. Or I'd chase the swallowtail butterflies, trying to catch them, or inspect the grass carefully in search of weird insects. Once to get a closer look, I unwittingly disturbed a bee's routine by sitting on it. This resulted in a sting on my behind that hurt just like the word sounds. I rushed to the house, and found Mom in the kitchen.

"You sat on a bee! That was a mistake: show me where."

I quickly, and carefully, took down my underpants. Examining the rising red spot she said, "Hold still. I'll remove the stinger."

"Remove the stinger? You mean the stinger comes off the bee when it stings someone? I want to see it."

She carefully pulled it out, and showed me the thin black line.

"Next comes a poultice of baking soda and water," she said, and added, "Unfortunately the bee dies after it leaves its stinger in you."

I felt bad about that. But soon the soothing wet stuff on my bottom made the hurt feel better. Mom had rescued me again. Her magic, her love, her kiss, and her pats made everything better. So I learned about first aid for bee stings.

Mom rescued me one other time. There was just enough space between the far corner of the Smoller house and the corner of their garage to form a nice passageway. It was a one-car garage and sat very close to the Herbert's garage which was a twin. In fact, the Smoller's roof slightly overlapped the Herbert's. They shared a common driveway.

Dixie Herbert and I decided one day to climb up to the roofs of the garages. Somehow we managed to get there. It was fun to run fast down one rooftop, then leap to the other roof, running fast up to the peak of it, turn around and do the same in reverse, up down, up down, up down. But on a turn, when I was at the peak of the Smoller's roof, my shoe slipped. No one had sneakers then. I slid feet first on my bottom all the way down the wooden shingles to the Herbert's overhang. That stopped me.

We girls wore dresses for play in those days, and it was no different that day. My bottom was filled with splinters. They hurt! I hightailed home to Mom.

She got the tweezers, put me over her knees, bottom up, and went to work.

"My heavens, child, how can I ever get all these out?"

It was a moot question. I thought she'd never finish, and my bottom stung, especially when she liberally daubed a worked-on area with alcohol.

Mom finally said, "Virginia, I've removed as many as I possibly can. The rest will just have to work their way out."

I decided once was enough of that kind of fun.

One summer afternoon Cornie heard shouts back of our yard and called, "Virginia, quick—the meadow's on fire!"

Together we looked out the kitchen door, saw smoke rising—saw neighbors beating on flames. We rushed to our shed. I grabbed a broom; she found some old shirts. We joined the neighbors, all trying to contain the fire. But the afternoon wind hadn't died down, and the grass was dry. Already the fire had spread as far as our baseball diamond.

Cornie shouted to me, "Let's work behind our shed!"

"Yeah! Dad would be upset if it burned down."

I felt good working with the adults and other kids who had shown up. But there was no way we could put the fire out. Soon the sound of the fire truck siren filled the air. Chief Roy Hedges ordered the hoses attached to the hydrant at the far edge of the meadow. A deluge of water put out the fire accidentally started from someone's ash pile.

As we surveyed the damage, the pungent smell of sodden burned grass and bodies of ants, bees, grasshoppers and other insects filled the hot summer air. By late August, however, green grasses were covering the burned spots. Soon all evidence of that exciting hour had disappeared.

The day galloped towards four o'clock, and I knew what the slow fading of the light and the gradual darkening of the clouds meant: one of summer's joys, a wild plain's storm was upon us! Cornie and I ran to the front porch and plopped onto the swing. When the atmosphere suddenly dissolved into an evil gray-green, we knew the fun was about to begin.

We started swinging. A cold west wind drifted over Otto's house. All La Vista Place trembled in anticipation. That was our cue to swing as high as we could. We heard the swift-rising wind, heard it accelerating; saw it catch the crown of our huge elm tree which began shaking itself wildly as if saying "No, no." Now raging, the wind answered, doubling its efforts to tear the branches from the bole.

Joining the melee was the first explosion of thunder. A cautionary sprinkle wet the sidewalk. Twigs began to fall from our elm. Now hard rain fell—La Vista turned black. All became a noisy torrent; spray filled the air and our noses. Lightning lit the neighborhood. Thunder smashed into our ears punching us down on the swing. Then the air turned frigid. Our elm tree gave in, bowing, swaying, moaning, losing leaves.

Never slacking, the west wind kept swirling and surging. But now, as suddenly as it came, it now gradually shoved the invading blackness east. The thunder and lightening now moved in concert, following the blackness, but left the pounding rain to mash down the branches of our Bridal Wreath, flatten the grass, flood our streets, and thoroughly soak us.

Suddenly the rain lessened to a sprinkle, and magically, the sky lightened. Cornie and I anticipating the next act, dashed up to our bedroom, two steps at a time, pulled on our bathing suits, and rushed out of the house to the street to wade in the knee-deep, above-the-curb water.

"All Hell broke loose downtown," Dad said at supper.

We all enjoyed the excitement of these sudden wild storms which freshened the air and littered the yards with debris.

One constant activity Cornie and I shared with our Dad was reading the Sunday newspapers. He'd sit in his brown upholstered chair, sports section in hand. Cornie and I flopped flat on our stomachs on the living room rug. I'd look at the news section until my sister was through with the 'funnies.' Besides meals and riding in the car with him, this was a weekly activity.

The Katzenjammer Kids, wild little boys who were always in trouble, was my favorite along with *Little Orphan* Annie—with certain reservations. She was such a goodie-goodie. Clark Kent and his own do-gooding were acceptable because he was handsome and had large muscles. But his body looked rigid to me; he didn't seem real.

When I was six, huge letters on the front page announced the exciting news that Charles A. Lindbergh on May 21, 1927, had flown solo from New York to Paris. I think the name of his plane, "The Spirit of St. Louis," helped make this event indelible in my mind because St. Louis was where my Aunt Biddy lived.

Later news of the kidnapping of the Lindbergh baby in the spring of 1932 kept my eyes glued daily to *The Des Moines Register.* I read every word of the investigation and charges against Bruno Hauptmann and his subsequent fate. It was my first awareness of someone trying to get money by doing an evil deed, and of the penalty paid if he or she was captured.

The newspapers furthered my interest in geography when they reported Admiral Richard E. Byrd's establishing a base, Little America, in Antarctica. I had followed the accounts of his flying over the North Pole in 1930, but learning of people living under the snow in the frigid north was much more exciting. In the late nineteen twenties and early nineteen thirties, Iowa had heavy deep snows, so I could imagine what it might be like to be living in arctic conditions.

While Byrd and his men endured hardships at the South Pole, in the Middle West we were experiencing terrible heat and drought. The summer of 1930 was unbearable with temperatures as high as a hundred and ten degrees for days. Mom's flowers withered; Dad's vegetable garden failed. Photographs of dying and dead cattle appeared in *The Omaha World* Herald. Story after story talked about the great Dust Bowl.

We didn't have to be told; we were living in it. All our windows were closed; all the shades were drawn. I'd pull a shade up a little and make pictures on the sill in the dust that had seeped in. My fingers got hot, and I wished for the wonderful cold winter mornings when Jack Frost left tracks on our windows in the shape of lacy designs. Instead, a fiery wind blew and kept us indoors; or no breeze stirred, and we'd sweat and struggle for breath. We prayed for wet weather.

Often, when the wind was still, I'd leave the dreary house and, since none of my friends wanted to play, I sat in the sparse shade of our thirsty elm. Its withered leaves were seared, curled inward and hung straight down, still green but dry as fall leaves. I leaned back on my hands, and the dried grass crunched and broke.

Dad often said, "At least we don't have to mow the lawn."

I listened to the silent neighborhood: nothing stirred. No delivery trucks or kids on bikes came by. Not even a bird twittered. Now and then a few small white clouds appeared. My hopes would rise. They simply floated away. One day a small black cloud came fast from the east, a small spot against the ice-blue shimmering sky. I moved out from under the elm to the sidewalk, staring as the cloud passed overhead. One rain drop, two rain drops—no more. I learned that sometimes weather controls our lives.

Finally, this dreadful time passed, the Iowa farms renewed themselves, and life went on.

A group called "Chautauqua" came to Atlantic, put up a huge tent, set up bleachers, and produced the first stage play I ever saw. Mom took us to the other side of the railroad tracks to see Uncle Tom and the impish Topsy. This play was my first experience with the problems of Negroes. One day the tent appeared: the next day it was gone. Mom told me Harriet Beecher Stowe wrote the book called *Uncle Tom's Cabin;* and the play, written by Mr. George Aiken, was based on it. Later, when I learned that two black families lived in Atlantic, Mom taught me to use the word Negro for people with dark skins; all other terms were outlawed.

The big event of every summer was the annual Cass County Fair, the summer's highlight, the event we depended on for fun. In my early years, someone in our family would take me, or Dad would take us all. Later, as Cornie and I got older, we would go with our friends.

Gramma Shrauger once took me with her when I was a very little girl. Grampa drove us to the entrance, and we walked down the dirt road, past the bleachers and the racetrack. Gramma knew exactly where to go. The midway with its rides weren't on her schedule, and the enticing smells of hot dogs and sweet cotton candy didn't affect her nose one bit. She marched me right along to the building where quilts were hung on poles attached to overhead beams. Gramma told me women from all over the county spent a year sewing and quilting them.

The only quilt I'd ever seen was our raggedy one made from old dresses belonging to Great Grandmother Bradley. Mom said it was called a crazy quilt because the pieces were oblongs, squares, triangles or shapes that had no name. The pieces came from elegant gowns of silk, velvet, and other kinds of materials. It was soothing to run my fingers over the smooth ones, tickly over the nubbly ones, and delightful over the nappy ones.

I'd never before seen a new quilt made of cotton. We threaded our way between the aisles, colorful tunnels of hanging quilts. I liked the bright designs, and Gramma pointed out the tiny stitches that held them together.

Going right along, we walked to another building and saw table after table crowded with jars of home-canned fruit and vegetables. Some had blue ribbons around their caps, some red or white. Gramma told me the blue were for first place winners, the red for second and the white for third. The jars were set out neatly in double rows: the clear red of the tomatoes; the deep blue-red of the beets; the yellow of the carrots standing like soldiers upright in their jars; and the bright green of the string beans exactly the same length, packed in tight. I thought they were a miracle. Mom's beans didn't look like that because she cut them into inch lengths.

She canned everything Dad grew in our garden. Once there was a terrible racket in the middle of the night: all the jars of green beans exploded. After Dad cleaned up the glass and mess, I never heard another word about it, except in a joking way. The event became a landmark: events happened either before or after the Great Fruit Cellar Explosion.

These jars at the fair were being tended by the farm women who, I supposed, had canned them. Standing behind the long tables, now that the hard work was done, they were smiling, looking cool in their colorful cotton dresses and neat aprons. It was a vacation for them. They were relaxed and happy chatting with each other, flicking well-bleached dishtowels to discourage the flies settling on the homemade cakes and pies.

As we left the food display, I noticed a contest was being held for prettiest baby. I wanted to stop there for my experience with babies was zero; but Gramma had done her duty calls on fruits and vegetables, pies, cakes, and quilts. Now she went directly to the Lotto tent, the reason for her coming to the County Fair at all. Here she settled herself intending to play until she won a blanket.

Sometimes, she told me, to win she had to come to the Fair a day or two, other times only part of one. This day I was stuck in the Lotto tent wondering why she so loved this game. We played Lotto at home; why would anyone want to come here to play when there were exciting rides, cotton candy, targets to hit, and sulky races to watch?

But Grandma knew what she liked. As she bent her head over her cards, wisps of thinning white hair hovered over her stern, lined face. Her summer cotton dress was perfectly pressed, and her black handbag hung by its handle over her wrist. Gramma's attention never wandered as she listened to the caller and stared at her cards.

I watched the man as he shook the box of numbers, pulled out one at a time, and shouted each number. "We have a six, we have a six, a six, six, six," he'd shout.

I examined the players with their sober faces tucked into their cards and wondered what intrigued them so. Lucky me, and lucky Gramma. This day she won her blanket in the first hour of play! But she didn't seem as happy as I was. I decided it was the disappointment in winning so soon that dissatisfied her.

As I grew older, I went to the fair with my girl friends, Armelda Welch and Jean Tomlinson. We curled our hair, put on our prettiest summer dresses and wondered if any of the boys in our class would be there. At the entrance to the fairgrounds we walked by some CCC men, the Civilian Conservation Corps, that President Roosevelt formed so unemployed men could work, earn money, and take care of their families. The men we saw were digging a drainage ditch next to the Fair's entrance. I thought of the rude jokes and cartoons about them printed in magazines and newspapers. They were lucky to have those jobs; my Dad often didn't have work in those days.

But I forgot about them once we paid our nickel admission. We marched straight to the Ferris wheel where we sat three in a seat locked in by a bar. It didn't seem very secure as we bumped along to the top of the wheel while the attendant helped others settle on successive seats. The higher we got, the crowd noise quieted. We stopped at the top. Now the fair was a faint murmur. We sat quietly, as still as we could, clutching the bar and each other if a slight breeze moved us, never admitting we were frightened.

With a start the wheel resumed turning. We leaned into each other as we descended and circled up again, and again, and again. Finally, glad to have the ride over, but not admitting it, the attendant let us off. In spite of being uneasy, or maybe because of it, we were thrilled with our ride to the sky.

Being Iowans, we always toured through the smelly animal barns, pushing through the crowd to watch the baby pigs searching out their mother's teats, sucking away, while she lay on her side, all 250 or more pounds of her, eyes shut, occasionally grunting when a piglet pushed a nipple hard. We stared at the velvet rabbits secure in their cages, aching to pet their black and white mink-like coats as they scrunched down on their bellies, their noses busy wriggling. We thought the special chickens clothed in orange, yellow, white, and black feathers unbelievable. Nearby roosters outdid the imaginative ones in our picture books having huge, tufted anklets. Unlike the rabbits, they stalked around in their barred cages and stared at us through beady, evil eyes.

We chose carefully how we spent our money. A favorite gamble of ours was trying to win a stuffed toy by choosing the right yellow baby duck out of the line floating down a metal river set on a counter. The trick was to pick the one with the hidden magic number. We might as well have given the man the nickel. Or we could buy a hot dog. But since we often had those at home, we usually bought sticky pink cotton candy which inevitably got caught in our hair. Then home we'd go, happy with our afternoon at the fair.

Once Dad took Mom, Harold, Cornie and me to the County Fair sulky races late on a Saturday afternoon. We sat on hard wooden seats high up in the crowded, covered bleachers. Everyone around us talked a lot and knew about the riders and horses. Dad and Mom chatted with them. I listened. All were strangers to me. Dad told me people came from towns and farms all over Cass County and other counties too.

The hot day began to cool as the sulky drivers warmed up their horses by slowly pulling the two-wheeled carts around the oval track. Their brown and black coats gleamed in the late afternoon sun. As the time for the first race approached, the drivers lined up their sulkies.

A gunshot! Off went the horses at full speed. I watched their strong muscles moving their bones, racing along, manes and tails flying straight out behind. Noise of the pounding hoofs rose to our ears; the sulky wheels were turning so fast I couldn't see the spokes. Leaning forward from their waists, the drivers urged the horses ahead with light flicks of switches. Clouds of dust spun up from the track.

Around the oval they pounded—two vying for the lead. At the last turn, the crowd rose to their feet, shouting names of the riders and horses. Not being able to see over the grownups, I missed the finish. So forever in my memory, I see the two horses, two drivers whipping, and two sulkies frozen, a photo—seconds from the finish line.

We sat close to The United States Marine band that had come to our fair from Washington, D.C. All the handsome young men, looking like rosy-cheeked farm boys, were in their dress blues. We heard them play Elgar's marches, their horns filling the air with pure, rich sounds I'd never heard before. This band opened my ears to new musical possibilities. Little did I know that one day I'd be a war-time Marine; but I never wore dress blues.

15

I loved going to Grampa and Gramma's handsome, roomy house sitting high on a hill at eleventh and Chestnut Street; I had to tilt my head back to see it from the sidewalk. Eleventh Street was a hard climb, so all the houses behind Grampa's sat on similar flattened lots.

Mom called their home a gingerbread house because it looked like our story-book pictures of Hansel and Gretel's house with its brown lathe crisscrossing the yellow paint on the second story.

A wrap-around porch extended from the gable-sheltered front door to the second entrance at the rear of the house. No one used the front door because of the fifteen steep and narrow steps leading up to it. Everyone used the driveway entrance. Greeting you was a reddish-brown terra cotta tile floor, such a pretty color, cool and welcoming. You were in a complete room, all windows and screens, looking in three directions. I called it the 'summer porch' because we sat out there in spring, summer, and fall. It was a do-everything room. We ate meals there, played games there, and just sat there sometimes, watching the birds that settled in the vines which Gramma had trained to climb up to the second floor.

Two side-by-side doors invited you inside. One, never used, (a mistake?) led to the dining room: the other opened into the living room. The fine brick fireplace with oak mantel was on your left where Gramma displayed her family pictures. Facing Chestnut Street, large windows made the room bright and cheery, and opposite them, sliding doors opened into the dining room; Gramma let me slide them in and out.

Big clawed feet supported her oval oak table. Over it hung a large Tiffany-type green and yellow light fixture made of stained glass leaves held together by lead strips and hung with gold tassels from the leaf tips where they scooped in as the edges drooped down toward the table.

On the far wall near the floor were built-in oak drawers for linens, and above them was a cabinet with leaded, beveled glass doors, the glass divided into squares and triangles. A shelf always held a dried, rosy-tan hydrangea arrangement which Gramma replaced each fall from her garden. Behind it was a wide narrow window which matched the cabinet doors.

Her oak buffet was to the left of the swinging kitchen door. Here she kept my treats, the fat pillow mints and horehound candies in their cut glass, stemmed, and lidded containers. The silver service was on a table to the right of the door.

Gramma had a curious kitchen, curious because it was so bare. It had no canisters or tools visible because Gramma didn't often cook, Mom told me.

Crowded into the corner just inside the kitchen door was a small dining table by a window where Gramma, Grampa, and Uncle Harlan, until he married, ate their meals. I recall watching Grampa bending over one of his favorite foods—a heap of hot mashed potatoes, a pat of melting butter running down its sides, topped by a mound of glistening cold "dutch cheese" as he called it—"cottage cheese" according to Dad and Mom.

Grampa also loved oysters. Each fall he'd go to Sauer and Dahlberg's butcher shop at 321 Chestnut Street to buy them. Once he took me along with him. Sawdust covered the floor. I had fun sliding my shoes under the sawdust; some got between my socks and shoes. It prickled.

The huge oyster barrel sat at the glass counter's end, jutting out a little, so everyone would know the oysters had arrived. As Mr. Dahlberg ladled out a quart for Grampa, we stood watching the oyster liquor drool down the sides of the cardboard container. A smile lit Grandpa's face.

Once, before the family schism, Gramma invited us to enjoy oyster stew with them. Dad loved oysters. Mom wouldn't touch them. I wanted to please Grampa, and I didn't mind trying new foods; but in looking at those soft, gray, bulbous, repulsive looking things, I couldn't bring myself to put even one in my mouth much less chew and swallow it.

But I loved the flavor of the cream part, so I spooned that up saying, "Grampa, this is soooo good," and hoped he wouldn't notice I was leaving the oysters.

I wanted to like them because he did, and I thought if I loved them he would know how much I loved him.

"Would you try just one, Virginia?" he asked me.

"No, Grampa, I can't eat even one."

I finished first. Until I was excused from the table, I stared at the family as they ate the stew, their heads bent over Gramma's white stoneware soup bowls. Since the lamp threw a dim light on their faces, and the spaces behind them were dark, I thought they looked like some of the pictures in Mom's art books. They spooned up the soup and the oysters, the only conversation being the clacking of metal on ceramic.

A small hall was beyond the kitchen table, and beside it was the enclosed back porch that formerly held Gramma's icebox. Grampa was one of the first men in town to buy a refrigerator, a General Electric I think, with a compressor sitting on its top. She thought it didn't belong in the kitchen, so she put it where the discarded icebox once stood.

But the little hall wasn't only a passage to the back porch. It held Gramma's gas stove. I later believed the unusual arrangement grew out of her pioneer past when fires were dangerous to houses, thereby causing the cooking to be done in an outside shelter. To the left of her stove under a window was a small table, and that's where she made batter for pancakes.

She let me stand beside her to watch the pancakes cook. My eyes were level with the pancakes. I saw the accidental dribbles she made when pouring batter onto the griddle; the dribbles became midget cakes. She saw that I saw, so she created a number of accidents. Scooping them up with the pancake turner, she'd drop them on the counter. Pop! Into my mouth went the crisp, teensy pancakes. That helped me be patient as the stack of big ones grew taller and taller.

I loved to watch the bubbles appear in the pale batter, watch them pop and see the shine of the batter become dull. That meant it was time to turn them over. My Gramma was an expert. The upside was now a golden brown prettily decorated with myriads of big and little brown and white circles. I breathed in their sweet scent. Mom never made pancakes—her specialty was waffles.

When they were ready, Grampa and I sat at the kitchen table and gorged ourselves, the delicious pancakes soaked with huge pats of butter and orgies of syrup. I'd drink milk. He'd drink coffee. Eventually Grampa paid for his overindulgence of sweet eating, being diagnosed as a "diet diabetic", as Mom called it. Supposedly watching his diet, he cheated regularly, but never used insulin. Gramma would try to control his eating, but it was her sister, my Great Aunt Cinny, who indulged Grampa's sweet tooth.

If I never mention watching Gramma eat, it's because I seldom saw her eating. She never sat with us at the little kitchen table. Then, after Dad emancipated Mom from Sadie's verbal abuse, as a family we never again ate a meal with them. Later, Mom told me Gramma had been nursing stomach cancer for years. She was living on ice cream, having given up real food long before.

When I went upstairs to go to bed while staying with her, I enjoyed running my hand along the rail next to the open space which looked down into the music room. Grampa designed a big open triangle to replace the wall above the railing, open to the ceiling, to let daylight flood through the two big landing windows, onto the stairs and through the opening, bringing extra daylight into the dark music room.

Gramma's upright piano sat along the wall below the triangle. She didn't play the piano, at least not while I was there. I played it when I learned my first piece. It was out of tune. The music room was a raised room, one step up from the living room.

At the top of the stairs was an open space from which one entered the bedrooms. Here, one day Gramma proudly opened her wide, deep drawers for linens above which were doors hiding shelves for all the many colored blankets she'd won playing Lotto at the County Fair. When closed, the drawers and doors formed a handsome wooden wall.

The windows in the master bedroom overlooked the driveway and gave a view of Chestnut street. Gramma's long dressing table, made pretty by a lacy runner, stood against the wall on the right; neatly arranged on it were her comb, brush, and powder container. I never looked in her dresser drawers. She was private about her personal possessions.

Once in her bedroom I saw a weird looking piece of wire, and asked, "What's that funny looking thing, Gramma?"

"That's my dress form, Virginia. It has the same dimensions I have. It's for fitting the dresses I make for myself."

At floor level, just outside the bathroom, was a little trap door covering a two-inch hole. This was proof of Grampa's avant-garde nature and love of invention. He had installed a central vacuum system in his house. Unfortunately, I never saw it used.

At the top of the stairs was the nursery. Mom and Dad so christened it because Harold, his wife, Fran, and infant Francie lived in Grampa's house for a while after my brother returned from World War II. I thought it was a good location for a nursery because baby's cries could be heard both upstairs and downstairs.

Later, when Harold and Fran were using the bedroom with the anteroom, and Mom and Dad's room was once Gramma and Grampa's room, one night, baby Francie cried and cried. Only Mom heard her. She rushed across the foyer in the dark and plunged down the five steps to the landing. That aroused everyone. Mom was taken care of as well as the babe. In all the falls Mom had during her eighty-nine years, she never broke a bone but had many bruises.

The long, hot summer days in the thirties made one want to get up and enjoy the early mornings. Grampa sometimes would make a date with me. We'd outgrown the baby sitting and ice cream game.

"Would you like to go for a ride with me tomorrow morning? Can you be up and ready to go at 6 o'clock?"

Of course I could and would. Each of us kids had an alarm clock of our own which got us up at whatever hour was appropriate. On one of these mornings, Grampa was late, very late. I sat out under the big elm tree on the curb, feet in the street, holding my chin on my knees, listening to the birds enjoying a chat. Nothing else was stirring. Already the temperature was seventy-five along with high humidity. I kept watching for his car to come around the corner. Thirty, maybe forty minutes went by. Finally I saw his Buick.

"I just didn't wake up this morning, Virginia. Don't know why."

"That's OK, Grampa." He did look a little sleepy. I noticed he hadn't shaved.

Today we went at his usual leisurely pace out north of town, dust sifting up behind the car. Drifting along in the cooler country air, we stared at the cattle in the meadows and looked at the drooping dry-leaved corn struggling in the drought. We seldom said anything. The smells from the barnyards were ripe. I counted windmills that pumped water for the farmers and their animals. I liked these peaceful drives, not at all like driving with Dad.

Grampa was chewing his Sweet Burley tobacco. Gramma didn't allow chewing in the house, so he stuffed his mouth full as soon as he got into his car. This particular morning he was driving and dreaming when all of a sudden he spat. Tobacco juice spattered his clothes. It dribbled down the closed window. He grabbed his big white cotton handkerchief from his coat pocket and, after dabbing his chin, his tie and suit coat, scrubbed round and round the glass. Finally he cranked open the smeared window and threw his hanky out. He didn't say a word. Nor did I. I didn't care, but I knew he was embarrassed.

Eventually Uncle Harlan married Gladys Anderson. One day Gramma brought the young bride to call on Mom. She planned to serve them tea and cookies in the living room. Excusing herself, she went to the basement for some jelly.

As she was coming up the stairs, she could hear Gramma saying, "And these and this we gave to Cornelia and Harold."

Mom came up behind Gramma and said, "Mrs. Shrauger, *if* and *when* I wish to show Gladys what is in my cupboards, I shall do so." It was always "Mrs. Shrauger."

Our gang grew larger when Howard and Jeanne Marshall moved to La Vista from elsewhere in town, bringing their three boys, Howard, Jr. a year older than

I, Robert, (Bob), a year younger, and William, (Billy), a couple of years younger than Bob. Mr. Marshall was known to the men in town as 'Skin,' as was his first-born and namesake. Now we had more players for baseball games. They now lived in the house across from our neighbor's, the Smollers.

It was early on a Saturday morning, already hot, and I knew in my bones the day would become what Mom called a scorcher. My bed was next to the window. As was my habit upon awakening, I put my chin on the windowsill to gaze up and down the street to see what was going on. I noticed a strange car in the Mar-shall's driveway. The different color of the license plate told me the Marshalls had company. They must have arrived the night before.

I ambled downstairs and began frying some eggs.

A chilling, ferocious noise interrupted me; it was coming from the front yard. I turned off the stove and rushed to the porch. The Marshall boys, Mr. Marshall, some boy I didn't know, a man I'd never seen before, and all the Herbert's were running toward two dogs who were embroiled in a fight in the Smoller's front yard. One was the Herbert's Airedale, a handsome young male we loved because of his friendliness and strength.

The Airedale, Mr. Smoller later told me, had strolled into his yard to sniff the newly planted petunias around his young elm tree. Both he and the dog heard a warning growl. Both saw a Pit Bull advancing from the Marshall's. When he mounted the curb, the Airedale attacked; the Bulldog was invading his territory.

Immediately and completely engaged, they set up a continuous and astonish-ing noise; their growling and yipping filled the neighborhood. Neighbors, still in their night clothes, stood on their porches. The men sent the boys for brooms.

Quickly returning, shouting the dogs' names, the boys advanced as close as they dared to the twirling, snarling, gouging beasts. They smacked the dogs' hindquarters with the brooms—or anywhere they could—with no affect.

The gashing, roaring dogs careened up the common Smoller-Herbert drive-way. Both men ran to their hooked-up hoses and doused the dogs with the full force of two streams of cold water. First the Airedale would be under the Bull Dog, then the Bull Dog would be under the Airedale. The water had no effect. It seemed to freshen the beasts—they were completely caught up in their intent to kill each other.

The men gave up trying to stop them. Everyone stood back listening to the fierce growls and yelping, watching the strong bodies move up and down the driveway, onto and off the yards—attacking, aiming for each other's throat but slashing at ears, legs, anything that separated itself from the mass of the other's body.

Panic seized me. I found it hard to breath. I ran to our porch and sat in the swing, holding my ears. As the cries of pain continued, I ran to the rear of our house as far from the noise as possible. Burying my ears in two pillows didn't help. There was no escape—no way not to hear the fighting dogs.

They fought for three hours, watched to the end only by Mr. Smoller, the Herberts, the Marshalls, and their guests. Mr. Smoller told me later, the exhausted dogs finally backed off from each other, still snarling, covered with blood, hardly able to stand.

Marshall's guests had to stay several extra days until their dog was well enough to travel. The Herbert's dog, recuperating in their basement, didn't show up in the neighborhood for several weeks. Ever after, the sound of dogs fighting set off fear in my gut.

The Adams family, recently moved from St. Louis, had rented the house across the street from Earl. Mary Louise was in Cornie's class, and Helen was a year younger than Dorothy and me. I felt like I was in a house of giants when I visited them. Mr. and Mrs. Adams were both six feet two, maybe more, and all their girls were exceptionally tall.

One December, getting on toward Christmas, I was invited to the play there. Playing with Helen was different. I came in through the kitchen, and plunged into the most wonderful aroma I'd ever experienced: Mrs. Adams was making candy. She was working fondant on a huge marble slab, and sweet-smelling steam was floating above several pots simmering on the stove. She told me she was about to dip pieces of fondant into chocolate and other surgery syrups.

I managed to keep my saliva in my mouth, then joined Helen in the adjacent dining room; we sat on the floor. She was setting up her doll kitche, and I watched while she arranged her toy refrigerator, electric oven and miniature plates. Finally she plugged in the oven. I didn't know miniature electric stoves existed.

Helen had a tiny metal plate, and on it she placed a fat, white marshmallow that fit it exactly. Into the oven went the marshmallow. We waited, and peeked, and waited, taking turns supervising the baking of our own. When I thought mine was done, I took it out, admired its toasted pale-brown outside, poked it to be sure the inside was all runny, then ate it, savoring its crisp skin, its warmth and lethal sweetness.

I saw that this method of toasting marshmallows produced superior results, better than turning one on a long handled fork over our stove's burners or trying to toast one on a stick over an open fire.

Having had enough marshmallows, I went through the kitchen and saw that most of the sweet smelling fondant had become chocolate-covered candies. Mrs. Adams, proud of her work, pointed out butter creams covered with a white sugary coating flipped into a curl on their tops and other kinds and colors. I wasn't offered one but consoled myself thinking that the smell was almost as good as a taste. Probably baked marshmallows were better anyway.

The Adams family was Catholic, and Helen couldn't play on Saturday mornings because they went to catechism. Helen couldn't explain catechism in a way I could understand, but I got the idea it was a school to learn about their church. Of course I wanted to visit.

"Helen, can I go to catechism with you one Saturday?"

"Oh, no, that's only for Catholic kids."

I had never thought of church as being a place where certain people weren't welcome, so I tried another idea.

"Could I go to church with you one Sunday."

"Oh, no, you're not Catholic."

"How about you coming and visiting my church?"

"My mother wouldn't allow that."

I could see that being a Catholic was very exclusive, and that somehow I had wound up in the wrong church. Their religion was secret, therefore desirable. I never thought to discuss this with my Mom. However, she was a good friend with their Priest, Father McDermott, so I decided it was OK for me to be friends with Catholics.

The Adams family included an "after-thought" baby, as Mom called children born to a couple in their later years. I was about seven when he was about three. I had come to see if Helen could play. Baby Rob was sitting on the steep hill in front of the Adams house, leaning back on his arms, and kicking up his legs as high as he could. I sat near him to watch. It was quite a sight, this blond haired toddler, with hair falling over his grown-up looking face, his extra long legs and extra long body leaping up and down like a wild pony.

As he stopped to rest, his legs akimbo, I could see up the leg of his summer shorts that he had no underwear on. I also could also see something strange where his legs met. Instinctively I knew that this was what Mom called "private parts." At that time I hadn't thought about the sexual paraphernalia of boys; I took advantage of the moment.

I tutored. "Turn over this way, Rob; now spread your legs."

But I never did get more than that first glimpse of extra wrinkly, pale skin. That day I couldn't further my education. But I stored that memory and built on it later.

One summer as the Fourth of July approached, someone in our gang observed that to properly celebrate the glorious day, we needed to earn money to buy more firecrackers, more money than we could save from our small allowances. We decided to put on a circus just like the traveling Ringling Brothers show. An older boy, Randy McDermott, had a pony which could do at least one trick. Earl agreed we could use his fine trapeze, and all of us had various talents. We visualized a big affair, lots of acts, and seats for our paying audience. Our mothers volunteered their household chairs for seating, and goodies to sell to the audience.

We started on the Saturday before the big day bringing props to the site. With immense effort we dragged Earl's trapeze around his backyard fence, across Dorothy's yard, through the meadow to behind my house—it seemed like a mile. The boys hammered some boards together making a platform for the tap dancers. Having discovered musical talents among the performers—a kazoo player, a trumpeter, and a drummer—we enlisted them to play during the opening parade and between acts.

Randy brought white chicken feathers from his neighbor's farm to put on headbands for our Indian warriors. This was important because every circus we'd seen ended with a rip-roaring cowboy and Indian fight.

Circus day arrived, sunny and not too hot. Everyone in the neighborhood knew the opening parade started at four o'clock. The customers streamed through our back yard to the meadow. Toopee Hill, a friend of Harold's, sat by our toolshed and sold the ten cent tickets; Dorothy collected them. As business manager, Harold would count the proceeds and see that we neighborhood kids got our shares. Our guest performers were performing for fun.

As visitors paid their ten cents, the sweet smell of fudge rounds, pink-frosted cupcakes, and raisin cookies tempted them. Sales were brisk. Enterprising Bob Marshall, who always had a money-making scheme up his sleeve, brought Wrigley's peppermint gum. Five cents each was the price of the refreshments except for the gum, which we sold for two cents a stick.

It seemed to me the crowd of arriving customers would never end. Everybody came, all the parents, most of the neighbors, and some of their friends. No one minded that we didn't have enough chairs.

Randy, mounted on his foxy black and white spotted pony, led the Grand Parade, the musicians followed, sounding a little odd, and the rest of us marched two by two in a large circle around our equipment and past the audience.

Our ringmaster, Skin Marshall, carrying a cane and dressed in his father's old tuxedo, a bent top hat perched on his head, blew a shrill whistle, then shouted, "Ladies and Gentleman, we are about to begin the Great La Vista Circus. Sit back and enjoy our youngest performers as they sing and dance."

Three little girls opened the show singing *Twinkle Twinkle Little Star* followed by a not-too-well rehearsed, unaccompanied tap dance on the make-do stage.

As they ran out of the ring, our clown, Earl, wearing his father's too-large old clothes and a squashed hat, his face disguised by looping lines of red lipstick and black eye shadow, strolled among the audience waving a bunch of dyed chicken feathers. He surreptitiously tickled lady's chins.

Skin reappeared shouting, "And now, Ladies and Gentlemen, here to give you a thrill with their daring feats are the La Vista Acrobats! Give them a loud welcome!"

The audience responded with enthusiastic clapping. Accompanied by the kazoo, the acrobats did a team performance, knee-swinging on the rings and bars, up, over, and pass-throughs while extraordinary heights were achieved by Dorothy on the swing.

Next, the older dancers tapped and spun, wearing their skimpy dance-class costumes. And last, our animal performer, Toopee's dog, did tricks; hind-leg walking, roll-overs, and Dead Dog.

As these acts came to an end, everyone rushed to the center of the ring and did whatever was their best: cartwheels, hand-walking, handstands, headstands and feats on the trapeze equipment. Our sympathetic audience applauded for everyone and everything, so we all outdid ourselves, performing beyond our abilities.

As a thank-you, Randy raced his pony around the equipment, making him rear up on his hind legs now and then for the enjoyment of the crowd.

Then came the finale. Those of us in the role of cowboys crept behind the straw bale barricades lent by the neighboring farmer. Just as we got settled, the Indians wearing their chicken-feather headdress attacked.

We cowboys shouted "Here they come," and shot off our cap-gun pistols.

Cowboys and Indians chased back and forth, kept reloading and shooting the cap guns, kept whooping and hollering until everyone was hoarse and, at last the Indians ran off, the cowboys in hot pursuit.

Then Randy took his pony at a leisurely canter around the circle, stopped, and caused him to rear up on his hind legs for one last time; then he raced off the field.

This ended the successful and only performance of the Great La Vista Circus.

To everyone's surprise, the next day a seven-inch article reporting our efforts appeared in our daily paper, *The Atlantic News Telegraph*. Of course it didn't hurt having the owner, Percy Chase, and his wife, Jane, living in the neighborhood. The reporter said we served pink lemonade, which we didn't, and he omitted our noisy finale. Maybe the reporter had gone home by then. I thought it was the best part of our circus.

On Monday before July fourth, Cornie and I ran down Chestnut Street to Chris Yeanos's Shoe Shine Parlor and spent our shares of the money. We bought lots of minnies—the long strings of three-quarter-inch crackers that made a wonderful, long-lasting cracking just like the ones we heard in the Fu Manchu movies. Chris also sold red bombs to set off under cans, the favorite of the big boys. We didn't buy those. But to be daring, we selected a few lusty crackers that were stuffed with enough powder to take a finger off or put an eye out if you weren't careful. We bought Red Devils, a really safe firecracker, a thin red disk which, when scrunched on the sidewalk with the heel of your shoe, rewarded you with a lovely confined crackly explosion with every twist of the heel. As a contrast, we bought plenty of sparklers so we could play fairies. I had enough money to buy more firecrackers than I managed to shoot off on that celebratory day.

On the Day of Independence, early blasts of giant firecrackers and sounds of tin cans hitting the sidewalk awakened me. Out the bedroom window, I could see that the neighborhood big boys had gathered in front of our house. I quickly dressed, and ran outdoors to join the fun. Standing back out of danger, I bravely watched Skin and his friends setting red bombs under the cans, lighting the fuses, then running as fast as they could to get out of the way. What wonderful explosions!

Mr. Allen came out on his porch and gave us dirty looks, and Mr. Smoller hollered at the boys saying, "It's too early for all that noise."

So they contented themselves by chasing me up on my porch and throwing lit firecrackers at me. For the first time in my life, I was really scared. I thought I was going to cry. As much as I liked adventure, I didn't want to get hurt. But they soon gave that up and went elsewhere looking for trouble. Cornie came out, our gang gathered, and we had a cracking good time until hunger drove us into our houses for breakfast.

In the next day's newspaper, we learned a boy in some other town accidentally shot off his hand, the firecracker factory in Spencer, Iowa, burned down, and the State of Iowa banned firecrackers.

A day or two later I amused myself by breaking open all my leftover firecrackers, piling up the gray and sparkly powder into a heap on one of our porch cement balustrades. In retrospect, it seems to me I had a heap at least seven or so inches high spreading out in all directions, almost to the edges of the wide cement block. I casually threw a match on the pile.

Instantly, a huge explosion! I sat immobile, stunned, heart thumping, ears deafened. I realized I had done the dumbest thing in my whole life. I looked at my fingers. They were all there. I wasn't even burned.

16

Dorothy's father was a dentist. Mom trained Harold, Cornie, and me, to call everyone Dr. or Mr. and Mrs. So-and-so; therefore, I never learned Dr. Hupp's first name. I knew Mrs. Hupp's first name was Blanche because Mom played golf with her. I overheard a lot about Mom's golf games. I knew Blanche as a dark haired, dark skinned woman who made wonderful jellyrolls but never gave me a taste of one.

I was invited into the kitchen one day when I came to the back door looking for Dorothy. Mrs. Hupp was spreading grape jelly on a sweet-smelling, thin and flat white cake. I watched as she rolled it up and powdered it with sugar. I suppose she made it for the family dinner and didn't think of breaking its symmetry for a kid.

But she allowed Dorothy to have me for dinner now and then. Dr. Hupp was known around town for his droll humor. Dorothy looked like him, being dark skinned, having rather chubby cheeks, and a somewhat immobile face. Once when his sister was visiting from St. Cloud, Minnesota, I was seated at their table. Mrs. Hupp had made a delicious vegetable soup. Dr. Hupp had the tureen in front of him.

As soon as we had emptied our bowls, he twisted his head to the side in a funny way and asked in a fake, squeaky voice, "Anyone for seconds? Please pass your bowels."

Silence reigned; then everyone laughed, realizing his unintentional mistake.

One Saturday when Dorothy and I were riding our bikes on the gravel road, I discovered my brakes weren't working. Since the road was downhill all the way to Chestnut Street, a quick decision made me pull into a driveway on my left. But my speed caused a skid as I turned. That dumped me against the cement culvert and tore a huge hunk of flesh from my shin.

When Dorothy she saw the blood, she said, "Dad's home. He'll take care of that."

Dr. Hupp washed my leg in their bathroom sink, soaped the wound, and made it sting fiercely with iodine. After putting a neat bandage on it, he sent me home. I was grateful; however, the wound got infected. Mom didn't notice, and I never thought to tell her. My shinbone hurt so much I prayed to God to please heal my wound. I promised I'd be a very good girl from then on if He'd help me. I guess He heard, because the gouge turned into a bumpy scar which eventually smoothed itself.

On another summer day, when Dorothy and I were playing in the meadow, I decided to climb one of the two weeping willow trees that bordered the swampy place further downhill. A breeze had come up and the willow leaves, slight and silvery, turned over and back, gleaming like pale daytime fireworks. As I climbed up, up, up, the soft rustle of the restless leaves enclosed me, and I soon detached completely from the fading earth sounds. On I went until the thinning tree trunk suddenly made a slight sideways bend, then shifted back. I realized my weight might be too much for it. But I lingered. The breeze was pushing me back and forth, gently. I was a baby in a cradle.

As I rocked, I looked to the west. I could see over the swamp to the farthest hills beyond Randy McDermott's house. From that brief moment I understood that depending on where we are, the world varies. This was Dad's vista! I was glad I'd made the climb.

Grampa was on the Atlantic Water Commission. He told me the City had put up a fine water tower around the loop near Mrs. Bibbys. So on another day, Dorothy and I decided to examine it. We walked down the dirt road that led from La Vista Place to town.

It was shaped like a circular quart ice cream carton with the bottom being half of a round ball; an inverted cone sat on its top. We saw an attached ladder that one could climb if one wanted to. I wanted to: so I did.

Quickly I passed the round bottom, and up the straight side I went. A wind came up, which hadn't been noticeable below. I gripped each rung, tight, and climbed as fast as I could.

"Better come down, Virginia, you're up too high," called Dorothy.

That was reason enough for me to go further, and I kept saying to myself in rhythm to my climb, "Don't look down. Don't look down. Don't look down,"

Then the edge of the cone was in front of me. I did not consider climbing further. Its slanting side rose high from the tip of my nose to the point. A ladder lay flat on the surface that I could take for the trip. But no, I'd reverse.

I clung there for a while, then felt for the rung below with a foot, couldn't find it, finally found it; one at a time I unglued my hands, eased down to the next rung, and the next, and slowly I made my way down to wise Dorothy who always kept her feet on the ground.

Sometimes I wonder what she thought of all my derring-do; but Dorothy never told of my exploits, for she always was allowed to play with me. My Mom didn't know either.

Later when I was in eighth grade and we were studying how to figure cubic volumes, Miss Wissler, our arithmetic teacher, assigned me the problem of working out the cubic feet of water in the tower. What would she have said if I'd told her I had once climbed it?

One day Mom arranged to have Dorothy stay overnight with me. We were in the downstairs guest room. With lights out, window and shades up, moonlight streamed through the screen spotlighting the lower half of the bed. We were having a frolicking good time, scrambling about, laughing and giggling, making howls like dogs baying at the moon, and generally being so delighted we almost fell off the bed.

Suddenly, in a stage whisper, Dorothy said, "Someone's looking in the window."

Sure enough, there was a man's face, hat on his head, glasses resting on his round nose which pressed against the screen. That meant his face was practically in bed with us for there was less than a foot of space between the bed and the wall of the small room!

I recognized Mr. Allen, our neighbor. Instantly I grabbed the cord and pulled the shade down. Dorothy and I hooted and hollered, and rolled about the bed in utter abandon thinking him harmless and being thrilled at the thought of having a voyeur at the window. Then we noticed his silhouette on the shade didn't vanish right away; so we quieted and kept watching his shadow until it disappeared.

This event reinforced my idea that those neighbors kept a pretty close eye on us. Later I wondered why he was wandering around so late at night. The Allens always went to bed early. I suppose all our giggling, and yipping had disturbed his sleep. After all, only the double driveway separated our homes. Curiosity most likely brought him to our window, so I didn't bother telling Mom about this.

"A Treasure Hunt! Who wants to go on a Treasure Hunt?" The minute Skin yelled "treasure," the question was answered. He'd never given us a suggestion before, so we immediately agreed.

Our whole gang was lolling under the poplar tree's thin shade in my back yard, wondering what we could do with this hot sunny July day: Skin, Cornie, me, Dorothy, Bob, Billy, Earl, Louise, Helen, Dixie, and his sister, who seemed not to have a name other than Sister. The thought of having a Treasure Hunt pleased us all.

"I read Treasure Island. I bet all of us have secret hidden treasures at home," I said.

"I know about wicked pirates who attack ships, crawl on board, and steal gold," said tall Louise, flipping her straight black hair that always hung over her eyes.

"And they buried it in Florida where my Grandpa and Grandma go in January," said Skin.

Knowing we had to be both hiders and hunters didn't deter us. First we scrambled home to our private stashes. I selected two look-alike miniature bottles. Cornie set up a card table in our kitchen while I found some old newspapers and dug out the ball of used string I'd been saving for emergencies. When everyone joined us in the kitchen, we pooled our little pieces of junk. I wondered how some of it could be called junk?

"How can you think of hiding that, Dorothy? That little doggie looks just like your dog."

"Blackie said it was Ok."

I coveted a little perfume bottle of Helen's that would be fine in my collection, and Bob brought a gold chain....

"Get to work everyone," said Cornie.

We selected the best treasures, put two or three on squares of the newspaper, then carefully wrapped, tied, and stuffed them in our pockets on top of the peanut butter and jelly sandwiches my Mom had provided. Cornie gave Skin a piece of paper and a pencil stub. They were the Map Makers.

Skin led the pack. We ran pell mell out the door in a beeline across the meadow, over the gravel road, straight by the willows and swamp toward the first country road off Chestnut Street. The older kids had raced ahead of the straggling little ones, so Skin called a halt at the culvert to allow them to catch up. Cows used to go under the road there, from pasture to pasture. Now it was crowded with rusting wire and old fence posts.

As we waited I noticed that the blossoms had fallen off the bushy hawthorn tree growing there. I could see that when we came hiking this way later on we'd have some good eating.

"You little kids stick some of your treasures in those cracks in the cement walls while we make the map," Cornie said as the little kids caught up to us.

I watched her draw our yard, the meadow, the gravel road, the mud bottom, the country road, the turn, and now the culvert. Skin labeled everything in clear printing. Then I joined the others and hid a couple of packets in culvert cracks getting a scratch from a rusty wire end.

Back on the road we examined every old fence post along the way putting our small treasures in weathered notches.

"Tell us where you're putting them," Skin called, "so this map will be right."

As we worked our way along, the sun got higher and hotter. We all began sweating. I was hungry.

"Hey, how about we hike on down to the Oak Grove and eat?" I said.

Everyone agreed. We decided to continue our game after lunch.

A full blooming carpet of tall blue Sweet William sheltering tiny white wild flowers greeted us as we walked into the woods and followed the little path that led along the waterless creek. It was wet only during the heaviest spring melts; now the bottom was cracked and dried into little gray diamonds and squares with edges curled up. It looked like a path of shattered doll plates with all the pieces lying just a bit apart, like a jigsaw puzzle one could push together.

We were in a low area, at the bottom of a sloping hill. A slight breeze drifted through the shady grove.

The heat of the hot July sun cooled as it filtered through the crowns of the full grown trees.

"Hey," called Louise. "I bet I can get my arms further around this big tree than any of you."

That started a contest with Skin judging. When it was my turn, I hugged the trunk spreading my arms as far around as they would go while I sniffed in the pungent smell of the gnarled bark, and put my fingers between the deep, rough ridges. But no one could beat Louise.

We gave that up and looked for a place to sit in the dense shade. There were plenty of choices among trees fallen because of old age, or pushed over by the wind during our winter storms.

"Over here, Virginia." called Dorothy.

Earl and I ran to where she stood by a thick, fallen oak bole stretched out flat and high off the ground alongside the creek. The rest of the gang followed our lead and found other trunks to sit on. We three struggled to settle ourselves, and fished out our squashed sandwiches. As we ate, I watched the gray-green shadows and shafts of sunlight that held mists of tiny flying insects, the color of onion-skins. For dessert we chomped on apples and cookies.

My sister and Skin climbed on a fallen trunk lying on a little slope across the dried-up creek from us. They were on a stage. The rest of us were an audience in a natural amphitheater. We wondered what they planned to do.

They began singing, deliberately off key, as they sidestepped back and forth along the bole. Their song sounded more like shouting.

Skin started pulling down his pants a little, and Cornie copied him. They pranced and danced. I couldn't decide whether they were amusing themselves or us. Their singing became giggling as inch by inch, down went their pants, further and further: down, up, then down, up, then down—just past curly hair that must have begun to grow recently. I was fascinated, but embarrassed for them.

As their pants began to reveal all, I stopped looking at Skin because I wasn't as curious about seeing his penis as seeing what my sister's crotch looked like. Even though we shared a room, I had never seen her undressed. I couldn't take my eyes off of her.

I began laughing. So did Dorothy and Earl. Near hysteria, we lost our balance and fell off the log backwards. All eyes turned onto us. Skin and Cornie had lost their audience. They stopped their performance. Our Treasure Hunt had ended.

After putting our trash in our pockets, we trudged silently back to the road and hitched a ride on a flatbed wagon with a passing farmer who was going up to the Country Club Road.

I don't recall what we did about the Map or the Treasures or if anyone went looking for them. Maybe our look at new kinds of treasures was enough.

Was it an accumulation of curiosity in my unconscious, and the stimulation furnished by the surprise Treasure Hunt entertainment which led to the search in the Marshall attic? Bob and I had gone up there to find a ball or bat or something. I don't know just how it happened that he was on his back, and I was leaning on my elbow beside him unsnapping his coveralls, enjoying the nice little click as each snap came undone. He didn't have any underwear on. His skin was soft and smooth, and I continued to unsnap and feel until I found that curious softness at the top of his legs, his treasure. It felt like I imagined a little mouse would feel.

"Bob, you two had better be coming down now," Mrs. Marshall called up the stairwell into the silence, coming to our rescue.

We did as we were told. For me this was a tantalizing revelation, but that was the end of it. As Bob re-snapped his coveralls, the sound wasn't as interesting. I had learned all I needed to know, for then.

One summer night Mom allowed Cornie and me to have the Adams girls, Louise and Helen, and, of course, Dorothy, for an overnight. We spent the evening playing board games and making popcorn and fudge before eventually going upstairs to bed. I looked out the bedroom window. The night was bright as day, and our front sidewalk looked like a white ribbon running toward the street. The moon was at full.

"Let's take the sheets and go out on the sidewalk and play Fairies!" I suggested.

Everyone agreed. Cornie and I ripped the sheets off the beds, and got an extra from the linen closet in the hall so we'd all have one. Down the stairs and out of the house we streamed into the glorious quiet and solemn beauty of the warm night.

Our big elm stood there, its trunk shaded and invisible in the brilliance of the moon, its motionless leaves a shining silver cap. Not a breath of wind stirred. All the neighborhood houses were dark. The magic atmosphere silenced us.

I began dancing and twirling my sheet in great swirls. It caught the light of the moon, and as it curled back on itself, parts of it were shadowy. I could clearly see its moving outline on the sidewalk and on the lawn, moving as I moved. I heard faint rippling sounds as it drifted through the air. I was one with my Fairy veil.

Cornie, Louise, Helen, and Dorothy came along behind me in single file flinging their sheets about. We split at the end of the warm sidewalk, danced to the lot lines, returned to the walk and made our way back to the porch. Quieted by the beauty of the night, without a sound we filed into the house and to bed.

Mom believed in birthday parties, so all three of us kids had a party every year. I remember nothing of Harold's. Mom let us invite whomever we wanted; sometimes there was a crowd. Cornie's last party was eventful because she invited her whole class. At least twenty-five kids arrived for refreshments (Mom's standard cocoa, toast, and cake), games, and fun. This time the games and fun got out of hand. One of the boys rocked Mom's nice little black, armless rocker right through a low, front porch window. Somehow lots of chocolates, a nice present, were ground into the living room rug. Quite a party!

I invited only my decorous neighborhood girl friends. With them I easily put away my overactive, competitive play behavior and rather enjoyed being a lady. If I had been asked to someone else's party, Mom and I, at the last moment, dashed to Chris Yeanos's Shoe Shine parlor to buy a ten-cent book for the birthday present—maybe one of the *Big Little Books*. Mom never remembered to prepare ahead of time, and that kind of thinking was beyond me. She'd give me a dime; or she'd give me two dimes—one for the present, the other for a pack of Camel Cigarettes. I'd quickly select a book, and off we'd go. I'm not sure if the present was gift—wrapped for the birthday girl. Serious omission.

I loved the parties and the girls who attended. It was always girls until we got into high school. Armelda Welch, my classmate, had parties that were very sedate, asking only two close friends. But her gatherings stand out because of the heavenly angel food cake her mother always served. I never got a second piece of

Mrs. Welch's masterpieces because I didn't have the nerve to ask for one: it wasn't offered. But to this day I can almost taste those few pieces I did have, delicate, light, with a thin, true, white sugar icing. ummmm.

I suppose not buying birthday presents until the last moment was a symptom of Mom's general disorderliness. Theoretically we had a Saturday cleaning schedule. Was she too busy with her many interests that she didn't notice whether or not Cornie and I did our jobs? We were supposed to dust and pickup the house on Saturday mornings.

But how many times did she come running across the porch at noon on Saturday, coming from organ practice at the church, calling, "Girls, quick, one of you get the dust mop and the other straighten up the magazines while I stir up lunch. Dicky and a visiting minister are on their way. They'll be here in a few minutes."

Cornie and I always responded to this crisis with alacrity. She took care of the magazines, while I wielded the dust mop and swished it where I saw inch-thick dust bunnies.

Along with my frantic mopping, I'd have religious thoughts like, "Is cleanliness next to Godliness?" and "What is Grace anyway?"

Then I'd hear Dicky, Mom's motherly name for him, calling from the front door.

"Cornelia, we're here."

Cornie and I had finished our tasks, and Mom almost had the soup, sandwiches, and coffee ready.

Mom practiced the organ every Saturday morning. Reverend Richard Chambers—just out of the Seminary, new to our church, twenty-six and unmarried—would be in his study preparing his sermon. If a visiting minister arrived, he always introduced him to Mom. She always asked them to lunch. My people-loving Mom no doubt wanted to fill in for Dicky's lack of a wife, knowing all about minister's wifely duties learned through her long career as an organist in Iowa City and Atlantic.

One of those mornings I had spent an hour or so meticulously arranging by dairy names my enormous milk bottle-top collection. Carefully I placed the round cardboard seals in straight adjacent lines across and down the nine-by-twelve foot living room rug happily covering it almost completely. I could now count them by multiplying.

Suddenly Mom burst through the front door, stopped short seeing the rug decoration, contained herself, and said, "Virginia! Quickly pick those up: Dicky's coming with a guest!" I did.

But Mom's general disorderliness had even more interesting facets. In my role of watcher and hanger-on-to-Mom, if she were going out, I'd often be sitting on the bed, chatting with her, reveling in the pleasant soapy smell of her body, watching her select a dress, watching her struggle into her corset, and observe her as she looked through the large dresser drawer where she kept her hose, nighties, slips, bras, and undies—all in complete disorder. She'd shuffle through the tangle of pink and flesh–colored garments. Then out of the jumble she'd pick up a pair of panties, sniff the crotch, throw them back, select another, sniff again, and with decision pull that pair up over her hose and corset.

Mom told me her sisters called her "pin Prentiss" because all repair jobs on clothes were simply pinned. (She was always hurrying.)

"And," she added, "Lil always used needle and thread but didn't bother to use the right color—and she, an artist! Only Biddy mended her clothes correctly—as always, perfection."

But Mom's untidy habit with her underwear and mending didn't invade her clothes closet. Her best dresses were removed the moment she got home, hung neatly on a hanger, and were returned to their assigned though crowded space, buttons buttoned, zippers zipped, very best to the left and then in order of favorite or newness to the right. The intricate puzzle of shoes on the closet floor caused anxious searches preceding her usual hurried exits through the front door.

By watching Mom I began to realize the importance of outward appearances. The hint was in the contrast between Mom's closet and her dresser drawers.

17

At some point in her life, Cornie decided she was her sister's keeper. She began to militantly see to it that I fulfilled my household duties. I had no intention of not fulfilling my duties, but my sense of time was quite different from hers. Perhaps my quality of being divertible was the stumbling block. We didn't find much common ground—I wasn't interested in finding any if she wished to shape me into her image. I don't think my Mom played any role in this.

Consider the Saturday morning duties. Aside from theoretically cleaning my share of our common room, dusting the territory of the living room and music room was mine. I rather enjoyed this, once dancing class was over, and there was time to do the work before lunch was ready. But I had a problem. The Queen Anne secretary held charming, miniature volumes of very short stories. Inevitably I'd peek into one, get interested, sit on the floor, lean on the wall under the windows and begin to read. The *Little Match Girl* was a favorite. Soon I was far away from dusting and home.

If I were lucky, I'd come to the end where the little match girl dies, and could have a good, private cry. But if I were unlucky, my sister would appear, note my inactivity, and storm at me.

"Why aren't you getting your work done? Do you always have to sit and read all the time?" Reluctantly I'd put the wee loved book away and continue grubbing.

I came to know every inch of that French Secretary, and I cherished its charm. I also enjoyed dusting the items on the mantel over our fireplace; an old inoperative Victorian metal clock topped by a brass lion, a never polished copper vase, monogrammed with Mom's initials, a handsome wooden box containing Dad's sweet smelling cigars, and a small, stemmed Tiffany mint dish, blue, laced with silver. Lastly, on the mantel sat a small picture of Grandpa Prentiss, which, if I felt charitable, I'd dust.

My other constant assignment was to set the table before dinner every night. I took pleasure in arranging the knives and forks just so, an orderly kind of thing to do. I needed practice in orderliness. Of course I always forgot several items, and had to get up from the table after we were all seated to fetch the salt and pepper, or butter, or dessert spoons, or all of them. It was what happened after I set the table and before supper that seemed to especially annoy Cornie.

I usually would take whatever book I was currently reading, settle down in Mom's comfy orange chair in the living room, and become engrossed in my story. Never, never, never would I hear Cornie calling me from the dining room. She'd burst into the living room, ranting, "Are you deaf? Can't you ever hear me calling you? Dinner's ready!" Reluctantly, without a word, I'd put the book aside and trundle off to eat.

One Saturday morning, Dorothy came into the kitchen calling for me. I hadn't yet done an extra duty assigned to me for that day, carpet sweeping in the living and music rooms. I made a move toward the back door, but Cornie caught Dorothy, shut her on the cellar steps landing, and leaned her big frame against its door. Trapped in absolute dark, Dorothy hollered and banged on the door.

Cornie shouted, Dorothy on one side of the door, and I on the other, "Dorothy, you'll stay on those steps until Virginia does her job!" and needless to say I did my carpet sweeping in short order.

Cornie and I did have one intimate conversation as we were getting a little older. It had to do with body measurements. In one of Mom's magazines appeared a list of 'proper' body measurements. I got Mom's tape and unhappily discovered that my muscular calves and thighs were much too large to be labeled correct. Cornie did the same, and she was even less correct. We actually walked home together from school the next day and talked about the fact that our legs were too big. It was the only time I felt close to her, commiserating about our unfortunate body builds.

The days of playing together in the dead storage had slipped away. She had solidified her gross resentment of me. I could never understand why she felt this hostility. Actually I didn't think about it much: I simply avoided her. Then it began to evidence itself in physical attacks. She would wrestle me down to the living room floor, just off the rug, onto my back, put her knees on my shoulders, grab my hair and bang my head against the oak floor. I would cry, of course, but no one came to my rescue. And I never tattled. We had been trained not to. Very early Mom had conditioned us, saying,

> *"Tattle tale tit, your tongue shall be split,*
> *And every doggie in the town shall have a little bit.*

Either Cornie chose her times carefully when we were home alone, or my Mom ignored what was going on, knowing that if she interfered she would lose her temper. Many years later I wondered if this were the case. Possibly this always happened on Saturday mornings when Mom was at church practicing her music for the Sunday service. However, time has a way of solving some problems. My sister matured before I did and stopped growing. She was big in the shoulders and very strong. Eventually she could hit a golf ball an enormous distance. But because I continued to grow, I outgrew her by several inches.

One day she got me down, and as she began to pound my head on the floor, I made up my mind I would not cry. I didn't. I was about nine at the time, she, eleven. Getting no reaction from me, she stopped. At least I decided that was why she stopped. Maybe without my crying she could hear the thump thump thump of my head hitting the oak floor. That might have scared her. Maybe she didn't get an adrenalin flow without the thumps: maybe she needed my loud protests. In any case, she got up and walked away. That was the end of the attacks and the head-poundings.

As adults we never discussed this. I didn't feel the necessity, and perhaps she conveniently forgot about it. However, I profited from this abuse: I discovered that if anyone pulled my hair, it didn't hurt.

We two were very different. She was steady, reliable, a hard-studying pupil, and a serious trombone student. She studied diligently in high school. I studied what interested me. She worked hard in math. Math was easy for me. We simply were on different tracks. All I wanted was to be left alone. I don't know what she wanted. Except for the size of our thighs, as we matured, we never discussed anything.

Mom, of course, knew we were very different. Harold brought his friends Jesse Marshall and Bill Herring to the house one day. Cornie and I were hanging around. Bill, an epileptic, had an attack as he stood in front of our fireplace. He fell backwards into it.

Mom called, "Virginia, quick, bring a teaspoon from the kitchen!"

I ran as fast as I could wondering, "Why a spoon?"

Mom put it in Bill's mouth, and held it there until his body relaxed. Later she told me about epilepsy, that the spoon was to hold down the tongue so the victim wouldn't accidentally swallow it and choke. She also said she asked me to run for the spoon for she had long known that Cornie was no good in emergencies. I guess I was. I didn't seem to get excited, and didn't mind seeing blood, or mice, or bugs, the usual accompaniments to life and living.

After supper one evening Cornie and I were doing the dishes. A nice little gray mouse scurried under the door from the room outside the kitchen that held the icebox. Cornie screamed, "A mouse, a mouse!"

Dad came running from the dining room, grabbed the broom, and swatted at the poor little creature. I guarded the basement door. Cornie hid her eyes. Dad wielded windmill-like strokes and, finally, the broom and the tiny mouse made contact.

As he tossed the dead mouse out the back door Dad said, "Now some other animal will have a fine dinner."

One of our gang's biggest projects came about spontaneously. Whose idea it was I don't know, but we decided it would be fun to dig a cave. Maybe we could make the entrance at the edge of the meadow by the gravel road where the drop-off of the cliff was the steepest.

"Look," said Cornie, "see where the roots of the meadow grasses are poking down through the layer of black dirt and into the clay?"

We took up hands-full of the pretty ocher colored clay from the side of the cliff. It was a little damp for some reason, so we decided it might be easy to dig. After a conference, Skin drew an outline in the clay marking the tunnel entrance. Its opening was to be about three feet below where the green meadow grass grew.

All the gang joined in this subterranean adventure, even Helen and Louise, who ordinarily avoided outlandish projects that required muscle. With them, Earl, Dorothy, and I, Cornie, Dixie and Sister, Bob, Skin, and Billy formed the construction team. We couldn't accomplish this unless everyone helped. Of course if you didn't help, you'd be excluded from joining the secret club we planned.

After discussing what tools we needed to dig the tunnel, off we went to gather all the shovels, hoes and buckets we could find. The bigger kids, Skin, Cornie, and Louise, took turns digging with the pointed spades. We younger kids scraped out the loose dirt with hoes, shoveled it into the buckets, and dumped it down the cliff. When the tunnel was about three and a half feet long, we rested.

"This is real work," said Dixie. "How can we ever dig a cave when it's taken all morning to dig this little tunnel?"

Who thought up the alternative? I don't recall. But someone said, "Hey, I know. Let's dig a hole in the meadow and then cover it."

Since the tunnel was already dug, all we needed to do was join it to a covered hole. Everyone agreed. That's why we referred to our work as digging a cave.

We smaller kids continued work on the tunnel, smoothing its sides, and cleaning away the excess clay while the bigger kids dug up squares of sod with the spades and stacked them to be replaced later. Then the serious digging began. On some days Skin's boyfriends from other parts of town came to help. I don't remember how long it took to dig the huge hole—it was about seven by seven by six feet deep. Somehow the clay wasn't too hard packed or else our Dads kept their tools sharp. But we managed. We were determined and stuck to it for days.

Finally the digging was done except for one thing. In no time at all, Skin and Cornie joined the tunnel to the hole. Constructing the roof was all that remained to do. We wasted no time in beginning it.

"Cornie, come on, and you too Dixie," said Skin. "Let's go look at all the trash dumps and see what we can find. And the rest of you, go along the fence lines and anywhere else you can think of to find materials to construct the roof."

In short order Dixie, Skin, and Cornie returned with several boards, a little burned but usable, which they arranged around the edges of the hole. Louise, Helen, Dorothy and I searched along the fence line. Deep in matted grass in a fenced corner where the mower couldn't reach, we discovered a pile of young tree trunks, evidently meant for firewood, but stashed and forgotten. We grabbed their protruding ends, and by twisting and turning we gradually loosened them. Everyone helped. We carted them to our cave, and arranged them in crisscross fashion as roof supports.

Earl, for once, came through with flying colors. In his garage he found two old doors minus knobs. The big kids carted them across the meadow and laid them flat on the crossed boards. So far we hadn't asked permission to use any of these materials, but when Earl said his folks had a new carpet, and the old one was waiting to be trucked away, we sent him to ask his Mother if we could have it.

She said, "If you kids can drag it off, yes."

We did. Luckily it was larger than our hole. We could overlap it onto the grass. The hole was covered!

Now came another hard job. Cornie ordered, "You, Skin, Dixie, and Louise, you shovel the clay over the rug, and spread it out as even as you can. The rest of us will haul the sod and put it on the clay. Then we'll all stomp the sod edges together so they meet."

Dorothy, Earl, and I wanted to have a fireplace in the cave, so, while the roof was being finished by the rest of the gang, we dug out a small flat place in the corner to the left of the tunnel entrance. Someone found an old piece of stovepipe in a trash pile, and Skin set that up for us. The pipe even had a little cap on it to keep the rain out. No builders were ever as awed by their success as our gang.

"Let's have a Christening," said Helen. We all agreed that was appropriate, like sending off a newly built ship.

Christening turned out to be having lunch in the cave the next day. We all came bringing sandwiches, and Dorothy, Earl, and I brought newspapers, matches, and firewood. We christened our fireplace by firing it up, planning someday to bake potatoes in coals. It drew well, so we didn't asphyxiate ourselves, but the cave was a little smoky. We traded sandwiches in the light of our flickering fire. Our summer was a success.

For the next month, now and then, Earl, Dorothy and I brought our lunches, and crawled in through the tunnel. The diggers had left a clay bench along the side near the entrance, so we had a place to sit. If we didn't feel like building a fire, some light came in through the tunnel. We tried to baking potatoes only once.

After completing the cave, gradually the Marshall boys, Dixie and Sister Herbert, Cornie, Louise and Helen lost interest and drifted off to other things. So for what was left of the summer it was only Earl, Dorothy and I who enjoyed the fruits of our labor.

As it turned out, the building of the cave was more fun than playing in it. Hiking in the country and swimming in the Sunnyside Park pool were more attractive than crawling in through the tunnel, getting dirt on our bellies, and eating in the dark. So our cave was mostly a secret.

Next winter Dixie told me he saw an old tramp going in and out of our cave. This was during the Depression when tramps left the railroad cars and fanned out over the town to the 'marked' houses to get something to eat. My Gramma's house was one of them, and she told me many hungry men stopped at her kitchen door. So we accepted this tramp's need for shelter and never told anyone about it.

The winter took its toll on the roof of the cave, and it began to sag. By the time the next summer was over, we heard the Herberts had begun to use the hole as a garbage dump.

One day, after the morning dew had disappeared, and when the sweet-smelling red clover had grown long stems, Dorothy, Helen and I went marching to the meadow to pick the longest stemmed, prettiest lavender-pink blossoms. We weren't in a hurry; we had until late afternoon to accomplish this summer ritual. We discovered that if you closed your eyes to a slit and stared at the meadow, it looked like a purple-pink carpet. So we always stood at the meadow's edge for a while, bathing in the warmth of the morning sun and sniffing the sweet scent of clover.

Then we spread out across the meadow and began picking and dropping perfect clover heads and stems into paper sacks. When we thought our harvest was enough, we set up shop under the elm tree in my front yard. While sitting in a circle, we braided three stems at a time, carefully tying them together at their ends. Then with a short string we knotted three of the threes below their purple-pink heads. Finally we tied the heads to other stem-ends to form long chains.

This manufacturing was preparation for our annual late-afternoon occupation. While we worked we had serious conversations: maybe about whether it was all right to tell white lies, or should we always tell the brutal truth. We never decided between what was kind and what was morally perfect behavior.

Pretty as our chains were, we didn't mind sending them to certain death. At about four o'clock in the afternoon, we tied one end around the elm tree and the other end to the tree on the opposite side of the street. We were anticipating the daily recreational drive of our rich neighbor, Mrs. Mullins, in her electric car, and Inez Van Motz, whose car horn sang songs instead of blasting out ugly noises.

As soon as we spotted Mrs. Mullins's car approaching, we stood mute-mouthed and staring as she silently drove her fancy black electric car through our chain, catching it across her fenders. She never acknowledged us, and disappeared from our sight like a black ghost in her black dress, her nose in the air under her large black hat and over her grand Victorian bosom. We supposed her yard-man removed our art-work when she got home.

Then, knowing Miss Van Motz would be on schedule, we scrabbled about, quickly stringing a second clover chain across the street. We looked forward to her arrival. She always drove by after she'd finished her work at four o'clock. Soon she cruised toward us off Chestnut Street onto no-name street, easily seen in her white Buick.

"There she is! Here she comes! Hi! Hi! Honk your horn! Honk your horn! Hi! Hi! Honk your horn!"

She never failed to oblige us with a smile and a wave of her hand while driving bravely through the clover chain.

Often Helen, Dorothy, and I would pack a sack lunch and hike around the roads south of town. One morning we decided to explore a country road to the north. There was no danger of getting lost as most of the roads were straight lines.

It was a sunny pleasant day, but "tuning up to be hot," Mom said as she made my sandwich.

The farmland out this way wasn't as hilly as it was on our south side of town. We could see a long straight stretch of road ahead of us. Eventually we got hungry and decided to stop under a large oak tree. We leaned against the tree, and opened our sack lunches. As we chewed, we stared across the road at a herd of fenced-in cows as they chewed their cuds and stared at us.

On the crest of the long sloping hill behind us was a flock of black-faced sheep peacefully grazing. Then for no reason we could see, they began baaing and circling.

"Something's bothering them," said Dorothy.

We stood up to watch, and Helen cried out, "Hey, they're starting to run—all of them—right down the hill towards us!"

Crowding together, baaing, and looking like a roiling white cloud, they stirred up a huge wave of dust; the entire flock now ran slantwise down the hill!

"Look! See that one left behind? It's trying to catch up, but for some reason...." Helen stopped.

At first we couldn't see Earl's white pit bull nipping at its tail. As the pair dropped behind the flock, we could see the dog move abreast of the frightened creature. He began slashing at the sheep's side with his drill sharp teeth. Crimson blood spread over its white wool, yet it kept running.

Dropping our sandwiches we dashed toward the farmhouse close by the cows, and hollered, "Help! Help!"

A woman working in her garden stood up and ran toward us still clutching her hoe.

"A dog's attacking your sheep!" we all shouted, pointing toward the meadow.

She turned and rushed toward the nearby barn. "She's getting her husband. Come on!" said Helen.

We raced back to see what else there was to see.

Now the dog had the sheep down on the hillside above the flock and was tearing away at its belly. The flock at the fence was milling around, baaing. Only the fence separated us from them, the savage dog, and the helpless bloody sheep.

As fast as we could we ran towards town, anxiously glancing back, even though we'd already seen too much. Finally, out of breath, we slowed to a walk, glanced back now and then, and discussed what we should do about this when we got home.

"What if it isn't Earl's dog?" asked Dorothy.

"The Montgomery's should know what their kind of dog might do," said Helen.

As the increasing heat, the excitement of the slaughter, and our long run made us thirsty, we turned into a long farm driveway near the edge of town planning to ask if we could use their well. Ahead we saw a large black object lying in the grass near the drive. Made wary by the attack on the sheep, we cautiously approached.

We saw it was a large horse, on its side, dead. Its belly was swollen. It looked as if it would burst.

"I wonder what would happen if we poked the belly with a stick?" asked Helen. I immediately envisioned a fountain of guck bursting forth. I wasn't thirsty after all.

Later Mom told me that the dead horse was probably put along the drive to be picked up by the glue factory truck and driven to Omaha.

She said, "It's a regular service given to the farmers."

That information made me take a long look at the glue we bought at the dime store.

Earl's dog remained in the neighborhood for a few days, and then disappeared.

18

Often when I was going home from school I felt what was called "stitches" in my right side. I'd breathe hard and try to ignore it until the strange sensation went away. But early one morning I awakened with a terrible bellyache. Mom immediately called our doctor, then moved me to the downstairs guest bedroom. Dr. Ralph Barnett came quickly.

He was a gentle man. The planes of his thin, bony face were as evident as lines on a map, and his thin lips had a lift at the ends. His forehead, deeply furrowed, was crowned by a tangle of dark hair, and black bushy eyebrows rested on the top of his glasses over his brown eyes. His hands were cool as he pressed my tender belly. He'd been a student of Grandpa Prentiss's.

"Cornelia," he said to Mom, "I think we'd better get this young lady to the hospital. She has appendicitis."

Until I was trundled into the operating room, Mom stayed beside me.

She told me, "Do what the doctor tells you, Virginia; follow directions and everything will be all right."

She patted my head before I was rolled into the small, all-white operating room to deal with strangers.

Soon a man's voice said, "Breathe deeply, Virginia," as something cold was put over my nose.

Immediately I was standing beside a railroad track. My head vibrated with a pounding, pounding, pounding as a huge steam engine, black smoke trailing over it, came thundering around a curve—straight toward me. The sides of it swelled in and out in time with the pounding. Steam roared from its stack. I found it hard to breathe.

Mom held my head—I was back in my hospital bed. Never had I felt so sick. I was throwing up, or trying to. Mom told me the ether made me sick.

When I could rest a bit she said, "Your appendix was about to burst, dear. Dr. Becker removed it just in time, so you'll be fine as soon as your incision heals."

She came every day to see me. When Dorothy visited me, she made wisecracks, faces, and jokes. We laughed so hard my taped belly hurt. One of Mom's friends brought a bunch of colored balloons and tied them to the head of my bed.

While Dorothy was there, three exploded, and three times she and I went off into howls of laughter.

One morning I was struggling to clean myself after a bowel movement. That wasn't easy for I was flat on my back and bound in an armor of tape across my belly and half across my back. I was lucky to be able to move at all. I thought all was well.

A crabby old nurse came for the bedpan, took a look and said, "Well! I should think a big girl like you should know how to clean up her bottom!"

She finished the job.

I was "mortified", to use one of Mom's favorite expressions. I had tried, but failed. I never told Mom about this, but it taught me that Angels of Mercy weren't automatically merciful.

Each day I felt better. Mom's friend, Gwen Swan, loaned me the whole set of the *Little Colonel Books*. My fourth grade class sent a grocery box covered with pink and blue crepe paper, hearts and ribbons. Everyone in the class wrote me a note. I was to remove one each day through the hole in the box top; it pleased me to think I was missed.

But these little pleasures were forgotten the day Dr. Roy Becker, my surgeon, and a friend of Mom's, came to remove the tape. Taking a corner of each strip, one by one he briskly yanked them from my belly. I was sure I was being flayed; I thought my intestines would be hanging out when he got through, sure that all the skin that kept everything in place (my idea of anatomy) was gone with the tape. A lot of it was. I exerted all my will power to keep from crying.

Then to divert me, I guess, he offered me a gift—my appendix in a little bottle of liquid.

"Here's your appendix, Virginia. Do you want to take it home and put it on your dresser?"

I shook my head, no. He put the bottle in his pocket, quickly cut the black stitches, and yanked them out. He left. I was absolutely knocked out for the rest of the day.

I thought I was being kept in bed forever. After about ten days in the hospital, I was sent home for a two-week stay. I wasn't to get out of bed at all the first week. This was very hard for me. Mrs. Swan brought another set of books, the red, yellow, blue, green, purple and all the other colors of fairy tale books. I entered this world of fantasy happily. Mom kept me company when she could; but being used to being active, I was terminally bored.

But the worst realization was yet to come. Evidently having my belly sliced open interfered with my running speed. My pride in my status as the fastest runner in my class was destroyed. I had always won all the races across the gym or playground, but I couldn't win anymore. Evidently cutting my belly muscles did that to me. It was a bitter blow. My high sense of competition drained away. From then on, if I competed in anything at all, I competed with myself.

Much later, after I was completely well, Mom told me that Dr. Becker told her I'd made a terrible ruckus when I was going under the anesthesia. That offended me. I thought I had cooperated in every way, doing as I was told. I learned that sometimes, even though you try, you can not please.

Mom used one illness of mine to foster my independence. I was having cramps, and I noticed that my feces had turned pure white. I duly reported this phenomenon to Mom who called Dr. Harvey Johnson.

She said, "Virginia, there's no reason you can't take care of this yourself. Tell Dr. Johnson what you told me."

As I stood before her, looking at her encouraging face, I thought, "Mom must think I'm growing up."

Although I was apprehensive, I had time to gear myself for the ordeal as I walked down Chestnut Street to his office. I had been there one other time when he recommended a stretch knee-bandage for my hurting knee. I climbed the two steps to his office. He was at the door waiting for me.

"Come into my office, Virginia. Tell me what the trouble is."

I mustered up my courage. I told him in the same words I told Mom, words that in our house were not embarrassing, but they certainly were for me outside our house.

The doctor ignored my flaming face, and said, "There's something I can do for you."

He brought out a small, brown bottle and told me to take a certain amount a couple of times a day until my bowel movements were normal again.

I thanked him, and left, saying to myself, "That wasn't too bad. I can do things like that."

Mom and Dad had their own ways of dealing with the sore throats that occasionally afflicted me. Now and then I would have a throat so sore I could hardly swallow. Mom always sympathized, and at bedtime or if I napped, she would apply a cold compress around my throat—a towel that had been dipped in ice water. Then she'd wind a dry towel around it. For some reason it helped. Maybe it was the tender loving care, or maybe it was the heat exchange. I would press the sorest side of my throat into the icy wetness of the towel and was soon soothed to sleep.

Her favorite lunch treat for sick kids was milk toast: crisply toasted bread in a flat-bottomed soup plate, swimming in very warm milk and loaded with white sugar. I could always swallow that.

Dad's method was more direct: he went straight to the source. His cabinet in the upstairs bathroom held not only his grooming items, but also a supply of tongue depressors, sterile cotton, Band-Aids, Q-tips and liquids in small bottles. The one he used for sore throats was iodine. Taking a tongue depressor, he wrapped it in sterile cotton, and dipped it into the iodine, which made the cotton turn a deep purplish brown.

"Open wide," he'd say.

He trained me to flatten my tongue and breathe in slowly as he quickly swabbed the swollen red throat. It always felt better after he finished.

Sometimes the summer sun exacted a penalty from those who worked or played too long unprotected. One hot and sunny summer day kept our gang in the swimming pool at Sunnyside Park from ten in the morning until four in the afternoon. That evening I began to be uncomfortable. By the next morning it was quite clear that I had been in the sun too long. I was a bright pink everywhere except where my swimming suit covered me. I felt as if my skin was on fire. In those days we hadn't heard of using tea, which someone later told Mom was a good remedy for sunburn. We didn't we have lotions to ease pain. So Mom put me on the old sofa bed in the living room. Dad set up a fifty-pound cake of ice in our big dish pan with a fan behind it directed towards me.

Grampa Shrauger came and sat across the room by the ice, his hands joined across his round belly, mouth munching his wad of tobacco. He brought more ice when it was needed, making me feel loved, sympathy written deep on his kind and wrinkled face. I lay on my unburned stomach, my head turned toward him: neither of us said anything. We both listened to the comforting hum of the revolving fan. I breathed in the grassy smell of the bed's covering, another hand-me-down from my great grandmother Bradley who had designed and woven it. Grampa's comforting presence was with me for two days as I lay there, gradually healing; then I resumed living.

A year or two later when I came home in the late afternoon, I learned that my fair-skinned Dad had suffered severe sunburn. Shirtless, he had cultivated his garden under a cloud-covered sky. By evening he was in terrible pain. A local doctor coated him with bee's wax, heavy on his back. It had the deepest burn.

Dad didn't say anything, but soon he began pacing around the house, walking the circle through downstairs rooms and the little hall. Long after bedtime he walked up the stairs, up and down the hall, back downstairs, around the circle, around and around, up and down. I listened and worried, knowing how terrible the pain must be.

In the morning he went to another doctor who couldn't believe that all that heat had been sealed in with a wax covering. He removed the torturing shield from Dad's back and treated him with some kind of salve. By evening Dad could tolerate the pain. He lay on his belly on his bed. I looked through his bedroom door, and saw huge blisters all over his back. By bedtime peace reigned in the house; his burn took a long time to heal.

From these two incidents I learned that sun is fun, but can be an enemy, at least an enemy to those of us who have fair skin: precautions must be taken.

Gramma had ambitions for her granddaughters. Cornie was to become an opera singer. With this in mind, in 1931 off they went to Omaha to hear Marion Talley sing. As far as I knew, my sister had never dreamed of being a professional singer. Two summers later, in August of 1933, Gramma took me to the Century of Progress Exposition in Chicago. She didn't say what example this could be for me. As I showed no talent, maybe she decided I would be a good enough companion. To celebrate such an opportunity, Mom bought me a navy blue wool skirt and a lighter blue loose-knit, short-sleeved cotton sweater. I wore these clothes to Chicago where I found the temperature hotter than Atlantic. Since it was August, I was in a constant sweat. Still I thought the new clothes beautiful. The woolen skirt got good use until my narrow hips began to mature.

When I tried on the skirt and blouse, Mom said, "Oh, honey, I so admire your breasts. They're pushing your blouse straight out. When I was growing up, the style dictated that we girls wear a kind of brassiere that flattened our breasts. We weren't supposed to have any! Because of that Lil, Biddy, and I developed our droopy, pendulous breasts."

Mom, over the years, talked about this abuse now and then and, I thought, "Today she brought it up again to make me feel comfortable with my changing body."

Gramma and I rode a bus to Chicago, and I felt captured. It took all day to reach the big city. Every once in a while the driver let us out at a rest stop, the object of which was to use the toilet facilities in some unsavory shack. Instantly long lines formed. The quick-lunch counter offered pie and dried-up looking sandwiches. All the adults—everyone except me—ordered pie and coffee. *Pie and coffee.* Didn't anyone ever want anything but pie and coffee?

We stayed in a hotel—my first time. We entered a tiny, poorly lit elevator barely room enough for our Bell Boy, our bags, Gramma, and me. Our room was small and dark, not at all like hotel rooms I'd seen in ads.

Each day we went to the fair. It seemed huge compared to our County Fair. Masses of people, bright colors, flags, and big buildings everywhere made me anticipate what we would see. However, what we did mostly was sit on a bench near the RCA Victor dog because Gramma was tired all the time. The white dog with the black ring around one eye opened and closed its plastic mouth as music blasted out. I came to think of that bench as Gramma's bench. Andthepeople- wentby; thepeoplewentby.

We did see the freak show, another first for me. Freak shows were always at our county fairs, but we didn't spend money on them. Here we saw, according to the barker, a "boy reared by wolves" whose skin looked like a creek-bed in sum- mer, squares of dried dirt all over his exposed arms, legs, and chest. I wondered why they didn't shape him up by giving him a bath. Or did he live forever with that dirty skin? A huge woman sat in a huge chair; we were told she weighed four hundred ten pounds. Too bad, I thought. The tallest man in the world wore baggy pants, and his head was at the top of the tent. I'd seen clowns on stilts inside loose pants at the circus. I was suspicious. There was a two-headed calf which wasn't new to me; pictures of such animals born on farms near Atlantic appeared in our daily paper. Seeing the freaks didn't seem to me to be worth the trip to Chicago because they were available at our Cass County Fairs. However, I was pleased that Gramma invited me along.

Uncle Bob would come to visit us when he was home from Hamilton College for holidays. We all welcomed him, for he was fun and full of tricks. Sitting in the living room after dinner, Bob would make a long face, and we kids would stare at him knowing what to expect.

Looking very sad, he'd begin to wiggle his ears—first one and then the other. He'd stop; then wiggle both.

This was the cue for us kids to call commands: "Left! Right! Together!"

We'd dissolve into giggles, continuing until he gave it up saying, "My ears are tired."

Resting, Uncle Bob would light a cigarette. In a room already filled with smoke, for all the adults present were smokers, he'd blow smoke rings which lazily spread and wavered, floating through the smoky air like weary birds. I never tired of this performance. But best of all, he'd tell ghost stories which frightened me. However, I was always ready for more the next night. Bob was a pretty nifty uncle! He was thirteen years younger than Mom, and he seemed to me more like an older brother than a hard-to-know relative.

Grandpa's unmarried cousin, Elsie Earle, came to see us whenever she was visiting Grandpa Prentiss, traveling by train from New York City. She was a short round ball who wore flowered chiffon dresses with ruffled collars. She amiably taught Cornie and me how to knit and purl, but didn't stay long enough to finish the instruction: so the solution to the mysteries of knitting departed with Cousin Elsie.

Mom gave a waffle and bacon brunch in Cousin Elsie's honor. She placed Cornie and me with Elsie so we two could get to know her. She ate in an intriguing way. Besides lifting her little finger when she drank her coffee, she took up her knife and fork in her bejeweled hands, and, holding wrists and elbows high, cut apart each little square made by the waffle iron. Then, putting down her knife, she'd shift her fork from her left hand to her right, and bring the speck of waffle to her little 'O' of a mouth. The flaccid skin drooping below her chin would jiggle as she daintily chewed. When she moved her hands, her rings glittered for, as I later learned, the jewels were diamonds—large diamonds.

The bell cuffs of her silk dress flipped up and down as she fed herself, revealing chubby arms, pale skin, and wrists decorated with numerous busy bracelets. Hardly able to concentrate on my waffle, I watched to see if her sleeves might dip into her syrupy plate. She was affable, but there seemed to be little to talk about. Since we never left the table until everyone was finished, it was a long brunch.

But later, after I had begun to be a stamp collector, I often received little notes from her. She enjoyed saving and sending me stamps taken from cards and letters she received from traveling friends.

Once when she and my Great Aunt Nettie went to Europe together, Aunt Nettie wrote Mom saying, "I'll never travel with Elsie again. She wants to sit in the hotel room all morning writing notes to her friends, while I want to go and see the sights."

When Cornie and I were little, clothes were never very important. Not until we were in high school did we think much about them. I suppose because there was so little money, to be clothed decently and cleanly was all that was important—high style, not mentioned: seldom new shoes; the old were repaired.

Whenever the soles were worn completely through, she would send me to Ira Welch's shoe store, which belonged to Armelda's father. I'd go to the back room, nod to Mr. Stover, a deaf mute, and he'd open his palm indicating that I should sit on the chair just inside his shop. I'd take off my shoes, hold the shoes upside down, and point to the gaping holes in the soles, unraveling seams, and the run-down heels. He'd nod. I'd amuse myself by watching him do the repairs while running my socks over the large slick, clean and polished piece of leather on the floor in front of me.

Mr. Stover put my shoes on his cobbler's last one at a time. First he cut the old sole threads with his razor-sharp curved knife; then he slashed the leather at an angle just in front of the heel. Completing the destruction, he ripped off the old sole and the worn heel with a special claw hammer.

Over my dilapidated destroyed-looking shoe, he placed a new piece of shiny leather like the one my feet were enjoying, and tacked it into place. Carefully he cut around the shoe with his curved knife. There was the new sole! He then repeated the process on the second shoe. Moving to his green industrial sewing machine he stitched both soles, and repaired the broken seams. After pounding on new heels, he gave the shoes to me.

I had a little trouble getting my feet into them. They seemed small now, and not nearly as comfortable. But with a little wearing I knew they'd relax, so I didn't think about it anymore. Forever I shunned uncomfortable shoes and seldom had a blemish on my feet.

Occasionally at Christmas time, Aunt Nettie would send clothes—something extraordinary and identical to Cornie and me.

An example of Nettie's taste appears in the family picture taken that wonderful summer of 1928, when I was seven and Cornie was nine. As well as Grampa Prentiss and Uncle Bob, pictured are the three Prentiss sisters and their children gathered in the Prentiss's backyard. Cornie and I are wearing handsome two-piece cotton knit dresses, white with a sedate, muted, checked band around the lower edge of the top and the collar, and the same band down the button front jacket. The skirts are a ribbed knit, and we are wearing knee socks. I don't remember these outfits, but they were certainly much nicer than the two new school dresses Mom could afford to buy for us each fall.

Great Aunt Nettie was the visitor I wished would come but never did. She made herself known to Harold, Cornie, and me through wonderful Christmas presents never seen in Atlantic: a Mexican stick and ball for all of us, Harold's chemistry set, my electric animal identification game, my blue leather diary, and my ballet dancer powder box. She never married, had no children, but intuitively knew what would please us at any age. We had no money to visit her, and after Grandpa died, she didn't come to Iowa anymore. But she wrote me about once a year from the time I was twelve until I was a junior in college. She became very ill then, and died soon after.

Here was this wonderful woman whom I had no recollection of meeting, but what she said to me in her correspondence made her alive, loving, concerned, fallible and funny. She was always an educator, as were her brother, Grandpa Prentiss, and her nieces, my Aunt Biddy, and Aunt Lil. Excerpts from my Aunt Nettie'e letters provide examples of her interest in me:

August 13, 1933, "I have a package of stamps tucked away among my papers that I bought for you when you were ill last winter. The trouble was that I was ill too, and things got into a mess and I have not yet sorted the mess out. When I do, I expect I shall find the stamps.... Wouldn't it be wonderful if we could all be together for two or three weeks sometime so as to get really acquainted. That was what I was able to do with Prentiss and Malissa (my Aunt Biddy's children) *last winter and what I am doing now with Cornelia Schwarz* (my Aunt Lil's older daughter) *although I shall have her for only ten days."*

March 26, 1934 "It was extraordinarily nice to have your letter of March 3rd. Your words were long, as you suggested, but I was able to understand them all. Now there are two of us who don't know whether we are suffering from "mental disability" or are "trying to be superior." Of course there is a third possibility, the fun of experimenting with words. In general I expect your teacher is right in saying we should use simple language. On the other hand a large vocabulary is tremendously important if it isn't used for size but for clear expression. I am sure that a dictionary is one of the most important books to own provided it is used as well."

August 15, 1934, "Do you mean to tell me there has been no rain in your part of Iowa yet? I read the papers every day for word of a break in the drought and thought it had at last come to Atlantic, although I had read of 115 degrees in Ottumwa. That's too much! I should think you would build a hole below the cellar and dig in for your stamp room."

December 22, 1935, "It's a terrific shrinkage when a box becomes a note but thank God, love is not limited by the size of a container and so with my Merry Christmas and Happy New Year wishes goes a mint of love...."

May 27, 1938, "I note your desire to visit me no later than a year from this summer. I hope that that visit may become a reality...."

November 12, 1938 "…. I have just bought a hat that I haven't the courage to wear…. It is a gay bonnet, rose and blue feathers on a beret and I look like an old virago in it…. I am afraid that all this discussion of my clothes is a sign that my head is empty tonight…."

December 29, 1938, "…. I so appreciated your letter of November 18th telling me of your work at S. U. I. It seems to me that wherever you are you find yourself well occupied what with your ability to sing, to dance, to swim and I suppose to act, but please, blessed lamb, don't overlook the fact that good hard study now makes for later strength.

February 27, 1939, "… I hope to goodness you don't put that cold slick slimy make-up cape over your bare shoulders, although your figure of 'snake around the neck' suggests some such pleasant compulsion. Put your dress on first and powder your nose second if you don't want to catch your death-o-snake…. I saw a delightful play called "Dear Octopus"…. It seemed most appropriate to me for the old lady in that play, who seemed about forty, to say, "You can have your face lifted but you have to lift your own legs."

May 29, 1939, "… If you want reflections on education read The Education of Henry Adams … no one seems to know, with any large supporting body of opinions, what education is. Certainly for women like you and me, the ability to earn one's living is essential. If we are educated, we chose a task which we love that we may be fulfilled. I have adored teaching…."

January 18, 1940, "… We know now that we have to leave this apartment, where I have lived since 1914 … I particularly have accumulated endless papers. I think it takes me longer to tear up a paper than it does to write one. If I could only say "spizzeringtum boo" and make a file of papers disappear in a moment how happy I should be…."

My Great Aunt Nettie died when I was a senior in college. We never had our three weeks together.

19

Eating was a favorite occupation for all of us Shraugers. Mom had been trained in the English style of cooking in her home and later earned a degree in Home Economics. There she learned how to prepare gravy for two hundred people, and white sauce to stretch vegetables for a family. Whether she made these for hundreds or five, her gravy and sauce were always tasty. She told me that learning to prepare these two things was the basis of all cooking.

Her skill as a quantity cook was put to work at our First Presbyterian church where women, often assisted by us older children, prepared and served dinners rivaling professional catering houses. The basement Sunday School room was transformed into a banquet hall filled with long tables covered with sheets of white paper, cups, saucers, utensils, salt and pepper shakers, and vases of flowers. In this way, the ladies earned money for their various church projects from outside organizations that paid handsomely for the service.

On election night in November, 1932, I was pouring coffee for early arrivals at such an event. As I placed a filled cup in front of a man while holding the pot up high behind him, the pot tipped, and hot coffee spilled onto his shoulder. I was devastated.

Seeing my distress, he protested, "No, I'm all right. No, my shoulder isn't burning; my suit coat is well padded. Now, young lady, just you forget about it, and take care of the other people."

He was reassuring. I felt better. That was my first table-waiting disaster, and the beginning of my appreciation for the skill of waitresses.

After dinner, I was helping to clear the tables. Someone turned on a portable radio to hear the election returns. Suddenly a great roar came over the airwaves; everyone rushed from the kitchen to listen to the broadcast.

"It is apparent that Franklin Delano Roosevelt has defeated President Hoover."

Excitement reined! I realized something important had happened! Never before had I been interested in politics or what went on in Washington, D.C; but from that moment on I began to pay attention.

Eating at home was always a pleasure. Mom made many dishes lathed with her tasty cream sauce. She served creamed cod that came dried and packed in little wooden boxes. This was a favorite of mine, for I loved to crunch the vertebrae. Family favorites were creamed peas and little onions, creamed chipped beef on toast, when in season, creamed asparagus on toast, and always creamed potatoes. A boiled New England dinner was a Sunday treat. Of course Dad liked steak, roast beef, meatloaf and hamburgers. Mom made delicious stews of beef and vegetables and another kind of beef stew she called "goulash" served on noodles. Her cooking was what I came to think of as tasty plain cooking. In those days no one had a freezer, so what Mom prepared was fresh. Fried chicken served as an occasional Sunday dinner, turkey appeared on Thanksgiving and Christmas, and ham—hardly ever.

She was a fine cook in general, but in particular she made delectable desserts. Just her mentioning anything with a crust would stimulate my salivary glands. Her lard crust was ragged, patched, askew, but heavenly tasting, light and crisp. She made a rhubarb cream pie that was so irresistibly rich, the mouth had to have another and another taste until foundering set in.

Her blueberry tarts were a specialty for our lunches in season, but somehow blueberries and I never became friends even though eating blueberries produced a desirable and lovely blue tongue.

But sweets weren't her only specialty. Eggplant sliced and twice dipped in beaten eggs, pressed into finely crushed cracker crumbs, was then fried in Crisco. This was the only fried food we were treated to except for chicken now and then, eggs, and her famous fried potatoes and onions.

Artichokes may have been a tradition she brought from her home in Iowa City. Every season when artichokes appeared in the local markets, Dad bought some. Eventually they became the required salad for all our Thanksgivings and Christmases.

I loved our summer salad lunches. Dad would bring new pickings from his garden as soon as they were ready, when each was young and tender. He provided leaf lettuce, carrots, radishes, green onions, tomatoes, and green peppers. What's more, he'd clean his basketful at the outdoor faucet and bring it like an offering to Mom in the kitchen.

The platter she prepared sat in the middle of the table, so each of us could serve ourselves. Ice tea was the remedy for hot weather, or lemonade made from real lemons. For the tea, the sugar content was whatever we added individually. My ice tea always had a sugary residue at the bottom of the glass—about a quarter inch of tea-flavored sugar—so delicious to sip or spoon up and grind between the teeth.

Mom's good friend, Jenny Meredith, tried to be there for lunch on weekdays during the fresh vegetable season. We all loved Jenny. She was so pretty with her brilliant blue eyes, her sweet relaxed smile and her always-tanned skin. Counting her, we were six. Day after day we'd have the same lunch: a great pleasure.

One evening, Dad said, "Mama, can't I ever come home for lunch and have only the family here? Must Jenny be with us every day?"

I don't remember Mom ever telling Jenny not to come; so, yes, often she was the sixth member of the family during that season.

We never had fresh fish at home: it wasn't available at the market. But Wayland Hopley had a big farm pond. One Saturday he asked Dad and several other men to come help him seine it. Why this seining happened only once, I don't know, but it prompted a great gathering. Most of the guests invited for dinner were strangers to me, but all of us Shraugers were there. Mom and some other women helped Mrs. Hopley prepare potatoes and vegetables. Cornie, Harold, and I milled around in the small backyard with the crowd of grownups waiting for the trucks to return with the men and the fish. Finally the line of trucks came up the long driveway, and we stood back while the men wrestled huge barrels off the truck and into the yard.

I ran up to Dad to look into a barrel; he took off the lid, sunk his hands in the water, and grabbed two huge frogs. He held them high by their legs, so we all could see the great black pop-eyed creatures shining with dripping water.

"These are bullfrogs," Dad said.

"But a frog isn't a fish!" I complained.

"Right," he said, "Now Hop and I are going to prepare these critters for our dinner."

"How do you eat a frog?" I asked.

"We only eat the legs," Dad told me. "Mom and Helen will fry them."

I was disappointed that we wouldn't have fresh fish for the first time, but, then, I thought, "We've never had frog legs either, so it's OK."

After being fried, frog's legs looked and tasted like chicken legs, so privately I wondered what all the celebration was about. At home we went back to our occasional fish diet of dried reconstituted dried cod, canned salmon, tuna, or sardines.

As Harold, Cornie, and I grew older, my parents thought it all right to leave us for a few hours early in the evenings while they attended impromptu card games.

Harold, in his early teens, would be home with us. On these evenings, Mom prepared a "pickup supper" for us.

Not taking time to wash, we ran to the card table placed in the kitchen. We wanted to rejoin our playmates as soon as possible; so we wolfed down the egg sandwiches, hurriedly drank some milk, grabbed a carrot, and off we'd go again, cookie in hand. The cool of the evening beckoned: we wanted to be in it. Wiping our mouths on our shirttails, Cornie and I bounced off the back stoop to join Helen, Earl, and Dorothy who often were already waiting for us. Soon the rest of the gang joined us.

We stretched out on the grass as the sun dropped behind the hills; moisture settled on our arms, cooling us. We watched the moon coming up changing the fading light magically, and planned what games to play as we saw the shadows grow.

Dusk was our favorite time to play night games. In July, when conditions were just right, fireflies would pour forth, filling the air with their miniature blinking lights.

Seeing them, we ran home, punctured jar lids with ice picks, and returned with the jars, receivers for our captured fireflies. By holding the full jar close to the face of a friend, a glow would appear on a cheek or chin. It was as if we turned on a tiny flash light. With our jars full of these puzzling insects, we sat in a circle and watched the pulsing, moving masses, marveling at this mystery, wondering how and why: then we released them.

When only moonlight was with us, hide-and-go-seek began. That was the best game of all, I thought, especially when the moon created deep shadows. Because plenty of hiding places existed around our and the Smoller's yards, a rule restricted hiding to those two places. If a rule-breaker tried to run in 'FREE' everyone would protest, "NOT FAIR!" Then that culprit had to become 'IT'.

The game began with IT hiding eyes against arms on our elm tree while everyone scattered as IT counted to ten. If IT failed to find and tag anyone, IT called out, "Ally ally outs in free." That would bring everyone back to the elm to begin another game.

One night, with just enough light from a waxing moon, we began another Hide-and-go-seek game. I went tearing between the two houses when suddenly I was stopped by Skin Marshall's voice.

"Virginia," he whispered. "Come here."

He and Cornie had come out from behind our big spirea bush by Mr. Smoller's garden. They continued walking toward me. I heard something in Skin's voice that made me wary. In the first place he never talked to me—so I was suspicious.

"Come on, Virginia, I have something for you."

Feeling I must because he was older than I, I slowly walked toward them.

"Put out your hand," said Skin.

I paused.

"Come on, nothing's going to hurt you."

That was a dare. I came up to them, and put out my hand. He took it and guided it to his crotch. I felt something very warm and velvety soft. It was his penis.

Off I ran, resuming the tag game. I wasn't frightened now, for my thoughts concentrated on them, not me, thinking of what those two might have been doing under the bushes. I was never to know.

A night or two later, I was sound asleep on my back, and I dreamt I felt a body settle quietly over mine. I often had clear memories of my dreams, but as I drifted up from a deep sleep, by the weight I knew this body was real and heavy.

It was no dream. I began to struggle for breath. Then I realized this weight was my sister's. Fully awake, I became conscious of my heart beating fast. What could I do? She was bigger than me. She was humping me! I lay inert, too frightened to say anything. She didn't stay on me very long.

That is what happened, and it never happened again. But from that day on, I never touched one of my girl friends, never walked, as girls do, holding hands with any of them. Not until many years later, when I finally figured out why being physically close to women made me uncomfortable, did I feel at ease if a woman friend embraced me.

Without conscious decision, our night games diminished and came to an end. The older kids drifted off, the Adams family moved away, and the rest of us were growing up. When my schoolmates and I became seventh graders, night games seemed babyish.

Mom, being the sensible and far-seeing mother that she was, prepared me for my coming menses explaining what would happen to me when my sexual organs matured, and what I could expect.

"Just let me know, and I'll fix you up," she assured me.

She had on hand a belt and Kotex when it happened. Cornie, being older, must have been instructed as I was, but since we weren't intimate, it was never mentioned.

When my body began to change, and I noticed light red hairs appearing under my arms and on my legs, I went to Mom.

"Mom, what can I do about this hair that's growing on me? And these freckles! Can I get rid of them?"

Mom, recognizing the symptoms of adolescence, replied, "Virginia, you can take your choice. You can shave the hair off if you want to—and I'll buy you a razor. As for the freckles, you can stop swimming or being out doors all day, and start wearing long sleeves and a hat when you go out. For freckles there's no other choice."

I resigned myself to freckling, and later began shaving my legs and underarms. One winter morning after dressing by the bathroom heat vent, I sat on the toilet. The next thing I knew I was flat on the floor surrounded by family. I had fainted. Four faces were staring down on me. I found this embarrassing, what with my bare rump exposed.

"I think you'd better stay home this morning, Virginia," said Mom; and the rest of the family went about their business.

"I'm fine, Mom, I'm fine."

She said, "This sometimes happens when girls get to be your age."

"But I'm all right, Mom. I want to go to school."

Fainting meant I really was beginning to change, I supposed, a sign more significant than the appearance of excess hair. Soon enough the big change came.

One evening Mom and Dad had bridge guests. I went up to my room, undressed, threw back the covers and sat on the sheet not yet putting on my nightie. I immediately noticed the bright red blood against the white sheet. I called Mom, and she "fixed me up" as she said she would. The next morning she suggested I stay home, but, feeling perfectly fine, I refused the invitation.

When we were settled at the table for lunch one day, Dad laughed and said, "I stopped in at Roy Metcalf's this morning. You should have seen the suit I saw hanging near the cash register."

The memory brought a great guffaw from him. I noticed Harold's eyes were glued to Dad.

"It was a gray plaid, large squares run through with faint red threads. And it had a belted back! A belted back! And it was double breasted! It was the silliest suit I've ever seen!"

My eyes quickly turned back to Harold, whose face had turned pink, and thought, "That's Harold's suit."

Since Harold was working at Metcalf's Clothing store, he had bought the suit, which was the latest fashion. It fit him perfectly, and when he wore it on his weekend dates, I knew he was the handsomest fellow at the dance. Of Dad's reaction when he discovered the "silliest suit" belonged to his son, I never learned.

Harold left his management job with Collier Publications resolving to save money to buy a car when he was old enough to drive at age fourteen. In winter he trapped small animals and sold their pelts. Later, after Dad taught him how to use a gun safely, he hunted squirrels. Once he came home reeking of skunk. As it disappeared down a hole, he shot at it. But the skunk got in the first shot. Unaware that his clothes could be washed free of the odor, Mom burned them.

Mr. Pellet, whose small farm was across the street from Dorothy's house, hired him to help operate the dairy, and deliver the milk. Harold eventually earned enough money to pay something down on a second-hand car. For that and $33.33 a month, Bill Linke sold him a yellow Model A Ford roadster. He told me he later used it to court Fran Kephart who eventually became his wife. He paid for it by taking part-time jobs at Antrim's grocery store, Balding's Economy Shoe Store, and Metcalf's Clothing Store. Working was never a problem with my brother.

Some years later I asked him why he never finished college. His being five years older than I meant I didn't know all the facts about him.

"I'll tell you, sis; I was too busy working my way out of college to study."

He meant he had to have dollars for dates, and didn't study.

By the time Harold was seventeen and I was twelve, he had become my model for what a boyfriend should be. He was cheerful, polite, respectful to adults, a hard worker, loving, helpful, and easy to live with.

One cold winter night, dressed in his beautiful plaid suit, he was ready to go to the County Fairgrounds Community Hall for the Saturday night dance. He was a wonderful dancer, full of rhythm and grace, and he could be found at the Fairgrounds almost any Saturday night. (I learned that later on when I had my one dancing date at that hall.) Many bands that became well-known came to play there. Red Nichols and his Five Pennies was one of them.

I was hanging around the living room listening to the Saturday night broadcast of the Top Ten Hits of the week out of New York City. Even though Mrs. Herbert had taught our dancing class how to waltz, fox trot, and two-step, I had never actually danced with anyone.

As Harold was about to leave, he said, "Come on, Virginia, let's dance."

I can't recall what tune the band was playing, but he took me in his arms and we danced a few steps. He swung me out and brought me back to where we started, and I found myself very close to him. I felt his penis against me. I backed off.

I guess he sensed my gesture for he said, "Great! You'll be a good dancer. Gotta go now."

He picked up his overcoat, and with a bow he said, "Thank you for the dance, Miss Virginia."

Off he went to his evening of fun while I listened to the radio, solo dancing around the room. Pausing, I stood in front of the hot air register letting the heat make my skirt fly out, and thought about Harold, about taboos, and about how lucky I was to have such a nice brother.

20

When our class entered sixth grade on the second floor of Jackson School, I felt as if I were really growing up. We were assigned desks in the back of the assembly room behind the seventh and eighth graders—the big kids. These would be our seats each morning as we awaited the opening ceremonies, the staples of which were "The Pledge Of Allegiance" and the singing of *America The Beautiful.* Here we sat during study periods, teachers being assigned to monitor us. At other times, we went to whatever class was on our schedule, practicing, I thought, for how it was done in high school.

In our class were several fast maturing, muscular, six feet tall boys. Later they became heroes of Atlantic High's football and basketball teams. One or two had transferred to Jackson from Grant School where our rigorous standards of orderly behavior hadn't been drilled into them. Or maybe it was just hormones.

One day when Miss Amanda Wissler's study period was disrupted by smart talk from one of these giants, she asked him to come up to her desk, and said, "I have a present for you, Heavy. It's a reward for good behavior."

Heavy Johnson did a double take and stopped grinning at the class as she offered him a hunk of paraffin and said, "Go face the corner by the windows in the back of the room. Chew this until the bell rings."

The rest of us sat in wonder when this happened. Miss Wissler always executed her orders firmly but with a twinkle in her eyes. So, with Mandy, as my Mom referred to her, the culprit always did exactly as they were told.

Just which class our memorization of poetry was part of, I can't recall, for Miss Wissler conducted it. She seemed to be a jack-of-all-trades teacher. School was easy for me unless I had to memorize something, but with effort I could accomplish that too.

My friend, Ruth Howorth, recited James Whitcomb Riley's *Little Orphant Annie,* a poem about a little girl who told hair-raising goblin stories.

When she came to the punch line, Ruth's bright brown eyes opened wide under her round, protruding forehead and blond hair; her face lit up as she glowered at us and shouted, "And the goblins will get *YOU* if you don't watch out!"

The whole class gasped. How I admired her performance.

Miss Wissler assigned me Henry Wadsworth Longfellow's *The Village Black-smith* that begins "Under the spreading chestnut tree ...," and only by going over and over the poem did I manage to get through it and not disgrace myself.

I had an extra incentive: Mom told me that the poet had been a friend, and maybe a prospective husband, of my Great Grandmother, Cornelia Fitch Bradley; so I thought I should do my best for her. Mom let me take the letters he wrote to her for the class to see.

Ruth's home was interesting and different. It was an apartment over one of the downtown stores on Chestnut Street. It was long and narrow with no windows except in the living room, which faced Chestnut Street, and in the kitchen at the end of the apartment, which faced an alley. The light from these rear windows made the kitchen bright and cheerful.

"How was school today, girls?" Mrs. Howorth asked, beaming out of eyes that were just like Ruth's, brown and sparkling.

Nothing special today, Mama," Ruth said as she gave her a hug. "But you've done something special. You've been baking!"

The scent of chocolate was flooding my nostrils. Mrs. Howorth pointed to a tall, layered cake smothered in thick shiny chocolate frosting. Ruth brought plates and forks as her mother sliced huge pieces. Mrs. Howorth's revered reputation as cook at Atlantic's Calumet Café was well established: her cakes were light, her frostings smooth as silk, and her homemade ice cream was never-to-be-forgotten.

We sat at the round kitchen table. "Now put those forks down, girls. I have some fresh vanilla ice cream, would...."

"Yes, yes, yes! You know we want some, Mama," interrupted Ruth.

I always felt completely welcome visiting this kitchen.

As a team, Ruth and I were two of a kind. We were both tall for our age, athletic and mischievous. She could write stories with trick endings and read them aloud with expression that amazed and defeated me almost to the point of my forgetting about writing. She got straight A report cards and was always elected to a class office, and eventually was valedictorian of our class. We both had enormous energy which, in spare time, led us to whispering, passing notes, and causing our teachers to monitor us.

When we moved upstairs to sixth grade, Miss Beckwith, and Mrs. Linn, lower grade teachers, had come along with us. They knew us well. And by the time we were in seventh grade, all the teachers had our number. After racing through the assignments for the next day, disrupting the study hall was our pleasure.

Eventually, by consensus of the principal and the teachers, we two acquired jobs and titles. Our titles were Errand Girls, and Operators of the Hectograph. Each day, we went to the principal's office to pick up master copies of assignments written by the teachers in special purple ink.

On the way to the copy room, we had to go through the big assembly hall. Ruth would take off walking as fast as she could, while I struggled not to drop my armful of papers. It seemed to be a game with her. She liked to be the leader. I didn't mind following. I followed her blond head and always tense shoulders as fast as I could—sort of quietly—but that was hard, for often I was racked by suppressed giggles. We passed the bent heads of our studying classmates as Ruth fast-walked, and I fast-walked trailing her.

The copy room was tucked over the stairway at the far end of the school. A few steps led to it. Up we went, two steps at a time. Gently we shut the door, burst into laughter, and settled down to work. We did a good job putting the master copies square on that thick gelatinous roll which I could never resist touching because of its cold, inhuman texture.

Eventually, wearing streaks of purple up to our elbows as a sign of privilege, we coursed up and down first and second floor halls delivering the ditto copies: word lists, tests, arithmetic problems, as required by the teachers.

But the proof of our badness really lay outside Jackson School. Saturday night in Atlantic was the night the farmers came to town to do their errands, meet friends, and rest from their week's hard work. All the stores were open for them. On one Saturday, a hot July night, Ruth asked me to have supper with her. I never refused an invitation to eat at Ruth's.

After enjoying Mrs. Howorth's special meat loaf and mashed potatoes with thick pan gravy topped off with apple pie and ice cream, then a little more, Ruth and I scrambled down the long flight of steps to join the crowd cramming Chestnut Street.

We paused a moment at the curb, looking at the brightly lit street packed solid with muddy farm trucks, old black fords, various sedans and a few shiny roadsters. It was a long shopping center starting at Second Street and ending at the square City Park between Fifth and Sixth Streets. That night cars filled the side streets too.

Ruth had only one store in mind for us to visit. Her eyes seemed larger than usual. I knew she had a PLAN.

"We'll go to Woolworth's Five and Dime," she said. "First we walk down the aisle on the right side all the way to the end, then circle around the display area in the center of the store, and return to the door up the other aisle."

"Why do that, Ruth? I've been sticky and sweaty all day. It'll be ten degrees hotter inside the store."

She answered by taking my hand. After carefully placing a straight pin on my palm, a tiny-silver-sword, she whispered to me, "Just jab it into people as you go by."

Becoming a trifle anxious, but caught up with the PLAN, I followed my leader, jay-walked among the parked cars, and crossed the street. Just as I knew, the heat was smothering as we pushed our way through the sweating mass of humanity inside Woolworth's.

"Now the War begins," Ruth murmured.

My leader forged ahead as the glitter of cheap jewelry hanging high on little rods diverted me. Bodies prevented my seeing any other tempting sights. Just then I heard a yelp from down the aisle muffled by the rustle of feet. The confluence of quiet voices, and the exhaling of many pairs of lungs was fluming to the ceiling.

I refocused on the War. Turning sideways, I slipped through the crush of women facing the display cases waiting their turns, the smell of accumulated sweat almost overpowering me. Being as tall as Ruth, I could easily see over the shoulders of the farm women to select my victim.

I chose a rather small motherly woman thinking I could give her an underhand jab and not be noticed. Coming up just behind and to one side of her, I delivered my jab. In went the pin—a tough entry at first—but the trusty sharp weapon pierced the corset and gained its objective.

Instantly I reversed its direction and increased the pace of my direction, never saying "pardon" or "excuse" to those I jostled. The outcry of my victim sounded far behind me. I, forcing my way through the pack, gained the turn, and saw Ruth's blond head halfway up the next aisle. Outside, she stood waiting for me by the curb.

Silently we fast-walked single file up the street—weaving through the shoppers, past the line of stores, past the mobile Popcorn Wagon parked across from Skelly's Gas; having safely reached the park, we threw ourselves down under a great oak tree, and collapsed into laughter.

Staring up at the glossy green leaves reflecting the lights, we didn't discuss our individual feats, or our creeping, apprehensive guilt. We just stretched out on the cool grass, thrust our silver swords deep into the Iowa sod, and sighed.

On the night of the August full moon, I headed for Armelda Welch's, just a couple of houses down Cedar Street from our school, to join our gang of almost-eighth graders. Jean Tomlinson, Ruth, Armelda, Bob Britton, and a new boy—brought along by Heavy Johnson—tall, dark eyed and dark haired Junior Gilliland, who became the magnet for all the girl's eyes. I don't recall who else was there.

Across Cedar stood a row of clapboard houses, but we didn't seem to disturb any of the occupants with our laughing and chatter.

As we aimlessly milled around the playground, Bob Britton suddenly gave us direction by saying, "Wish we had a cigarette."

I had biked to Armelda's, so I said, "I can get some." And I did. I rode as fast as I could over the hills to my house. Knowing my folks were out playing cards, I ran directly to Mom's carton of Camels located under the table at the end of the daybed. I took a full pack and paper matches from the open carton and stuffed them in my pocket.

Back at school the subject hadn't changed, so those who wished took a cigarette. As we giggled, laughed, and coughed, we tried out appropriate gestures, aping the adults we had watched. I tried one. I felt my throat burning, hated the taste and never smoked another until I briefly experimented again in college. But Armelda and Jean, as they told me much later, began their lifelong habit that night.

The huge elm trees on the curbs up and down the street spread their leaves to catch the moonlight, the gravel of the schoolyard seemed almost yellow, and all of us, seething with hormones, careened around, talking and giggling, some puffing away.

Somehow Armelda's underpants were being kicked around underfoot until Bob Britton discovered them, grabbed them, tied them to the flagpole on the grassy area in front of the school, and pulled them to the top of the staff. Our hoots and hollers awakened the night as we coped with our embarrassment. When the novelty wore off, Bob let the pants down, untied them, and threw them up to the wide window sill of Miss Bell's first-grade classroom.

"Now, how to get them down," we asked each other. "No, no! It wouldn't do to leave them there!"

Heavy Johnson, already over six feet tall, tried jumping, but the pants eluded him.

"Let's ask a neighbor for a broom," someone said.

"Good idea," we all agreed.

So Bob and Heavy went up the street to the house near the corner where lights were on, knocked on the door, and asked to borrow a broom for a few minutes. The accommodating couple brought the broom, left their porch light on, and stood trying to see what the boys were going to do with it. I don't know what excuse they gave, if any, but the broom did its work, they returned it, and we retreated to the boy's playground.

A little later Bob came running from behind the building and stage whispered, "We can get the coal-chute cover off! Who wants to go inside the building?"

I guess we all did: I certainly was for it. A couple of the boys helped Bob pull the cover aside, and one by one we edged down onto the heap of coal which formed a convenient ramp. Out through the furnace-room door we dashed and up the stairs to the first floor.

"What was I doing here," I wondered. "We are breaking and entering!"

I ran as fast as I could through the wide hall. Brilliant moonlight flooding through the open doors turned the slick floor into alternate black and gleaming yellow stripes. Moonlight poured through the small square six-over-six panes of classroom windows transforming their shadows into skinny oblongs which snaked along the backs and seats of the desks. We raced the length of the hall to the stairs, hustled down the steps, then turned back, rushed down the basement hall to the coal room, up the coal ramp, and out to reality. The boys put the cover back on.

The strain of our thrilling illegal behavior spoiled the evening and caused us drift off. We all loved going to Jackson School, for it was our second home. Although we had toyed with its dignity that night, we did no harm. I thought the janitor probably found coal-dust shoe prints on the hall floors next day, but nothing was ever said. Bob Britten had put the pack of cigarettes into his pocket.

A few days later I learned why Armelda lost her underpants. She and I were walking through the City Park on our way to Dick and Janie's for a ten-cent Short and Heavy Sundae (two scoops of vanilla ice cream covered with marshmallow, then flooded with delicious chocolate sauce, crowned with a gob of real whipped cream, and topped with a maraschino cherry) when she tripped. Looking down we saw her pink panties entangled with her shoes. She quickly picked them up, and showed me their fastener: a single button.

"The button hole is too big, and I can't keep these darn pants fastened; they fall off all the time. I can't seem to make the hole small enough."

On a lovely warm Saturday in early fall day, the gang gathered on Marshall's empty lot to break in Earl's new football. Bob Marshall, his brother Skin, and a boy who was visiting him joined us so we could have five players on each side. Bob and Billy Marshall, Bob Britton, Earl, and I played on one team, and Skin Marshall, the visiting friend, my sister, Dixie, and one other, I don't recall who—maybe no other—for all the big kids were on that side.

My team lined up to defend as the opposition called their signals. I saw the ball carrier coming around my end of the line and managed a spectacular tackle, getting my arms completely around both the runner's legs at his ankles. Down we went. As I sat up, feeling elated at my expertise, the boy I tackled—Skin's guest—sat up and stared at me.

Something about the way he kept looking at me, moving his eyes from my eyes down to the front of my tight knit shirt, hovering there, moving on down to my waist and slowly back up made me wonder if I should be playing football. For the first time, I became self-conscious about my developing body. It turned out that he was the champion quarterback of the Red Oak, Iowa, football team. He made me feel I shouldn't be there. I resented that deeply. However, as a result, I never played sandlot football again.

As Graduation Day approached, Mom thought the ceremony so important that she bought lovely pale yellow crepe material from the Brandeis store in Omaha. Mrs. Smoller made me a simple, short sleeved, A-line dress with a white Peter Pan collar. Mom had Mrs. Smoller make Cornie an identical dress even though Cornie was finishing her second year in high school. I thought mine the most wonderful dress in the world. Only one other dress had been made especially for me, the one I had worn as an attendant in both my aunt's weddings when I was five years old.

Each spring for two years, I had admired Nadine Watson's beautiful white Oxford shoes that celebrated the change of season. I had asked Mom each spring if I could have a pair, but we could never afford them. Mom knew how hard I was on my shoes, how battered they became, how the toes curled up and how I'd clean and apply brown shoe polish on them only before Sunday School—if I remembered.

Come Graduation Day, dear Mom had not forgotten my deep desire for white Oxford shoes. She had been saving her pennies and surprised me with a trip to Welch's shoe store where she bought me a pair of those beautiful shoes just like Nadine's. So on this great day, a day I considered my 'coming of age day,' I proudly stood with my classmates at the front of the assembly room before all the teachers, parents, and the seventh and sixth graders in my pale yellow dress with its white collar, my white shoes on my feet, feeling happier than I ever remembered being. This was my last day at Jackson School which I loved, but like many loves to come, I was willing to put it behind.

It was Jean Tomlinson's Dad who put up a tent in Sunnyside Park, so we girls could celebrate leaving the eighth grade. Knowing the tent usually sheltered Tomlinson's burials didn't deter us. Eight or nine of us set up housekeeping for the night after eating the picnic supper our mothers' had prepared. I think my sister, Cornie, and a friend of hers were chaperoning us. The tent had a canvas floor, so our makeshift beds were protected from all "creepy crawlies," as my girl friends labeled insects and worms. No one owned camping equipment, so we used our regular sheets, blankets and pillows, and laid out beds side by side as if there were camp cots underneath.

Naturally some of our male classmates showed up, but we didn't invite them into the tent. After a while they went away. Heavy brought Carlton Hanson, a new arrival in town. He slouched against a tree, smiling his crooked grin, dark straight hair falling down over his wrinkled forehead and piercing blue eyes. We girls agreed he looked like Clark Gable. He must have thought so too, for later on he took on some of Gable's mannerisms we observed in the movies. Of course, Carleton became part of our high school gang.

Night came along. We decided to play strip poker as a fun way to undress for bed. Someone had a deck of cards. This might have been my idea, for the Adams girls, Dorothy, Cornie and I had sometimes readied for bed this way on an overnight. Maybe because I was an experienced poker player, I seemed to have most of my clothes on while the others were quite naked.

It was then that someone suggested we put on our bathing suits and go to the swimming pool. Armelda told us she tipped off the handsome new lifeguard that we might show up. Would the entrance be unlocked? We put on our suits, grabbed our towels, and off we went, down the hill to the steep road which led us to our new PWA pool.

Sure enough, the door was unlocked. We stripped beside the pool and quietly slipped into the cold water. Oh, the joy of it! Thrilled by our daring, we began to swim, and to dive to the bottom of the clear cold water, coming to the surface like seals.

Jean suddenly shrieked. We all shushed her.

"But look," she moaned, "I forgot to take off my watch."

This was her graduation present from her Mom and Dad. She quickly got out and sat on the edge of the pool in tears.

"Just put it in a glass of water, Jean, and take it to Mr. Carroll tomorrow. He'll take it apart and dry it off. It will be just fine," counseled Armelda who always had an answer for everything.

Mr. Carroll was the expert jeweler who worked at Cole's Jewelry store. Whether the watch was rescued or not, I never heard.

Our little dip was spoiled, so we went back to our tent, filled a paper cup with water, and into it went Jean's new watch. To divert everyone, I showed off my new lipstick, a graduation gift from Jenny Meredith, our family friend. It was truly elegant: a square tube of terra cotta with fittings of gold-colored metal—and a trick opening! It contained terra cotta colored lipstick. Jenny told me that she bought it to complement my bright red hair. In trying to open it without first learning how, Armelda broke the locking mechanism. That taught me a lesson about sharing treasured possessions.

All of our parents seemed to understand this emancipating camping act. In retrospect I wonder at their allowing us to do such a thing. Trust was strong in those days. Our world was safe. Realizing what their permission meant, we only slipped a little bit by skinny dipping. It was a first for all of us, and something unforgettable: the freedom of the naked body in water, swimming with water soothing your whole skin, sensuous, beautiful. A first, but not a last.

That summer, when I decided to be serious about writing, Grampa gave me an old typewriter from his factory. Dad brought up the battered table and matching bench that long ago had been used as a breakfast table in the icebox room. Now I had a large business-like desk and bench to use. I hadn't been given a watch for graduation as Cornie had been, but I—unlike her—didn't ask for one. Now, however, I felt I was even.

Just how Cornie fit into all this I can't recall. She was to become a journalist eventually but never felt the urge to write at home. I stayed home more than she did, so perhaps she didn't have a need to establish a special space in our shared room. She never complained. But when she went off to college she was given a new typewriter by a family friend. We each had what we wanted.

LIST OF PICTURES

Author tif Virginia Shrauger Jones
Cover tif Cornelia Prentiss

#1 44.tif David Ogden Bradley
#2 1. tif Cornelia Fitch before marriage, Cornelia's Grandmother Bradley
#3 40.tif D.O. Bradley Home in Dobbs Ferry, NY
#4 7. tif Grandmother Henrietta Driggs Prentiss, 1896
#5 3. tif Lue' Bradley Prentiss
#6 2. tif Dr. Henry James Prentiss
#7 5. tif Dr. H.J. Prentiss and Lue', Honeymooning
#8 6. tif Cornelia Prentiss, Dobbs Ferry, NY Age 13 months, 1896
#9 8. tif Lue's Sky Parlor, 239 W. 103rd St. NYC, NY, 1896
#10 9. tif Dr H.J. Prentiss with Hank (seated), Cornelia and Lil, 1901
#11 12.tif Cornelia's Aunt Henrietta Prentiss
#12 13.tif Elsie Earle, Dr. Prentiss' Cousin
#13 14.tif H.J. Prentiss holding infant Cornelia, 1896
#14 25.tif Prentiss Home in Iowa City, Iowa, 1909
#15 18.tif Lil Prentiss's sketch of Dr. H.J.Prentiss
#16 24.tif Lil, Hank, Biddy, Mother Lue', and Cornelia 1905, Iowa City, Iowa
#17 11.tif Sisters, Lil, Cornelia, and Biddy Prentiss, 1914
#18 16.tif Lilian (Lil) Prentiss
#19 10.tif Cornelia's Brother, Henry Prentiss, Champion College Boxer c 1918
#20 17.tif Lue' (Biddy) Prentiss, 1946
#21 37.tif Harold Francis Shrauger, in college
#22 28.tif Cornelia Prentiss, age 19, 1915
#23 15.tif Cornelia, her mother, Lue', infant Harold, 1916
#24 14.tif Dr. Prentiss in profile, in preparation for his bust
#25 23.tif Henry (Hank) Prentiss, WWI 1919-1920
#26 26.tif Lue' Bradley Prentiss
#27 22.tif Backrow: Harold (Sunny) Shrauger, Jr., Biddy,
          Cornelia, Lil, Cornie Shrauger; Front Row:
          Virginia Shrauger, Elsie Earle, Dr. Prentiss
          holding Cornelia Mary Schwarz—Lil's daughter;
          Robert J. Prentiss, and Prentiss Childs on
          Chair, Biddy's son
#28 29.tif Dr. Robert Jerome Prentiss, 1963

#29 36.tif Darius Edgar Shrauger Home in Atlantic, Iowa

#30 34.tif Darius Edgar Shrauger in his prime

#31 35.tif Sarah(Sadie) Shrauger, Cornelia's Mother-in-law

#32 31.tif SHRAUGER & JOHNOSN "ALL THINGS METAL", factory
      in Atlantic, Iowa

#33 39.tif Chicago, Rock Island and Pacific Depot, Atlantic, Cass County, Iowa

#34 39.tif Home of The Harold Shrauger's, Atlantic, Iowa, 1997

#35 40.tif Cornie, Harold Jr., and Virginia Shrauger, 1928

#36 41.tif Harold Shrauger, Sr., Staff Sergeant Harold Shrauger Jr., (sitting)
      D.E. Shrauger and Granddaughter, Francie Shrauger 1944

#37 42.tif Harold (Sunny) Shrauger Jr., Staff Sergeant,WWII

#38 43.tif Cornie Shrauger Day, 1940

#39 32.tif Darius Edgar Shrauger, c 1940

#40 Virginia, Cornelia, Harold, Cornie Shrauger, 1925

#1 44.tif David Ogden Bradley

#2 1.tif Cornelia Fitch before Marriage, Cornelia's Grandmother Bradley

#3 40.tif D. O. Bradley Home in Dobbs Ferry, NY

Grandma Henrietta Driggs Prentiss.
1896.

#4 7.tif Grandmother Henrietta Driggs Prentiss, 1896

#5 3.tif Lue' Bradley Prentiss

#6 2.tif Dr. Henry James Prentiss

#7 5.tif Lue' and Dr. H.J. Prentiss, honeymooning in Venice, Italy

Cornelia,
Thirteen months old.

#8 6.tif Cornelia Prentiss, Dobbs Ferry, NY Age 13 months 1896

Our "Sky Parlor", 239 W. 103d St.
Cornelia's home from Sept. 1900,
until Aug 16-1904.

#9 8.tif Lue's Sky Parlor, 239 W. 103rd St. NYC, NY 1896

#10 9.tif Dr. H.J. Prentiss with Hank (seated), Cornelia and Lil, 1901

#11 12.tif Cornelia's Aunt Henrietta Prentiss

HARGRAVE & GUBELMAN, 38 & 40 W. 23D STREET,

#12 13.tif Elsie Earle, Dr. Prentiss' Cousin

#13 14.tif Dr. H.J. Prentiss holding infant Cornelia, 1896

#14 25.tif Prentiss Home in Iowa City, Iowa

#15 18.tif Lil Prentiss' sketch of Dr. H.J. Prentiss

Nov. 1905. Iowa City, Ia.

#16 24.tif Lil, Hank,Biddy, Mother Lue',and Cornelia 1905 Iowa City, Iowa

#17 11.tif Sisters, Lil, Cornelia and Biddy Prentiss, 1914

#18 16.tif Lilian (Lil) Prentiss

#19 10.tif Cornelia's Brother, Henry Prentiss, Champion College Boxer

#20 17.tif Lue' (Biddy) Prentiss, 1946

#21 37.tif Harold Francis Shrauger, in college

Jan. 1915

#22 28.tif Cornelia Prentiss, age 19, 1915

July, 1916.

#23 15.tif Cornelia, her Mother, Lue', infant Harold 1916

#24 14.tif Dr. Prentiss in profile, in preparation for his bust

#25 23.tif Henry (Hank) Prentiss, WW 1 1919-1920

#26 26.tif Lue' Bradley Prentiss

#27 22.tif Back Row: Harold (Sunny) Shrauger, Jr., Biddy, Cornelia, Lil, Cornie Shrauger; Front Row: Virginia Shrauger, Elsie Earle, Dr. Prentiss holding Cornelia Mary Schwarz, Lil's daughter, Robert Prentiss, and Prentiss Childs on chair, Biddy's son. 1928

#28 29.tif Dr. Robert Jerome Prentiss, 1963

#29 36.tif Darius Edgar Shrauger Home in Atlantic, Iowa

#30 34.tif Darius Edgar Shrauger in his prime

#31 35.tif Sarah (Sadie) Shrauger, Cornelia's Mother-in-law

#32 31.tif SHRAUGER & JOHNSON "ALL THINGS METAL", factory in Atlantic, Iowa

#33 39.tif Chicago, Rock Island and Pacific Depot, Atlantic, Cass County, Iowa

#34 39.tif Home of The Harold Shrauger's, Atlantic, Iowa (1997 photo)

#35 40.tif Cornie, Harold Jr., and Virginia Shrauger 1928

#36 41.tif Harold Shrauger, Sr., Staff Sergeant Harold Shrauger Jr.,
(sitting) D.E. Shrauger and Granddaughter Francie Shrauger (four
generations)

#37 42.tif Harold (Sunny) Shrauger Jr., Staff Sergeant, WWII

#38 43.tif Cornie Shrauger Day 1940

#39 32.tif Darius Edgar Shrauger c 1940

#40 45.tif Cornie, Harold, Cornelia, and Virginia Shrauger 1925

PART III

21

All About Dad

My Dad adored my Mom. I knew. I felt it. At noon on summer days, I often stood by the cellar door and watched Mom prepare sandwiches. Into the kitchen he came and crowded up behind her as she stood at the sink or counter. He hugged her, then briefly put his hands on her pendulous breasts, and lightly rubbed his hands along her bare arms—she in her sleeveless, flowered house dress. I could see his face, relaxed in a smile, and sometimes he'd turn towards me—then wink.

When Mom recalled the first few weeks of my brother Harold's life, she would laugh and sparkle and tell about the times Dad brought his friends home to view his newborn son. Dad put Harold on the changing table, display him as he changed the diaper so his friends (all of them were about twenty-one) could see this wee man, evidence of Dad's prowess. If Harold made a fountain of urine, the fellows would laugh. Once during a demonstration, little Harold's face reddened and he defecated the typical yellow feces of breast-fed infants. This produced roars of laughter from the young men which startled the little heir into fierce crying. Then they laughed all the more.

Late on a fine fall Saturday afternoon, Dad was racing Mom, Cornie, and me along a dry country road sending whirls of dust into the blue late October sky. We were headed to the Wayland Hopley farm for dinner. The sun was surprisingly warm, but a cool breeze soothed Cornie's and my faces as we stared out the open car windows to see what was going on in the fields; we watched cows grazing, their calves sucking, and crows pecking where winter wheat had recently been planted. Quietly we anticipated playing with the Hopley boys; Dad was getting us there as fast as he could.

Dad and Hop, as his friends called him, had gone through Atlantic High School together; his wife, Helen, and Mom met at the University of Iowa. Wayland Jr. (always called Junior) and George Peter, kids about our age, were waiting for us. We loved visiting them. Everything was so different on the farm.

Dad had turned off U.S. Highway Number Six onto the long dirt road that eventually took us to their red brick house. In summer we couldn't see it. It was hidden by a thick oak grove at the end of the long driveway. But by now enough of the leaves had turned a leathery, deep brown. Some were fallen, some shrunken, so we had a clearer view.

"There it is, Dad," I shouted.

"Slow down, or you'll miss the driveway, Dad," said Cornie.

Dad swerved into the drive, and hardly slowed as he raced up to the house. Cornie and I piled out running at full speed toward the front door where George and Junior were waiting for us. As if we'd previously thought out our plan, off the four of us ran back to the dirt road and down to their hired man's house and barnyard.

"Any new piglets?" Cornie asked George.

"Yeah, brand new. Whole bunch. They're in the barn."

New babies were always in the small barn; it was a kind of hospital. The sows and their new-born lived there until the piglets grew big enough to be called shoats and could keep out of the way of grown hogs. They were then fed at the big barns several miles away.

Each sow had her own wooden enclosure and filled her space to the edges. These beasts were enormous, white, and pink eyed. They lay on their sides, pink skin showing through their white hair, their great bellies protruding upwards. Dad told me they weighed from two hundred fifty to three hundred pounds; although Dad was pretty big, that was a lot more than he weighed.

I counted eight pinkish white babies with pinkish eyelids and pink-edged flat snouts. If the Mom had been standing, I think her back would have come almost to my shoulders. Dad also told me that sometimes the heavy sows would accidentally roll over onto one of their little ones and, of course, crush it. Life there was pretty chancy.

In front of the pig barn stretched a large fenced-in yard. Here we saw the behinds of ten pregnant cows. Running to the gate that closed them in, we hung on it under the pure yellow leaves of an old maple tree, the four of us vying for space in front of a huge wagon full of shucked, golden corn. The cows were standing along a wagon, lined up like soldiers, shoulder to shoulder, pushing their noses deep into the kernels, crunching and munching, sometimes looking up, drooling, watching us as we watched them.

"Race ya to the grapevines," shouted Junior, having had enough of staring at cows. We all took off and ran through the woods, chasing and racing, shouting, yelling, and tripping over vines. Finally our stomachs told us it was time to go back to the house.

Eating at Helen Hopley's table meant having prime, farm-raised Angus beef—usually a prime rib—with potatoes, peas, and salad from their vegetable garden. Dad said Helen always overcooked and, therefore, spoiled the good beef. He couldn't understand why Hop allowed that to happen. But it was always the same. Maybe Mr. Hopley liked overcooked beef. I liked it both ways—pink in the middle, or juicy and brown. Mrs. Hopley's special chocolate cake made with tomato soup and covered with thick frosting was desert.

After dinner we kids played Chinese Checkers while the grownups settled down for bridge. At eight o'clock sharp, since I was the youngest, Mom took me upstairs to sleep in the guest room.

I don't remember being carried to the car or the return drive, but I knew we were home when I felt Dad's strong arms holding me tight against him. The warmth of his body kept me warm. My nose was next to his neck and his starched collar. Both smelled good. I drifted back into sleep, not remembering being put into my bed. It was the awareness of being taken care of by my big, strong Dad that I never forgot, for it seldom happened; and never again in that close, hugging way.

Because of Dad's lifetime friendships in Atlantic, my life among them produced some memorable outings. Often in spring, summer, or fall, we'd go with these friends for picnics out in the Iowa farmland.

As dusk fell one warm September evening, the Hopley's, Mom and Dad, Cornie and I, along with their Saturday night dinner crowd, went to a neighboring farm which belonged to Tom Hopley, Hop's brother. It was a nice setting among old trees near a small stream and a cushy green grass space next to it. We were anticipating a steak cookout.

The men built a huge fire in the middle of the grass. The women laid out blankets for all to sit on while eating our salad, fried onion-and-potatoes, and steak.

Cornie and I were running in and out of the light of the fire near the little stream when something in the water moved—the head of a cow! It lay on its side. We knew it was in trouble! We ran to Dad, and he and Hop investigated.

"Why, it's one of Tom's cows," Hop said. They immediately drove up the road to his brother's house, then returned with a big Ford pickup and thick chains. The rescue began.

"Sarah, what are doing in there?" Mr. Tom Hopley quietly said to his cow. "She's a young one, Hop, a valuable one, about three quarters grown; she's a beauty. Looks to be a real good one."

We all watched as the men put a big chain around Sarah just behind her front legs. Hop hooked the chain to the rear of the pickup, and got behind the wheel. Slowly, slowly he began dragging her. Tom stayed beside Sarah, talking to her as she began to resist. He patted her head, soothing her, keeping her relaxed, Mom told me. Gradually the yellow mud gave Sarah up. There she lay on level ground, soaking wet and caked with mud, not moving, exhausted.

"That's sticky clay in that run," said Tom. "The water's so shallow—I guess Sarah waded in to drink. Musta slipped, musta fell, couldn't get her hoofs under herself. Thrashing about got her mired."

Tom rolled big barn blankets around Sarah; somehow Dad, Hop, Tom and two others lifted and shoved her along a ramp onto the bed of the pickup. Tom drove Sarah home.

Next spring I was hiking past Tom's farm and there was tan Sarah, hunkered down in front of the barn, taking in the warm sun. Tom's wife, who let me have a drink from their well, told me Sarah spent all winter in the barn recovering from her near-death experience.

"But she's pretty well now. She'll be just fine."

The picnic continued after Tom drove off with Sarah, Mom frying her famous onions and potatoes, and the men roasting the steaks. When Hop passed Mom's plate to her to serve herself some potatoes, Hop demonstrated his earthy humor by putting a large cow patty on it. I noticed she didn't laugh; but Hop did.

On a warm spring Sunday evening, we Shraugers were invited for a picnic with the Hopley's on one of their lush meadows. It resulted in a trip to the doctor for me. In the adjacent plowed field as George Peter, Junior, Cornie and I chased each other through the ruts, I tripped and fell into the separating barbed wire fence. A barb pierced me in the exact top of my head. Blood streamed down my front.

Mom and Helen wrapped my head in a dozen dish towels. All preparations for the meal were delayed while Dad rushed me into town to Dr. Johnson who met us at his office; Hop had called ahead. The doctor shaved and cleaned my wound, and pulled squeaking strands of hair from the hole in my scalp before sterilizing it. He finished by crowning me with a two inch gauze bandage. This caused a lot of excitement at school the next day. Everyone wanted to know why I had a round white bandage in such a strange spot.

My Dad, Harold Francis Shrauger, was given his middle name in memory of his grandfather. Mom's dictionary told me that Francis meant "warrior," and that two Harolds had been Kings of England, the second defeated by William the Conqueror at the Battle of Hastings.

But the battles Dad engaged in were his struggles with alcohol and gambling. I never knew what caused him to drink; but many years later, when I was grown and gone, he stopped drinking—cold turkey—after two single-car accidents.

"Mama," he always called her Mama because she was a Mama nine months after she became his wife, "I'm going to stop drinking before I kill myself." And since he had a strong will, and a strong will to live, he did.

But his bad habits were ongoing for many years and continued long after I'd grown up. When Cornie and I were still little girls, Mom once burdened us with the reality of Dad's gambling. She called us to the living room to sit with her on the old Bradley daybed. Feeling desolate and with a premonition of disaster, for this was an unusual happening, I waited. We sat on either side of her, her arms around our shoulders. I looked up at her kind face as she spoke.

"Girls, I thought you should know that last night your father gambled away the last two hundred dollars we had in the bank." She looked first at Cornie, then at me, her face sober.

The deep Depression of the early Thirties had been affecting us for some time. We all knew we were poor, but I don't remember falling to pieces because we were now penniless. I filed the knowledge away and went on with my life. I was sure that somehow everything would turn out all right.

This attitude echoed Dad's who always believed things were going to be better, that something would turn up. My Aunt Biddy said he was a living Mr. Macawber. Actually, both Mom and Dad shared eternal optimism. She often used as a preamble to her day dreaming, "When our ship comes in...." I guess by osmosis I became cheerful about what the ship might bring.

Dad was almost six feet tall, and with his shoes on, he was an even six. I thought that was a good height for a man to be. Broad shouldered and big boned, he had played football for Atlantic High School and briefly, before he dropped out to marry Mom, at the University of Iowa. Often he identified himself as an athlete.

Drinking hot coffee in the broiling days of Iowa summers when everyone else wanted iced tea, he'd say, "Hot coffee makes you sweat. That's healthy for athletes."

His dark brown hair complimented his hazel eyes that were framed with exceptionally long lashes. For years I listened to Mom tell about the time she first saw Dad. Seated across from him in the University library, ostensibly studying, she studied Dad's eyelashes. He noticed her. That began a courtship.

She was in her mid-eighties the last time she repeated this eyelash-loving story, so I asked her, "Mom, was that the only reason you married Dad?"

"Of course not." She smiled. "There were many reasons. For one, I was in love with your Dad and he with me. And he was kind to me."

I knew her Papa had made her life difficult, so I was glad she had told me. Dad gave her obvious love and kindness—which she never had from her father.

University training hadn't made him a reader. He limited himself to three newspapers: the *Atlantic News Telegraph; the Des Moines Register; and* sometimes the Omaha *World Herald*. He read two magazines, *Field* and *Stream*, and *True*.

Once as we were growing up, a terrible crisis developed over a broken lawn mower. My brother and sister accused me of being the destroyer, but I knew in my heart they had committed the crime. Because we had so few dollars, every break of necessary items was a major event.

Although I denied knowing anything about it, the only confrontation I ever had with Dad took place. He marched me to the upstairs bathroom where he shaved every morning and said, "Virginia, own up to it. Your brother and sister both say you broke the lawn mower."

"But I didn't do anything, Daddy," I sobbed, full of fear, but knowing I was innocent.

"Do I have to use my strop to make you tell the truth?"

He held the razor strop in front of my face in spite of the fact that he and Mom, before they married, had pledged never to lay a hand on any children they might have. I stared at the strop, imagining how it would hurt getting hit by it, and burst into blubbering. He finally put up the strop, and that was the end of the incident. I never did understand what happened, but I defended myself as only a little kid can do, with tears and protestations. I received no consoling words.

In those early days I didn't long for another kind of father. That came much later. If I thought about it at all, I learned day by day what kind of a father I had. It was long after he caused me great pain that I realized he could be improved upon. That idea came to me when I was eight or nine years old.

One summer morning Mom again called Cornie and me to the living room and had us sit beside her on the old daybed. Cornie sat next to her and I sat beside Cornie.

"I have something serious to ask you two," she began. She paused. "What would you think if I divorced your father?"

Cornie immediately answered. "I'd never speak to you again."

I said nothing, squirming inside, puzzled that Mom would ask me such a question. I had no idea how to answer it. I knew what divorce meant, but no adult I knew of in our family had divorced, except Great Aunt Emma, my dead Grandmother Prentiss' sister; and she was considered eccentric so hardly counted in my mind. No ordinary people—no good people—divorced, I had decided. I had nothing to say.

Mom always taught us to "solve your problems. Don't run from them." Now she was considering running. So I knew she must be feeling awfully bad. But afterwards nothing changed. Life went on, but with one exception.

I began to pay attention when Dad wasn't home for supper, which was a noticeable happening because he was regular in his habits. Mom always went right ahead and served dinner at six o'clock. I don't remember her saying anything about his absence. But I noticed she didn't talk much during meals when he wasn't there. So we were all pretty quiet. Mom saved Dad's portion. In later years she told me that she always tried to get him to eat when he stumbled into the house; but he wouldn't.

From then on if Dad didn't appear at dinnertime, I would be uneasy when I got into bed. Light sleeping, not usual for me, became a habit on these nights. I'd hear the car come to a stop by the stoop at the end of the porch; my body would tense, my stomach would start hurting. I'd wait, listening for Dad's footsteps to cross the porch right under me. I heard the front door open—I heard the sound of Mom's quiet voice. Then the door shut quietly.

I'd hear Dad's voice, but never the words. Soon they'd walk slowly up the stairs to their bedroom. The house became quiet. My heart would begin to slow down. After a while I'd get back to sleep.

In the morning I'd tiptoe down the hall, glance into the folks' bedroom and pass by quickly, hearing Dad's heavy breathing and smelling the sour air coming from the room. With a heavy heart, I'd continue right along downstairs to have breakfast, and start my day.

Only once did I see Dad drunk. It was a cold winter night. Cornie and I were in the downstairs guest room bed under the covers, Mom between us. We were cuddling into her soft body, enchanted by her low voice as she read aloud from *The Wizard of Oz*. Her warmth seeped into me. In this pleasing word-world I was lulled into a deep sense of security.

Suddenly harsh laughter interrupted. Dad stumbled into the room. He stood just inside the door for a moment, weaving like a cobra's head. He staggered to the end of the bed and balanced himself, a hand on the footboard. We three froze like prey. He cursed and said something I can't recall, careened around the bed, and brought his huge hand across Mom's face.

Instantly brother Harold was at the door shouting in his maturing voice, "Get out of this room, now!"

I felt myself melt into Mom's body, heard screaming, then realized the screams were coming from Cornie and me. Mom was sobbing. Harold and Dad were struggling in the little hall just outside the door, Harold not half the size of our father. They fell to the floor, a tangle of arms and legs.

Harold was crying and shouting, "Leave my mother alone!"

Dad, undone by the liquor, flailed uselessly. He finally gave up. Rising up on my elbow, I stared at them, frozen with fear of my father, and fear for my brother.

Dad was collapsed on his back, panting and mumbling, "All right. All right. All right."

Harold stood up, put out his hand to his father, put an arm under his shoulder. Dad lurched to his feet, and let himself be led toward the kitchen.

This incident was a step out of childhood for me. Mom, Cornie, and I never discussed it.

In the last years of Harold's life, I asked him if he remembered that night.

"How could I forget it," he said.

Dad put our long back yard into grass so we kids could have a big place to play at home. It was wide and long enough for all our night games, and a good place to get under the sprinklers when the weather was unbearably hot. Dad mowed the lawn, even under the little triangle of sumac trees. This made a private room where my friend, Dorothy, and I sat and had solitary conversations.

He bordered the yard on the east side with white and pink peonies, and propped up the new growth with two-foot chicken-wire fencing. Gramma Shrauger loved them and pronounced their name "pie-oh-nees." After she died, in spite of the family schism, and later, after Grampa died, on Memorial Day Mom and Dad faithfully cut big bunches of them and laid them on their graves in the Atlantic Cemetery. After I was grown and gone, when spring came late, Mom, distressed, would write to me that they were afraid the peonies wouldn't come into bloom in time for them to be laid on the graves.

Dad loved a nice lawn, and he cultivated ours carefully. Each spring I'd see him take his rake, scratch the soil in bare spots, drop a little top soil from a sack, sew fresh grass seeds, and finish by scratching them in. Later I'd notice robins and sparrows combing the yard, and wondered if any of the new seeds would be left to throw up shoots. A fine yard was his pride and joy, long before this was a fashionable idea. Every spring when the dandelions were showing themselves, he'd bring me a small, sharp knife and a basket.

"Now, remember, Virginia, cut deep under the plant, like this, then pull the whole dandelion up, root and all. But first, pull off all the yellow heads. We don't want them to go to seed. Scattered seeds equal more plants. I'll pay you five cents a half peck. Keep track of how many baskets you dig."

Behind the house, camouflaging the stoop, was his favorite shrub—a dogwood which had shiny, brilliant red branches, and small white flowers which became white berries in the fall. Dad brought us kids a dog, and Topsy's house nestled under the dogwood shrub by the cement steps leading up to the back door stoop. For our cold winters, Dad lined the little house with old pieces of rug and placed straw bales at its base to keep drafts out. Inside he put a bed of yellow straw for her to snuggle in. Dad didn't believe in having dogs in the house.

On hot summer days during the 100 degree heat, she dug a refuge for herself, a narrow trench under Dad's red-leafed barberry bushes he planted on the Smoller side of our house along the dividing strip of grass. There she lay cooling herself, out of my reach, ignoring calls to "come."

Topsy was a cur. She had large brown spots in her long white hair. Mom told me that being a cur meant she was a mixed breed, and usually these dogs were of even temperament. She fit Mom's description, for Topsy was gentle and sweet. Now and then, I'd kneel down in front of her. She'd be stretched out on the sidewalk, panting, letting her firm, pink tongue droop down sideways between her brown lips. I'd catch it between my thumb and forefinger, and gently hold it.

Looking at me with her kind eyes, she held very still: I held very still. Then I let it go. She'd lick her mouth, wet her tongue, and begin panting again. She never got up, walked away, or reprimanded me in any way. She just lay patiently on the sidewalk in front of me as I hunkered down to play our game, this little testing. We parted, still friends.

Dad was in charge of the Department of Dogs. All the dogs that came after Topsy were hunting dogs. He trained them, if they had any training, fed them beef and bones and household scraps, and hunted for game birds with them.

At the end of our driveway strips, just behind the house, Dad dug a plot for Mom's cutting garden. She loved to have flowers in the house in the summer, preferring small ones, pansies, cosmos, short zinnias, something blue—and accumulated a large collection of little vases to hold them. Later, when we kids were grown and gone, Mom developed allergies to dirt and sun. Dad took over the flower garden for her, planting each kind of flower in a separate row; and then he tended it, watering and weeding.

Dad's garden down the street was an old-fashioned garden, Grampa told me. It was all business. Dad laid each vegetable out in straight lines, mounded the dirt around the roots, kept everything meticulously hoed. He fed a family of five.

Dad built a playhouse for Cornie and me. It was near the Allen's garage, right behind Mom's little cutting garden. It was as big as a small room with plenty of space for toys which were always scattered around on the floor for there were no shelves. The walls were made of gray painted shutters as was the door. Sunlight came through the shutters making striped patterns on us and our toys; I was charmed by the stripes. Ignoring the toys, I moved around among them to see the patterns change on my dress, my legs and my arms. Dad built the playhouse sturdily, with a solid roof. Cornie and I seldom played with dolls; their staring eyes made them seem so dead—building forts with blocks was our favorite occupation.

Dad built the playhouse when I was very little, for by the time I was about seven or so it sat in the meadow adjacent to the rear of our back yard. Now it was a shed and held tools, and then grain for feeding pheasants the year Dad decided to raise them. Being a small animal and bird hunter all his life, it seemed the next step was to raise pheasants here at home. Then we could enjoy the delicious birds in any season.

So he put up a huge cage behind the shed using two-by-fours and chicken wire. Inside he built perches and placed nesting boxes. This experiment took place during the early days of the drought of the 1930s. Since Dad was at work all day, he paid me to water the pheasants. I did this chore once in mid-morning and once about four o'clock. Harold did the evening watering after his work at Pellet's farm. I carried two pails filled from our spigot by the driveway, lugging them back to the pheasant cage. I got inside, emptied the dirty water in the pans and refilled them. For this I earned fifty cents a day, good pay for a person accustomed to a nickel-a-week allowance.

A few times, as a surprise Dad brought some of the tiny pheasant eggs to the house for breakfast—so tiny one easily fit in the palm of my hand. Mom fried them gently in butter. Their wee size delighted me. All of us enjoyed this treat, especially Harold. I was allotted two. For me there was a particular pleasure in eating those miniature eggs, although I thought they tasted just like chicken eggs. A half dozen would have filled me.

22

Of course the pheasant experiment—it lasted only a short time—was Dad's idea. He was the boss about these matters with no consulting or asking of opinion. Except for outlining her needs for the house and trips to Iowa City, never did I hear Mom say "we" planned or "we" decided. It was always Dad "thought" or Dad "wanted." But her influence was subtle and in unnoticed departments. Besides, she was too busy with her papers, books, and clubs to interfere with what Dad wanted to do.

Dad's interests were mostly outside. His first loves were cars and driving. His secret desire had been to be a racecar driver. But he discarded this daydream when he fell in love with Mom. Actually Dad practiced racing all his life. There was no speed limit in Iowa at that time, or for years. So eighty miles an hour was customary on his business trips to Omaha. On some of the trips, he got the speed up to a hundred, he happily told Mom.

"When I went with him, I was scared to death," she told me. "My defense was to go to sleep the minute we got under way." He didn't drive that fast when any of us kids were in the car.

Along with Grampa, he shared a love for all things innovative and new. In later years when I began housekeeping and he was in the appliance business, he furnished my washing machine, dryer, refrigerator and stove at wholesale prices.

He told me about planned obsolescence. "Plan to replace these in a few years. Get the latest models," he said; but in earlier days, he had cars, and Mom had an icebox.

I especially remember three of the automobiles. The Buick touring car had a top that folded down and flaps that had to be snapped in place when it was raised. How we all loved riding in this car. I thought it racy and romantic, but it was hard to keep the cold air out in winter.

Later, in the 1930s, when Dad was selling cars after leaving Grampa's factory, he bought a boxy blue Chevy with solid hubcaps. Harold told me Dad drove it 80,000 miles which was a lot for a car in those days.

This was the car that caused Dad to fly into a fit of anger one frigid February morning. It wouldn't start, and he was to drive us kids to school. Noticing I hadn't put on my long underwear, he ordered me to do so.

"But, Dad, they're wrinkly around my ankles. They're ugly. I hate them."

"Do as you're told!" he said in a grim voice, while cranking the cold engine. "Go to your bedroom, and put on your underwear!" he ordered.

Tears did no good. He ignored me. I stomped up to my bedroom, put on the underwear, and when I returned, the car was still silent. So we three sat slumped in the back seat while the cranking continued.

No wonder he finally exploded. Although not a profane man, when really pressed, he'd loudly proclaim, "God damn it!" which he did that morning—several times.

But God blessed it instead. The motor started, and Dad carted us off to school. I was grateful the car was the object of his anger and not me.

Dad sometimes offered ideas about safe driving.

One was, "When you decide to make a move and begin it, finish it! It's changing your mind that gets you in trouble—and never try to pass a truck going downhill. The heavy truck will accelerate, and you'll never pass it. Pass on the uphill."

About speeding, he said nothing.

Quick getaways were his specialty. Wherever we went, whatever the occasion, he placed his car in a position that enabled him to leave ahead of other drivers. Sitting in a slow-moving line of cars didn't suit his temperament.

During his stint as an automobile salesman, he managed to convince his friend, Owen Meredith, to buy a Chevy, not to buy a Buick, his usual brand. Convincing Owen to change was a mark of Dad's persuasive powers. Owen wasn't an easy man to move. Unfortunately the Chevy developed problems right away. Owen had drawn a lemon. Eventually there was some settlement made.

I listened to Dad as he sat in his easy chair, his hands folded over his belly, his legs crossed, right leg moving up and down a little as he explained about lemons.

"It simply happens," he said. "A percentage of a factory's production results in lemons. It's nothing to get excited about. It's bad luck of the draw."

Owen understood that too. He didn't blame Dad personally.

Mom told me later, "Owen loaned Dad money at a time when we were completely without funds. What's more, as far as I know, Owen never made any attempt to collect the debt." He was one of Dad's hidden benefactors.

While driving eight summers with Dad to Iowa City for our annual August visits with Grandpa Prentiss, I had opportunities to see what a skillful driver he was. Weather never interrupted our plans. One rainy morning we departed in our Chevy, picnic basket on the floor behind Mom, I in the middle of the back seat between Harold and Cornie. For this trip, I had the best seat. I could see down the road between Mom's and Dad's shoulders.

At this time U.S. Six didn't have a hard surface, and as we got east of town we realized it would be a slippery ride. For a while all went well. We kids began our game of License Plates—competing to count the largest number of out-of-state plates. The rain became a downpour, causing Dad to modify his speed and Mom to drift off to sleep.

About halfway to Des Moines, the ruts became deeper, and soon were in as deep as ocean waves in a storm-tossed sea. Here and there cars sat stranded on either side of the road. Three had skidded into the cornfields! More and more were stalled in the ruts. I watched fascinated as Dad weaved through a bottleneck formed by one derelict halfway off the road on the left, another halfway off on the right. A third rested with its nose in a ditch, its rear end high in the air. Never letting up on the accelerator, Dad went with the car, letting the wheels spin, getting momentum again, and then racing along as fast as the car could take us.

On we went, the intrepid spirit of his pioneer ancestors heavy upon us. He paid no attention to his cargo; his eyes were on the road and on the other cars, like the best of racing car drivers. Luckily there was no oncoming traffic, so he kept plowing the ruts. As we approached the outskirts of Des Moines, we got out of that morass of a road and onto a firmer base.

Dad said, "It hasn't rained as much around here."

Mom slept through it all. I knew my Dad was the best driver in the world.

One humid, cloud-covered Saturday, Dad drove Mom, Cornie, and me to Carroll, Iowa, where our dancing teaching had arranged an afternoon performance on an outdoor stage. I was about ten years old and Cornie, twelve. We were in the middle of the last tap dance number. The sky was turning dark. Heavy black clouds rolled over our heads. We kept tapping away even though it got so dark someone turned on the platform lights which drooped on wires over our heads. The leaves of the trees surrounding the stage began to tremble—then sway—and suddenly a strong, cold wind blew over us making the light bulbs swing crazily. Just as the music stopped, a gentle rain began. We didn't wait for applause nor did the audience. The sky brightened with lightening, and thunder ordered us to our cars.

Dad took off in his usual way, ahead of the pack, and Cornie and I relaxed in our skimpy satin costumes in the back seat while Dad tore down the dirt road. The rain broke loose. We could hardly see out the car windows.

Mom said, "The clouds have opened."

Soon the dirt road turned slippery, then muddy, and finally the car was axle deep in mud. With his usual determination, Dad ground on until at last we bogged down, a complete stop. I was sure we'd go to sleep and wait until morning; but no, my Dad wasn't about to be stuck there or anywhere as long as there was gas in the tank.

So he backed, and rocked, and rocked and backed, pressed forward and backward, and gradually—gradually found a firmer layer of something—hope perhaps—under the mud. Slowly, too slowly for me, the car began to go forward again. Our rear end fishtailed, but we kept moving; and inevitably, Dad won. He straightened the car, and we were once more on our way!

I didn't feel relief, I felt sick: sick and tired of mud and being stuck in mucky muck while being desperate to get unstuck. Silently I resolved never to travel on a dirt road again. Lucky for me, about that time all the Iowa roads began to be graveled or paved.

In those earlier days, fathers were expected to provide for their families; Mom often said, "Your Dad is a good provider."

He not only provided the money for our food, but he also did all the shopping.

Mom usually gave him a shopping list when he left for work, but sometimes she'd phone for him to pick up another item or two. Being a restless man, he never objected stopping to shop on his way home for lunch. Later, when he had his own business, he welcomed being interrupted.

Actually Dad loved to grocery shop because he loved to eat; he especially enjoyed selecting the beef we ate and eagerly instructed me: "Look for a good color, red, but not too red, nicely striated with white fat—white fat only—for the color means it came from a corn-fed animal. Never buy beef if the fat is yellow. That tells you it comes from a grass-fed animal. And if you're buying steak, be sure it's of an even thickness."

Even in times of no job and dwindling money, his knack of planning ahead kept food on the table. But what Mom was really talking about was his love of eating; and as Ecclesiastes iii, 13 says, "Every man should eat and drink, and enjoy the good of all his labor; it is the gift of God."

He brought Real Cheese from Omaha, so we didn't often have the Kraft cheese spread that came in little decorated glasses. Secretly I loved to make a sandwich of the pimento kind that Harold brought home from Antrim's Grocery. Cheddar and Limburger cheese came to the house via Omaha; but the smell of the Limburger repelled me and, for once, Dad didn't insist I try it. I think he was delighted to have it all to himself. He introduced us to fresh baked whole wheat bread which couldn't be bought in Atlantic.

About five o'clock, his come-home time, I'd be sitting at the piano, theoretically practicing, or under it, reading. He would stroll from the kitchen through our little pantry and the music room, big belly leading, on his way to his comfortable Turkish chair.

In one hand he'd have a huge hunk of Real Cheese and in the other a fistful of soda crackers. Sometimes, in a different mood, he'd carry a sack of salted peanuts from which he'd take handfuls, throw back his head, and toss the nuts into his mouth. He never missed. This was his usual 'pre-dinner lunch.' He'd turn on the radio, and read the paper, content until Mom announced supper.

One year in early spring, conditions were just right for morels to pop up on the grounds of Atlantic's Golf and Country Club. Word of this phenomenon caused Dad to be up at dawn to find the morels just showing themselves, moist and sparkling with dew. When he came back with his peck basket full of the lovely fungus, he gave them to Mom to clean, smiling, and proud of his ability to provide something special.

At lunchtime, back he came with beefsteak. All five of us sat down and devoured steak smothered with morels. I didn't know this dish was a luxury, but I discovered that steak and morels made me gluttonous.

Through a number of Mom's illnesses, when she was unable to cook, Dad would see that we were properly fed. He did the cooking, simple but good; steak and potatoes I think. Even during the hard times when he was without a job, we always seemed to have plenty to eat. Grampa Shrauger saw to it that we had oranges. He wanted to be sure we kids had our vitamin C. Gramma Shrauger must have had something to do with this, for she often spoke to me of the importance of 'vih-tih-mins'. She pronounced the word with a short "*i*" in all the syllables, as her immigrant English forbears did.

Of course there were apples, but they didn't taste good to me. One result of our limited variety in fruit was that I got awfully tired of dried prunes served for breakfast along with our cream of wheat or oatmeal even though Mom knew just how to simmer the wrinkled old things, with plenty of sugar and lemon.

At lunch one day, sister Cornie took it into her head that she didn't like green beans any more and wasn't touching her helping.

"Eat your beans, Cornie," said Dad.

"I don't want to. I don't like them."

"Since when don't you like them. Eat your beans."

There ensued a wrangle about Cornie eat and Cornie won't eat until my stomach began to ache. I don't remember who won the argument, for they were a matched pair when it came to determination.

Dad often said, "I will not put up with finicky eaters."

He insisted that we kids try anything new that appeared on the table. So we ate kohlrabi, a variety of turnip, and salsify, a root native to Europe, as well as all the common vegetables. We were introduced to artichokes early in life. We might be hesitant, but always complied, and Cornie's fuss was the only occasion I recall of battling at meals. Mom and Dad made two exceptions: baked stuffed peppers and stewed tomatoes. They were considered too sophisticated for children's taste buds, being in the same category as green olives.

Years later Cornie pointed out to me that there were exceptions for Mom. She never ate liver or any 'innards', as Mom referred to them. Dad introduced us kids to baby beef liver. We three kids and Dad thought liver delicious, sautéed lightly in butter, pink in the middle. Mom prepared it perfectly. I was so busy trying to get my share I didn't notice she never ate a piece.

Cornie said, "Mom is privileged."

I came to think nothing was as important to Dad as eating. Shoes could be left in disrepair, clothes were worn threadbare, holes appeared in the rugs, but we would not only eat, but we'd eat well. Nothing raised his ire as quickly as being a guest at the home of a parsimonious hostess. Now and then he'd come stomping into the vestibule, talking all the way from the car, speaking to nobody in particular and to anyone within earshot, spouting aloud his annoyance.

"You'd think a grown man was a boy of ten, the way she holds back on the helpings," he'd shout to Mom who was trailing behind him. "Cornelia, don't you ever agree for us to go to Grace's (or Peggy's, or Janet's) house for dinner again! Hear me?"

"Yes, dear," she amiably answered, knowing full well that as the occasion arose, they would indeed be back at Dianne's or at anyone's house who invited them to dinner. 'Stirring up' a card game and social eating was a big thing with Mom and Dad's group of friends and occurred any night of the week.

One evening we hosted a festive dinner party at our house. I wondered why the adults were standing about in the kitchen sputtering and laughing. They were in very high spirits, giggling and poking each other. Mom had scalloped potatoes and salad ready, the table was set, and she was tending something frying in her two cast iron skillets—round balls she kept turning over and over. Whatever it was, we kids weren't served any. The next day I asked Mom what she had been frying.

"Oh, a specialty called Pig Nuts."

"Pig Nuts?" I questioned.

"Yes, Pig Nuts. That's slang for testicles. Another name for them is Rocky Mountain Oysters. Mr. Hopley thought up the party and asked me to prepare them because Helen wouldn't have a thing to do with it."

So I missed out on "the reproductive glands from certain male animals" as I later learned from the newspaper's food section. I'm sure Mom didn't eat any of those.

To extend the supply of food Dad had grown and Mom had canned, each fall he would come home lugging case after case of vegetables from the local Cuykendall Canning Factory. This was a big operation that employed four hundred and fifty men and women around the time I was born, fewer in later years. The wage was thirty-five cents an hour for husking corn, stoking boilers, watching the machines that crimped the tops on cans, and packing up the finished products. After two fires, Mr. Cuykendall bought up-to-date machinery that enabled him to use fewer helpers. Farmers from miles around would bring their peas, corn, beans, tomatoes, and pumpkins for ready cash during the summer and early fall months.

During the season, Dad hunted pheasants and ducks with his friend, Frank Poch. They were good hunters, and lucky too, never returning with an empty bag. Once or twice I joined Dad in the basement where he was cleaning his share. He'd be sitting in a chair before the open door of our coal furnace with a pile of bird bodies, either pheasants or ducks, in a heap at his feet.

The roar of the fire surprised me. The coals were a simmering red, and an occasional flick of blue licked toward the top of the furnace. The bright ruddy light streaming out the door filled the room with a rosy glow. Dad's face and hands were as red as the coals, and I imagined I could see smoke coming off his flannel shirt. Spreading overhead in all directions were the round, white insulated heat runs of the huge furnace which looked to me like the arms of an enormous octopus which moved in the flickering light.

One at a time he picked up a pheasant or a duck, and I saw the beautiful iridescent colors of the pheasant feathers or the shimmering green feathers of the Mallard ducks. He busily plucked, then tossed the feathers into the fire. They had no time to hover over the coals. Caught up in the red and blue flames they disintegrated instantly with a faint crackle. Dad didn't seem to notice how the feathers magically disappeared. Pluck, toss, pluck, toss.

Overcome by sadness, seeing this destruction, I asked, "How can you kill those pretty birds?"

He thought about the question and finally said, "Virginia, you eat chicken don't you? It's a feathery bird, isn't it? It's good to eat, isn't it? It's killed before it comes to market, and someone has removed the feathers. Why is my preparing these birds any different?"

His questions smothered me. I didn't have an answer; so I accepted his explanation and learned to enjoy eating the wild game Mom prepared. She cooked a braised squirrel dish, roasted the ducks, made a pheasant casserole, and fricasseed rabbit. Even the ducks I saw aging for days on an improvised line under the gutters along the back of the house didn't repel me.

During those early days, our neighbor, Glen Allen, often punched a bag he hung from the overhang of their garage, but I didn't know he was a serious boxer until Dad invited Cornie and me to watch Glen perform at the Legion Hall. That night I found myself in a smoky foyer crowded with men laughing and talking. Dad guided Cornie and me through the crowd to our seats. Glen had given Dad the tickets, and we were seated in the second row.

A wrestling match was the first event—even I could tell it was faked; I decided wrestling was a joke, but Dad said, "No, the wrestling is to entertain us until all the late-comers arrive."

I recall nothing of Glen's match. But later I learned Glen had made a reputation for himself as a fine boxer. For me, the important thing was that Dad had taken me to a special occasion. Aside from circuses, it seldom happened.

The evening was the beginning of my awareness of professional sports and games. In high school Harold tried hard to be an athlete. One spring afternoon my girlfriends and I went to the high school track and field meet. I especially watched for Harold to return from a run through Atlantic's streets with the long distance runners. When he appeared, he was very near the last of the pack.

As he panted his way to the finish line, I thought, "He does this only to please Dad. What he really likes and does well is dancing."

Throughout my school years in Atlantic, as a family we'd gather around the radio to listen to sporting broadcasts. In 1937 we heard Joe Lewis fight James Braddock and listened in 1938 when he knocked out Max Schmeling. Mom was always engrossed with sports as a spectator, not only because she loved games, but also because all those events meant so much to Dad. I often wondered if she would have been such an avid fan had she married another kind of man. But she had played tennis as a young woman, and I knew she was a good golfer.

Occasionally, and at the last minute, Dad would rush into the house calling to Mom, "Pack your nightie, we're going to Indianapolis to see the races."

And off they'd go, usually leaving Mom's hat behind which meant she'd come home sunburned. Once they arrived in Indianapolis so late the night before the Memorial Day car race, they found all the hotels and motels full. Finally one helpful clerk called ahead, found a room, and reserved it for them.

They located the place, found it not too savory, but Dad said, "It will do."

After dinner they returned to their room and, while settling down, were amused by all the traffic in the halls; Mom said, "I suppose everyone is having an especially good time in honor of the races."

But the noise continued, and they found it difficult to sleep since the motel was thin-walled.

Suddenly Dad said, "Cornelia, this has got to be a whore house!"

"Oh, well," answered Mom, "all we want to do is sleep; we'll be out of here first thing in the morning. No matter."

It was as she said, and she relished telling the story.

23

Circuses were another of Dad's great loves because they brought animals of all kinds to Atlantic. So we were taken to many circuses with him. When Mom and Dad returned from a trip, if they visited a zoo, he told us about it first thing. In this way I learned that a wonderful zoo was where Mom's brother Bob lived, San Diego, California.

At crack of dawn one summer day, Dad took us kids down to the railroad tracks to see the Ringling Brothers circus unload. This year, the ads promised, there were to be new and unusual performers.

"Get up, Cornie, Virginia, we're leaving right now!" Dad rooted us out of bed at three o'clock in the morning. The Milky Way glittered, making a dim light as we three kids piled into the car and zipped down Chestnut Street. We parked in front of the railroad station, the car headed for home. Stumbling along in the dark behind him, we crossed the tracks. He found a spot in the grassy field from where we could see everything.

Men with lights at the end of long wires were shouting to each other and to men guiding elephants to the train. The small moving lights revealed only elephant parts—a wrinkled leg, a profile of a head and trunk, a curly tail. As the sky lightened, we could see the long line of circus wagons waiting to be unloaded. On some were bright painted pictures of fierce animals and with words confirming what was inside: lion, tiger, or bear. The elephants stood to one side holding ropes in their trunks. As soon as their keepers prodded them, the huge beasts pulled the wagons forward toward a ramp, and as each wagon rushed down to our level, the beasts let go of the rope. Other elephants then pushed the wagons to the camp areas.

Gradually the rising summer sun brought brilliance to the busy scene. Everyone knew his job, and all were in a hurry. Beyond the tracks was a large meadow. When Dad noticed the roust-a-bouts were there laying out the three-ring circus tent, we rushed to that area. I wondered how the workers knew exactly where to pound in the stakes that soon held the supporting ropes. Teams of men pulled huge center poles upright. In no time the tent top was up in its full, huge glory.

Since the flaps weren't yet attached, we could easily see inside. Working fast, shouting to each other, teams of men secured ropes to the many stakes. The space which a few minutes before had been open meadow had changed into a large enclosure with the tent top soaring above our heads: so high, so promising.

"Mom's fixing waffles and bacon for breakfast," Dad said; so back to the car we ran, and since it was parked strategically, we had no trouble getting underway.

We flew up Chestnut Street to La Vista Place. Mom had set the table, and the waffle iron was hot. She brought us plates of the promised waffles and bacon. As we devoured our sweets, we felt our early morning outing was perfect.

Dad went off to work. At eleven Cornie and I stood waiting in front of the Strand Theatre. Drifting up from the railroad station was the sound of drums, flutes, clarinets, and horns. Soon the circus band marched by us, accompanied by clowns, their painted faces and colorful clothes garish in the sunlight. Behind them lumbered the elephants. Riding high on their shoulders sat practically naked circus girls in brilliant, sequined costumes, bangles on arms, feet bare, toes pointing. The thick makeup and powdered bodies seemed unreal in the harsh light of noon.

Being drawn by a pair of horses came a caged lion. We saw his box unloaded that morning; now its sides were gone, and behind the iron bars he rested quietly. Equestriennes rode their restrained but prancing horses just ahead of a group of walking performers: the Japanese tightrope artists, trim in their light gray trousers and close fitting jackets; the famous balancing Wallendas, carrying poles; various others, and finally, the contortionist wearing brilliant orange and green tights. Those walking watched for the piles of elephant and horse manure and delicately stepped around them.

Clowns intermingled with the thin line of people who had come to see the parade. Not many onlookers were there, for the farmers were working at their chores. They would come to the afternoon or night performances. Some clowns rode little bikes, the size Cornie and I had; their's had solid white disks instead of spokes, and the handles and supports were painted rainbow colors. The clown's noses were false, and the grease paint on their faces was wet with sweat, for we were in the middle of the hottest Iowa summer we'd ever had. We knew the parade was over when we heard the calliope coming.

That afternoon we five Shraugers joined the slow moving crowd: farmers in their overalls, their wives in cotton print dresses, some holding their children's hands; people who lived in Atlantic; and folks from nearby towns.

Passing the long row of sideshows, we saw a mean looking man in a dirty gray fedora hawking the freak show. Then I heard the man shouting, "Plenty of time to see the girlies, right this way—twenty-five cents, Gents!"

Later Mom told me he was one of what were "common circus attractions." He was dressed in a checked black and white jacket, tight purple pants, and a filthy yellow derby pushed back over his greasy hair. From his elevated platform he held high over our heads a string of yellow tickets. As we crowded past him, out came the girlies, and I saw they were next to naked. Holding Mom's hand, I looked sideways at them.

Dad led us past the cotton candy vendor saying, "Not now, it's too sticky. After the show is OK."

Dad found our seats right away in the middle of the tent on the second row. He always got us good seats.

The band blared, the sound almost lost in the chatter of the people crowding in. The noise began to hurt my ears. The tent seemed smaller now with the bandstand and bleachers set up, and the crowd jamming in. The three rings made of curved, thick, heavy sections of wood fitted together, were in place; ropes and nets hung near the top of the tent and on the many supporting poles. Shouting to each other, workers raced around, checking to see that all was in order, pulling on ropes, and looking up at hooks.

Then the ringmaster appeared, dressed in high black boots, black jodhpurs, white shirt and red bow tie, black cut-away jacket decorated with red sequins, and a red cummerbund. On his head was a black top hat.

Cracking his bullwhip, he roared, "Ladies and Gentlemen! Welcome to the Greatest Show on Earth! Strike up the band!"

I was ready for anything!

The band played a march and in came the parade of all the performers, not just some of them as Cornie and I had seen in the morning. Their painted faces and colorful costumes were perfect, for they belonged under the muted light of the big top, not under the blazing Iowa sun.

As the procession left the tent, the trumpets blared, and the Ringmaster called our attention to the right-hand ring, now filled by a large cage.

"Ladies and Gentlemen, now witness a fearless man who's trained a dozen fierce lions to bow to his commands." The lion tamer entered the cage. He was dressed like an equestrian, wearing jodhpur boots, jodhpurs, and a tan shirt with a triangular red scarf around his neck. In his left hand he carried a long whip, and in his right, a pistol.

The audience exploded in anticipation, shouting and clapping. After he bowed left, center and right, he turned his attention to his assistants. Standing along a caged tunnel they urged the lions to walk through it. Slowly they came, one behind the other. The assistants saw to it that there was a good distance between them. They prodded the slow ones and put the prod under the nose of the faster ones. The trainer guided each lion to its perch where the animal casually jumped up: seeming bored, they sat looking at the crowd.

But the trainer began snapping his whip when the last lion, a true King of Beasts, leapt into the ring, his great mane flowing towards his tail. The huge roaring growling beast stopped, and showed his long sharp teeth, snarled and batted at the trainer's whip. Then he sped around the inside edge of the cage, and resisted mounting to his perch. Finally the trainer fired his pistol, and won the battle. The King of the Jungle then casually leapt onto his center perch, and settled down like all the female lions—and yawned.

The most exciting thing about the lions, I thought, was their jumping through the large hoop set on fire by the trainer—it made a colorful picture. As soon as each animal had its turn of "leaping through the terrifying ring of fire," as the advertising blurbs nailed on every telephone post in town told us, they loped to the tunnel and, one by one, disappeared.

While the cage was dismantled, the ringmaster announced the acts to appear next in each of the three rings. My eyes didn't know where to look. Men juggled bats and balls, girls balanced on tiny platforms, twisting their bodies into strange shapes; a trained bear danced and twirled; clowns invaded the stands. When these and other groups finished, out they scurried. Their helpers cleared the gear away just in time for others to arrange ropes and pulleys, nets and ramps.

When the aerialists began their act, watching was easy. Everything else stopped. I anticipated what was to come as each member of the team quickly mounted the wiggly rope ladders and paused to bow to us from one or the other of the two platforms set high and far apart in the upper reaches of the tent.

On their way through the air, they were fairies floating, and I could feel myself flying with them. I loved the flying people better than anything else, except, maybe, the cotton candy.

The Ringmaster brought the crowd to silence when it was time for the great Wallendas to appear. Even the circus dogs were quiet.

In less of a shout, he announced, "In the center ring, Ladies and Gentleman, today you are privileged to witness the greatest balancing act in circus history. Forty feet in the air you will witness The Great Human Pyramid, a balancing act on the high wire with nothing but a token net beneath them."

The Ringmaster paused. He continued quietly, "I'm asking you to be completely silent as the Wallendas perform their hazardous act."

An absolute hush fell over the packed crowd, but all gave a rousing cheer as the Wallendas in their white and maroon tights ran to the poles supporting the wire. Two husky men, holding bicycles, quickly climbed the long rope ladder to a little platform. Each balanced his bicycle on the high wire. Then, in tandem—firmly linked themselves together with a bar resting on their shoulders. Slowly they rode the bicycles backward and forward, getting the feel of the wire. The staring crowd was absolutely silent. We barely breathed for fear of distracting the performers.

Another Wallenda, holding a chair, ascended to the platform joining his companions; he then slowly climbed up and over the shoulders of the nearest Wallenda, and positioned himself at the center of the crossbar. These three paused as the wire swayed. Carefully the man with the chair balanced two of its legs on the bar's center, then seated himself to complete the second layer of the Pyramid. Again the wire swayed, but came to balance once more.

Quickly climbing to the platform, tiny Helen Wallenda wire-walked to the first Wallenda, climbed up and over him to the cross-bar, and walked to her teammate on the chair. With great poise, she carefully climbed onto his shoulders, held a crouching position as, once more, the slender wire swayed. When all settled into equilibrium, she unfolded herself and slowly came to a full stand. Then, waiting until all were once more perfectly balanced, Helen Wallenda, carefully raised her arms, and stretched her hands to the tent top completing the promised Pyramid. The crowd was absolutely silent.

Helen then turned her head, acknowledging us. The band burst into gay music, and the audience became almost hysterical, waving and shouting as the Wallendas quickly dismounted, bowed, and disappeared.

A dozen clowns rushed up into the bleachers and broke the tension by sitting on laps and making people laugh. Hawkers resumed their selling of popcorn. Dad treated us to hot dogs. Finally the clowns left the tent.

Again the music stopped when the Ringmaster cracked his whip. "And now, ladies and gentlemen, you are about to see the most extraordinary act in all of circus history."

The audience quieted.

"You will now be thrilled by an aerialist who defies gravity and will amaze you with her daring and strength. She is the only circus artist in the world who performs and has ever performed this feat. Here she is, Ladies and Gentlemen, the unparalleled "Queen of the Air," Lillian Leitzel!"

Trumpets announced her arrival. A tiny blonde woman entered from behind a canvas flap holding a tan cape closely wrapped about her body. She stood there a moment. Then, to the accompaniment of quiet music, she made her way to the very center of the tent where she dropped her cape to reveal sparkling white tights. Grasping a long rope, she allowed her assistant to pull her almost to the top of the tent.

The band began a waltz as she seized a ring. Spotlighted, with all other lights extinguished, Lillian Lietzel made a series of graceful twirls with a single arm holding a ring, and then with both arms holding rings.

Again the trumpets blared as she traded the rings for a short rope, and allowed herself to be pulled almost to the very top of the tent. The trumpets quieted. As the band played soft music, she secured a short harness around one slender wrist and began swinging herself back and forth, like a pendulum, pointing her feet towards the tent top.

She quickly gained momentum, her feet leading; nearer and nearer she came, feet first, to the top of the tent until finally—turning on her shoulder—she completed one full loop. In silence all of us stared. At this point the music stopped, and a drum began to roll. We were seeing the performance never done before and never by anyone else.

Momentum now took her up, a shoulder turn, down, and up, and over her shoulder, and down. As she ascended, yes, she threw the slim line of her outstretched body up, over and around her shoulder. Now, as her body completed the circle, toes pointed to the floor, the drummer was emphasizing each completed circle with "rat-a-tat-TAT"—"rat-a-tat-TAT"—rat-a-tat-TAT. The audience was quietly counting in sync with the TAT, "seventeen, eighteen, nineteen." As the number of twirls grew larger, our voices grew louder: "forty-five, forty-six, forty-seven." Down she came, up and around she spun, like an insect trying to escape a spider's web, and the crowd was chanting "sixty-seven, sixty-eight, sixty-nine...."

It seemed as if the drum's rat-a-tat-TAT, and the counting encouraged her. My mouth hung open. My soul was shaken. She was hardly human—spinning at the tent top, doing such an inhuman thing.

When she reached one hundred, I was sure her arm would separate from her shoulder. But she slowed, swung back and forth, gradually reducing her arc, back and forth, quietly back and forth until finally she came to rest.

As she grabbed the long rope, her assistant quickly lowered her. Applause vibrated the tent as she descended, and clutching her cape around her, she bowed, and immediately made her exit.

In anticlimax five huge, heavy, gray and white horses, with wrapped and fluffed tails rearing above their behinds, looking like question marks, came pounding into the center ring with the flashy equestrians on their backs, all bound by gravity to the floor.

I had to strain to see past them to our left, past the horses running around the inside of the middle ring and past the many dangling ropes. I was trying to see the Japanese gentlemen balancing on the tight wire aided by their big toes. To me, feats of highly skilled balancing and juggling were especially satisfying. Jugglers, a trained bear, and other acts filled all the rings. Suddenly the band made a musical signal, the tent emptied, and it was time for the last act.

The mock Cowboy and Indian fight signaling the end of The Greatest Show on Earth began as gunshots resounded through the tents. Indians dressed in feathered headbands and colorful supple leather shirts and pants hunkered down on sleek horses rushed by us, and Cowboys, slipping in behind straw bales for cover returned shot with rifles. No one fell dead and finally, when the fighters streamed out of the tent, we knew we'd seen the circus for another year, Dad's special treat for us kids. Now it was time to get our cotton candy.

At any other time, Dad's sales experience would have made him a good living as a car salesman, for he knew and loved cars.

Mom told me his good friend, Bill Linke, the local Chevrolet dealer, hired him immediately, but not too long after he let him go saying, "Harold, you're a damn good salesman, but I can't afford to have you. If the rich people in town who buy my cars would only pay up, I could keep you on. But they don't."

For a time in 1932 Dad worked for the State Gasoline Tax Department driving all over Southwestern Iowa collecting taxes. Mom and Dad had been Republicans, but when he was hired through a Democratic friend, they changed parties.

Mom justified her action saying, "I'll accept any political party that will give your Dad a job; but at heart I'm a liberal, and I'll always be a liberal no matter what party has my name on its books."

I don't know why this job came to an end.

Then he worked with Don McCrae, an Atlantic Ford Dealer, who, since business was poor, was also selling Blatz beer and soft drinks made in Omaha. Once when I came home for lunch I saw the giant beer truck parked in our driveway and felt ashamed that Dad had to sell beer for a living. I should have been grateful that Dad was such a scrambler. During those terrible days when so many people had nothing, he almost always brought home some money.

Every September, when school started, we kids had to fill out a form asking, among other things, what our Dad's did for a living. I couldn't make myself write down beer salesman, so I omitted the word 'beer'. Perhaps I was ashamed because most of my parents' social friends were professional people—doctors, lawyers, dentists—and others seemed to have no money worries. But I knew that my friend Dorothy's father, who was a dentist, was too often given a bushel of pota-toes or fresh garden produce in the summer. That fed them, but it didn't pay the gas bill.

On one of the wonderful warm days of summer, our family of five gathered around the oak table for lunch. Dad sat opposite Mom. I was on his right, my brother on my right, and Cornie sat opposite me. Sunshine poured in through the fluffy glass curtains covering the south casement windows making the yellow flowers nestling in leafy greens on the wall paper seem real. The sun surrounded Mom making her hair a copper glow.

In the buffet behind Dad were Mom's silver flatware and all her nice linens. On top of it sat three pare-point silver serving trays, and an ornate pair of sterling silver candle sticks. Aside from the table and chairs, the buffet was the only other piece of furniture in the room.

On the wall next to a small closet hung a photo of Lil's watercolor—a white-washed house built on a steep incline in Anticoli, Italy where Aunt Lil and Uncle Frank had lived while honeymooning there.

A royal blue cloth crisscrossed with one-inch yellow and green stripes covered the table. Aunt Biddy brought it as a present from Sweden to Mom when Uncle Mark took his family there. He was researching the Swedish social system for a book he was writing. The whole room was so cheery it made my heart glad.

In the center of the round table sat our huge, white turkey platter loaded with Dad's homegrown garden vegetables which he'd harvested from his garden, washed at the outdoor faucet, and brought to Mom to prepare for our lunch.

This time she made an especially pretty arrangement; she heaped rich green lettuces in the center of the platter, and edged them with a thick pile of sliced, deep-red beefsteak tomatoes. Rounds of shiny green peppers overlapped them, dripping their silvery juices. Slivers of sweet onions covered everything. Blue-red, marble-sized radishes along with slender white ones and tiny carrots filled all the crevices. As usual, the platter being too heavy to lift, we passed the serving fork and spoon instead. In turn, each of us reached to the table's center to serve our-selves as Mom's homemade mayonnaise made its way around the table. The only other food we ever had with this common summer meal was bread and butter, milk, or iced tea.

My favorite piece of bread was the heel. I think it was my favorite because Mom praised it as special, and in those days I always followed her lead. I also think she encouraged me to prefer heels so everything was eaten, important in those depression days.

I had my usual buttered heel balanced along the edge of my plate. As we all munched away, Harold launched into a story. I turned my head to listen. When I turned back to reach for my heel, I was surprised. My bread was gone!

"Who took my bread?" I cried out.

There was no time for an answer—the back of Dad's huge hand struck me across my face. My nose stung; I burst into righteous, indignant tears, and fled. I never questioned my father's words or his actions, so I didn't ask for an explanation. Everyone ignored the incident. But I never forgot.

After 1929, my fun of watching Mom prepare for a big evening became a thing of the past. Instead of the formal parties Mom and Dad and their friends had enjoyed in better days, they settled for co-operative dinners and, in the summer, picnics. Of course, card playing went on forever. They all were young, high-spirited, and fun loving, so they laughed and joked, and forgot their financial troubles when socializing. I heard no discussions about employment.

Although I knew we were poor, and that Dad was changing jobs often, deep down I never lost my sense of security. As a result, living through the Depression simply made hard workers out of Harold, Cornie, and me. During those days in Iowa, young people could be employed at age fourteen. In order to have spending money we had to earn it. Living through those times didn't destroy us in any way; it made us stronger.

Dad was a born salesman and eventually became one permanently. He had a book filled with line drawings of faces. Each had an analysis under it, giving clues to a salesman for reading the faces of prospective buyers. He was working to achieve success. I admired that.

Around 1935 automatic coal Stokers came on the market. Skilled as he was with mechanical things, it seemed natural that he could sell such a product because everyone who had central heating burned coal. Keeping a coal fire going took skill.

With great pride he showed me the stoker he had set up in our basement. He explained how it worked, how it conveyed the coal into the open maw of the furnace. I sensed he was practicing his spiel on me.

"This is a great back saver," he told me. "No more heavy work, no more remembering to check the fire—it's thermostatically controlled."

He sold them to anyone able to buy; but few could afford the price, and muscles didn't cost anything.

After a time, he turned his attention to smaller, less expensive household items. The repair of electrical items like irons, toasters, waffle irons, washing machines and other electrical household appliances came naturally to him. This eventually led to his selling new appliances.

By the early forties, his appliance business was large enough to rent more space. He leased the store owned by Mary and Costas Papathakos at 509 Chestnut Street where they once sold candy. His repairing of old items, then selling them like a pawnbroker, caused Mom to joke, "Now we're in the three-ball business."

When new appliances were again produced after WWII was over, he gained the franchise to sell the Hot Point line. He rapidly became a champion. At the annual sales meeting in Omaha, he often was awarded the Best Salesman prize. Many times he also had the winning number for the door prize. "Old Lucky Nuts," Mom called him. Of course he'd sell the items.

24

All About Mom

My Mom adored Christmas. She confided in me that she believed in Santa Claus until she was ten years old and was heartbroken when the fantasy was ruined. I don't know who or what disillusioned her. However, she mentioned it so often I knew it was a permanent injury.

It was her Mother's enthusiastic participation in the Christmases in Iowa City—making special cookies, entertaining friends—the whispered secrets among her siblings, their fun and giggling while they planned and made special presents, and the annual decorating of their tree which sealed Mom's love of Christmas. She built our Christmases on these memories. Yes, the Christmas Holiday and all her traditions made it the happiest time of year for her: it was all about love.

She saw that Christmases were always gay occasions in our house. Even when Dad was out or work, no matter if little money was at hand, there was always a tree—maybe misshapen or bedraggled, perhaps a last minute give-away rescued by Dad from somewhere; he always made sure we had a tree. He set it up, and we kids got out the ornaments. But I don't recall him opening presents with us.

Harold, Cornie, and I decorated the tree. Harold draped the lights, and Cornie and I cut and pasted together colored paper ring–chains. Since Harold was the oldest, artistic, and careful, he was privileged to place the fragile, hand-made glass German ornaments, saved from better times, on the branches. For ten cents, Woolworth's furnished a bunch of foil icicles.

Always packages with fine things in them appeared under the tree Christmas morning, mailed to us from our aunts, or given by Grampa, our local Santa Claus.

As for me, I don't think I ever believed in Santa Claus. With an older brother and my particular sister, who would have a chance to live in that fantasy world.

On Christmas morning, still in our nightclothes, we raced to the tree. Harold turned on the lights; we three always stood for a while, admiring the tree, the lights making the foil icicles gleam like a thousand stars. We knew to wait until Mom joined us and didn't touch the pile of presents dressed in their Christmas greens and reds, filling the space under the tree. But we were allowed to bring our stockings from the mantel. We sat by the tree and poured the contents into our laps. Out rolled the ubiquitous oranges, colorfully wrapped hard candies, red and white ribbon candy, and marzipan in fruit shapes which Mom said was a special treat. I never developed a taste for it.

"Santa always left some in my stocking when I was a child," she told us every year.

One year in mid-December, Mom gathered Harold, Cornie, and me together and asked, "Now children, tell me why we celebrate Christmas." Silence.

"Sunny, you know. Tell me." Silence.

"Cornie?" Silence.

I wasn't asked for I was too young, I suppose.

"Well, do you know what Easter means?" Mom asked Harold. Silence.

"Cornie?" Silence.

"I am shocked. What *have* you learned in Sunday School?"

She proceeded to tell us the story of the birth of Jesus and of his death and resurrection. I listened and learned so that if Mom asked these questions again, I'd know the answer.

A unique pleasure for us kids at present opening time was to watch Mom open the package sent to her from her Godfather, Dr. William Hubbard, a close friend of her Papa's. Mom would lift the gift high and say, "Come and see what my Godfather sent me this Christmas."

We'd gather round as she tore it open, a look of anticipation on her face. The present I most vividly recall was the last one she received. It was a dilapidated flower to be worn on a hat, or suit lapel—an ugly faded red; Mom never wore red.

"Good Heavens, look at this! An old misshapen, raggedy RED fake rose, obviously a hand-me-down, as usual. Dr. Hubbard never makes the selection, but turns that effort over to his wife. Everything I've ever received has been something his wife didn't want any more. Always it's been unusually ugly or in bad condition, like this one."

She explained the situation as she dangled it so we were sure to see it.

This last "offering" (her word) prompted her to write Dr. Hubbard. As she held the crushed, artificial red flower with its bent petals, and raveled stem, she wrote,

Dear Doctor Hubbard, I've appreciated your remembrances to me at Christmas time all these years, but as your wife seems to know nothing as to what would be appropriate for me, I suggest that you discontinue the effort. Sincerely …"

From then on, each Christmas he sent her a check for five dollars.

One Christmas morning, when Cornie and I were six and eight, and Harold, eleven, we joined Mom singing "Onward Christian Soldiers" as she led us marching downstairs to the tree. I marveled at the depth of her contralto voice. Later, the choice of song seemed odd to me.

As we came off the last steps, Cornie and I spotted two small-sized bicycles with training wheels, on standards, beside our tree—one red, one blue.

Delighted, we shouted to Mom, "Look, look, look what Santa Claus brought us!" We climbed on the seats, and spun the rear wheels of these prizes beyond our wildest dreams.

"Grampa is the Santa Claus," said Mom, smiling, sharing our joy. "He brought the bikes here last night, and was so pleased he could give them to you. He said he'd come this morning to see if they fit you."

And he did come later; we thanked him, and together we celebrated the day with Mom's good Christmas sugar cookies and milk or coffee. Grampa was my Christmas Star.

We were totally surprised. Having bikes never occurred to us. Whatever else we were given that year was of no importance. "Freedom!" I thought. It didn't take us long to learn how to ride the bikes. As soon as the snow disappeared, out we went. Soon, off came the training wheels, and we were racing around the loops. It became a daily occupation.

When Cornie's and my legs were much too long for riding our small bikes, what should appear at Christmas but two full-sized bicycles. Of course Grampa had again played Santa Claus. How we appreciated Grampa's thoughtfulness and generosity. How I appreciated him giving me wings.

Cornie and I didn't know he'd dug into his savings to give them to us. Much later Mom told me that. Most people in Atlantic were in financial trouble in those days. As was usual in our family, the problems of the adults weren't subjects of daily conversation. And Grampa wanted to give us something useful. I wonder if he ever realized how much we rode those bikes.

The next Spring, Harold taught me how to fix flat tires and replace the chain when it came off its sprocket. Our front porch was our garage. If oil spots were left, no one complained. Probably no one noticed.

Cookie-making time reined in our house for weeks before Christmas. Mom made thousands it seemed to me, not only for our enjoyment but for all her friends and relatives. This happened even through the Depression years. Cornie and I were enlisted to wrap the cookies in foil, then pack them in gay Christmas boxes selected by us from Woolworth's.

Harold and I delivered the local boxes. He drove, and I dashed out of the car to the doors of all Mom's friends, and many older church members "who needed remembering" as Mom said. Dad sent off large boxes to the families of Bob and Alice, Biddy and Mark, and to Lil and Frank.

As our cousins grew and went off to college, Mom decided one year not to send cookies to her family. Letters of complaint were quick to come.

Brother Bob phoned and asked, "Where are the cookies, Cornelia? Don't you know we begin our Christmas morning with your cookies, hot coffee, and then presents? Christmas isn't Christmas without your cookies."

She never missed again as long as she made cookies at all.

All through the hard times, Mom had her organ job at the church, still earning a dollar a week for the Sunday service and the choir rehearsal. She also played for weddings, sometimes getting paid, and for funerals where her pay was built into the cost of the service. But skullduggery (hard to hide in a small town) on the part of one director often deprived her of some of her rightful income. With this money she made monthly payments to Sam Marshall for Cornie's and my clothes.

Once she told Sam, "I wish I could pay you more, but we just don't have the money."

"Cornelia," he said, "if everyone would pay me a little each month like you do, I could stay in business."

They either didn't or couldn't, and Mr. Marshall eventually had to close his store and went on the road selling women's handbags and jewelry. Later, before he joined the army, brother Harold became his apprentice.

My sister's best friend, Jeanne Howorth, told me that Mom said when visiting her mother, Mrs. Howorth during the Depression years, said, "The struggle goes on and on, and there never seems to be an end to it."

"But Mrs. Shrauger," said Mrs. Howorth, "You have a college education. Can't you go out and find a job?"

"Oh, I could never do that, Mrs. Howorth. Harold's ego would be destroyed."

I think Mom understood my Dad's feelings, and she quietly managed to earn some money and remain in her role as a dependent housewife.

In 1930, when Grandpa Prentiss died, Mom's stipend stopped. During Dad's out-of-work times, in desperation she asked longtime family friends of the Prentiss's for money—ten dollars could be stretched a long way in those days—and they would send what they could afford.

"Pride goeth before a fall," Mom said.

And until her death, Great Aunt Nettie sent her a small check from time to time.

Aunt Nettie mostly helped Uncle Bob through medical school. Grandpa died the first year of his studies; his will stated that Bob's education came first. Dad, as executor of the Prentiss estate, with the help of Harry Swan, his lawyer, discovered that Grandpa's banker had sold Grandmother Lue's inherited Tarrytown National Bank stock and replaced it with worthless securities. Eventually there was little to disperse to the Prentiss girls. Mr. McChesney had stolen other people's securities as well as funds belonging to the University of Iowa. This scandal was covered in detail in the Iowa City and other Iowa newspapers.

McChesney, a close friend of Grandpa's and of the whole family, fled to Daytona Beach, Florida, hid for two weeks, and finally committed suicide.

Mom told me Mr. McChesney, shortly after her marriage, had said to her, "Cornelia, if you would divorce Harold and marry me, I am sure I could become a millionaire."

Lil, who was a good friend of Mr. McChesney's daughter, when she heard the news regarding the theft, said "Mr. McChesney is a dead man walking."

Lil was desperate for money—the loss of her anticipated inheritance was especially bitter because there was no market for Frank's paintings, and she assumed the role of family breadwinner through her employment as an art teacher.

That Grandpa Prentiss had named Dad executor of his estate was ironic, since he had little respect for him in earlier days.

Dad enjoyed being responsibile for the basement. He arranged it, swept it, and kept it clean as possible. He tended the furnace, he had an office there, and he built a shower using two-by-fours and aluminum sheet metal from Grampa's factory. I showered there now and then, but I thought the basement creepy, so it was an occasional occurrence.

Dad said, "Athlete's always shower."

This was his private space, and it was in this basement that Dad did his last best thing for me. He established a quiet place in the cellar where I could work on my new hobby of stamp collecting, which I began around the age of nine or ten.

In showering there, I noticed a small space under the basement stairs that looked secluded and cozy into which I believed an old desk of Dad's might fit. He moved the desk there and finished the job by building shelves for the supplies. I was delighted.

Before settling down, I took inventory of the jumble stored at the back of the room: an old chair, a tire, and some abandoned boxes. To my dismay, in the window-well above these things, I discovered a huge black snake coiled cozily under the dogwood shrub beside the back stoop. It was immobile, settled, so I knew I had to tolerate its proximity. I backed away. Pushing down my fear, I turned on the bulb Dad had put over my desk and began arranging things.

Every time I'd go to the basement to work on my stamps, I'd glance at the window, but never checked to see if Mr. Snake had made that place his permanent hunting ground. His was an evil presence that hung in the background. I chose to ignore him. The moment I got busy, he left my mind.

Mom gave me the stamp collection that had belonged to Hank, her long-dead brother. The oldest stamps dated around 1850. They had to be from the collection belonging to Mom's Grandmother, my Great Grandmother, Cornelia Fitch Bradley. I had read in some of my Great Grandfather's courting letters to Cornelia Fitch that he was bringing her stamps when he next came to visit from New York City. So Cornelia Fitch Bradley's daughter, my Grandmother Lue' Bradley Prentiss, had brought the collection from New York State when she and Grandfather Prentiss moved their family to Iowa City. Then Mom brought it to Atlantic after Lue' died. I felt the collection a connection to my roots.

Working with foreign stamps was my introduction to geography in a way that interested me. My Great Aunt Nettie encouraged me by sending a huge bright blue Scott Stamp Book in which were maps and flags of all the nations, and spaces for every United States and foreign stamp that had been issued up until that time. I studied the maps and became familiar with the location of the countries that issued the stamps I had, particularly enjoying the brilliant colors and exotic designs of stamps from the African countries. Why are U.S. stamps so plain, I thought.

My efforts taught me how to organize things, how to place orders for stamps, and how to buy a money order at the Post Office. It was quite an advance, since my only other experience in dealing with money had been, with nickel in hand, asking a clerk, "May I please have a Clark Bar?"

This space gave me sanctuary away from whatever was going on in the family, and away from prying eyes. My stamp books contained no secrets (my sister in later years told me she'd read my diary even though it had a lock!), so no one ever bothered my first experience with orderliness. Stamp collecting also taught me the joy of utter silence. Here in my little space I could sit and work and be lost in another world—a complete rest from my usual frantic mobility and noisy impulses that I exercised when playing outside.

Primo Levi—considered one of the essential voices of the Twentieth Century—said somewhere,

"A home need: space, warmth, comfort, silence, and privacy."

I had all of those in my stamp corner, and my Dad had given it to me.

As time went on, I depended on my Dad mostly for occasional transportation. It was Mom's character, wisdom, and counseling that was available to me. Her full name was Cornelia Fitch Prentiss Shrauger. I didn't know her grandmother's maiden name was Mom's middle name until I saw it printed on her Memorial program—Fitch, plus her maiden name, Prentiss. The women who bore those names, the first Cornelia and Lue', were story tellers, and through their stories, shaped Mom's story: they defined what she was.

She passed the tales along to me. I also saw pictures of great houses, heard talk of wealth, of elaborate entertainments, of travel abroad, of exceptional artistic talent, lawyers, professors, and skilled medical men.

All of this convinced me I was a member of an important family. I felt it in my bones. But none of this was apparent in my home. Mom never stopped talking about the mood swings of her father, Henry James Prentiss, whose belief that 'sparing the rod spoiled the child' caused her to become "mortally afraid" of him. Memories of her mother and grandmother supported her when she was in trouble with her Papa, and in grave moments during her life with my Dad.

Grampa Prentiss' mother, when her husband fell into alcoholism, solved her family problem by moving the family to New York City, established a business, supported a family of five and educated her children.

I gradually came to realize my female forbears were a line of strong women.

Several months after Lue' died, Mom joined with sixty other Atlantic women to participate in a charity minstrel show in blackface—a popular way to raise money in the nineteen-twenties. A professional company came to Atlantic and directed the production.

In a gay mood, Mom would entertain us at home by rolling her eyes, dancing and singing just as she did in the show, "It takes a long, tall, dark-haired gal to make a preacher lay his Bible down."

Mom told us that after the performance, Mrs. Finkbine, a "self—appointed official important lady," had called her down saying, "Cornelia, the idea of performing in a benefit so soon after your Mother's death! It isn't proper!"

I told her, "Mrs. Finkbine, my mother had a long illness. I spent one week out of every month caring for her. On her deathbed, Mama thanked me, and told me to go on living as usual when I returned home to stay." And she did.

By the time I was in eighth grade, I could easily see that some of Atlantic's families had a better hold on their well-being than we Shraugers did. But lack of prosperity and my earlier family history seemed to have no connection. The roots of my female line were so woven into me that I didn't have a realistic picture of where I stood in the world. The effect upon me of Mom's steadfastness and her conviction that my family heritage was special carried me through my growing-up years.

Mom often arranged for me to explore whatever interested me. On my request, she sent me to summer school for drawing lessons. Using pastel chalks, the teacher had us copy a print of ducks taking off from a swamp. I thought mine was quite presentable, but I told Mom that wasn't what I wanted—I didn't know what I wanted; but copying pictures of ducks wasn't it.

After finishing eighth grade, because I was tall, the high school music teacher asked me to learn to play the bass viol; I would join the orchestra in September. I soon discovered I had no aptitude for the instrument, so I gave it up for singing. I sang forever.

During a summer vacation, Barbara Busse, a local college girl, announced that she was teaching a class in voice training. My friends and I eagerly enrolled knowing Barbara was studying speech at Iowa University. Here I listened while she lowered Barbara Ann Jones's high tessitura a tone and a half. Here I watched her try to teach Louise Morrow how to trill her tongue. Louise never mastered it, but in spite of a lazy tongue she became our best actor. What I learned in Barbara's class, was to enunciate, and how to project my voice.

Mom was a natural athlete, loved dancing, and settled for golf, Dad's game, after she became his bride. She covered herself from head to toe because of her very fair skin. Her friend, Jenny Meredith, always looked cool and tanned in her short sleeves and bare legs; Mom in her hat, gloves, long sleeves, long skirts, hose, and zinc oxide-covered face looked like a ghost-faced mummy. But that didn't spoil her fun. One summer she was almost Southwestern Iowa's golf champion. She was runner-up.

Eventually, around 1934, she got a driver's license. She was not a good driver; she had no mechanical talent, and always drove too fast—no doubt conditioned by being a long time passenger of a speed demon.

She had only one accident; the car fishtailed on a skim of ice on a bitter February day. She jammed on the brakes. The car whirled around, made a complete circle, sideswiped a telephone pole and broke it in two. The car suffered little damage; she was unhurt.

I think that was the only accident she because we had only one car, as most families did at that time and Dad drove ours so work. So she walked in all good weather, 'shanks mare', as she called it, to most engagements.

I often observed my Mom reading; she read all the time when she wasn't doing housework. She had been asked to become a member of the library board when she moved to Atlantic at age nineteen, and remained active for thirty-six years. She came home from board meetings overloaded with new books to read. Her habit was to put a book in each room, reading a few pages in each as her work took her about the house. She read Faulkner, Thomas Wolfe, Thomas Mann, Virginia Woolf, and James Joyce not to mention books of history, biography, autobiography, politics, psychology, sex—anything and everything. She'd read sitting in the living room when she had an extra hour or two, and always late into the night, often until two in the morning. In this way, she read each month's supply by the time the next month's meeting came around. I guess that's why she sometimes napped late in the afternoon. For relaxation she became an expert at crossword puzzles, and created her personal crossword dictionary.

One day after school, I came home to find her sitting in the living room in our old Boston rocker with a book on her lap, the light of the swing-neck lamp shining on her golden red hair. Mom drew deeply on her cigarette, leisurely exhaled the smoke, and without looking, tapped the ash near a large free-form lavender glass ashtray. She made a mess because her power of concentration was enormous, and she never interrupted her reading. She gently rocked, smoking, her other hand idly scratching her head with a hair pin.

I began telling her of an incident at school. I stopped in the middle of a sentence as I saw she continued to nod her head and say "uh huh" from time to time as she kept reading, even when I stopped telling. I, for the first time ever, was being ignored. This caused me to realize Mom had strong interests other than me.

Despite always being on the go and appearing healthy, Mom had many illnesses. The first I was aware of was trachoma, an eye disease common in China but rare in our country. This she contracted at age six when living in New York City, possibly from the nurse Grandmother Lue' had hired to help with the babies. The disease was cured by Dr. M. L. Foster who operated on her eyes. Our well fed, earnest, and pleasant neighbor, Dr. Earl Montgomery, diagnosed tracoma's return. Doctors at the Iowa University Hospital eye clinic confirmed the diagnosis and called Dr. Montgomery "brilliant" for recognizing a blinding oriental disease he had never seen, but knew about.

Mom's treatments began before I can remember. She went to Dr. Montgomery's office every day, then every other day, then every third day, and so forth for months and months, twelve years altogether. The inner membrane of each eye was burned with Blue Vitriol.

It was awful. When I returned from school on treatment days, I'd see her lying quietly on the guest room bed, eyes covered with a hot, wet towel. As I grew older, I helped her down the stairs from Dr. Montgomery's office and into Dad's car while she held a hot towel pressed to her eyes.

Years later when I looked at Mom's pictures taken as a young woman, I'd think of how she looked after twelve years of harsh treatments. Stress had caused her skin to break out, her eyelids to droop until she metamorphosed from a raging beauty into an injured beauty.

She also endured two hemorrhoidectomies with her sense of humor intact; she told us, "Today I ran into Joe Steffens down on Chestnut Street, and we enjoyed a good organ recital about our similar surgeries."

Additionally she frequently burned herself on the oven or cut herself with a kitchen knife. When she caught her right hand in the wringer of our washing machine, Dad got rid of it.

25

Mom Continued

Mom's magazines were scattered on every tabletop, open invitations for us to read. The Collier publications were always present. I poured over Aubrey Beardsley's drawings in an old copy of *The Yellow Book* fascinated by his long, black, curving lines and tall, elegant, evil-looking women. Her music magazine was *Etude*. I learned about Anna Pavlova and her dancing partner, Nijinski in *Theatre Arts*, and about plays and actors performing in New York City. Alfred Lunt and Lynn Fontanne seemed special to me because they were married and acted in plays together. I always examined *The New Yorker* cartoons. Mom's sister, Biddy, and her Aunt Nettie gave her most of the periodicals as Christmas gifts. Biddy also sent her political magazines.

One year Mom gave Cornie and me a wonderful treat: she saved enough money to take us to see *Green Pastures* playing in Omaha. She told us the story was from a book called *Ol' Man Adam and His Chillun*. The cast was black; the energy and singing of the minister and his flock sent chills up my back. Seeing this play began my love for the musical stage.

Another time Jenny Meredith drove Hazel Marshall, Mom, Cornie and me to Omaha to see Maurice Evans in Shakespeare's *King Richard the Second*. Our tickets were spread about the auditorium. I didn't mind sitting alone in the front row, stage right, second seat from the end, because during one of King Richard's monologs, there I was, right under him, looking up at his golden hair and black velvet costume through a spray of spit as he clearly and forcefully enunciated every word in his magnificent English accent. That afternoon my lifetime love for Shakespeare was launched by Richard Evans.

Before fire silenced the deep-voiced bell that rang out the hour and completely destroyed the old Cass County Courthouse, Mom served on the local jury. She relished telling me about the happenings.

"Mr. Cockshoot was the prosecutor in a bootleg case. He didn't want me on the jury because I was a personal friend of Harry Swan, the defense lawyer. Between the two of them, the lawyers eliminated all the other prospective jurors, so I was reluctantly accepted.

"Mr. Cockshoot needn't have been concerned. The men on the jury took a swig of the evidence, pronounced it booze, and the prosecution won."

Shortly afterwards, Gilly Gould, the town taxi driver, asked, "Mrs. Shrauger, what'aya tryin' to do, put us guys out of business?" Iowa was a dry state at the time.

She presented her last paper to the DAR in Washington, Iowa; the subject was the Greek philosophers. She was eighty-one at the time and living in Halcyon House.

After her presentation, she told me, "I've decided I've come to the end of this phase of my life."

She wasn't active in politics. Instead she joined the League of Women Voters and studied issues because, she said, "In this way I can become an informed voter."

But the DAR was of great interest to her because it had been central in her mother's life. In later years Mom prevailed on both Cornie and me to join the organization, and, to please her, we did, she doing all the paper work. By that time the DAR had changed the rules, so the lineage that both my Grandmother Prentiss and my Mom had used to be admitted wasn't acceptable for our generation.

Mom told us, "Our predecessors lived in this country for a long time; several were involved in the American Revolution. I can document this for you girls." She did.

I was never an active member, and Cornie, always rejecting exclusivity, chose service organizations to work in; the YWCA, UNICEF, and Planned Parenthood. She also fostered many enterprises in her hometown of Washington, Iowa. Mom seemed to be satisfied that we were simply DAR members. It was a continuation of her habit of never pressuring either of us to do what *she* wanted. Perhaps she felt that her duty to her mother was done. Both Cornie and I paid dues to the organization until Mom's death.

Before Lue's death, which was just before Mom's twenty-sixth birthday, Lue' told her, "Cornelia, if there is any way to contact you from the other side, I will do so."

Mom never received a sign, she told me, or even imagined one. Since her bond was so strong with her mother, her faith wavered because of this silence, and from then on questioned whether or not there was a hereafter. All her adult life she went to Sunday Bible classes, studying and wondering, shaken in faith, but fascinated with the history.

When Mom became bedridden because of her leg amputation,(due to gangrene which began in her right baby toe) she wanted to know what I felt about the mystery of life after death. She taught me to be intellectually honest, so I told her that I was too much a creature of the scientific age to believe in the hereafter; for me, Jesus had laid down a way of life that was peaceable and good, so I tried to follow his teachings.

I added, "But after learning of the phenomena of space and studying the mystery of the beginning of life on our planet while in college, I believe some kind of omnipotent power exists."

Mom said, "I wish I knew what to think. Papa married his religious background and his scientific training so that they were both valid, as many Victorians did; but he never explained the marriage to me."

Her wavering faith was a great sadness to my Mom.

Considering all of Mom's major activities, I believe her work as a member of the Carnegie Library Board interested her the most. In the early nineteen hundreds, Atlantic—one of 2800 lucky recipients—had received a grant of $12,000 from Andrew Carnegie to build a library. The word 'free' had to be used in literature regarding the gift. In return, the town had to contribute ten percent yearly for the cost of upkeep, staff, and book purchases. During the years Mom was on the board, the town gave the library one mill on each tax dollar each year. Every month all the board members read book reviews and made recommendations for purchases.

Mom resigned from the library board after serving for thirty-six years commenting, "I'm glad I resigned before they kicked me out." She knew she had offended some board members when she vetoed censorship which took the form of hiding so-called offensive books from the borrowers.

Miss Kluever, my high school Latin teacher who also was on the board, sent her flowers which Mom appreciated.

She said, "Imagine, receiving flowers when one isn't sick—or dead!"

The Board gave her a plaque noting her thirty-six years of service.

Just when she developed her ideas regarding censorship, I don't know. Perhaps they evolved as a result of an incident involving her younger sister. Biddy returned home to Iowa City from her studies at the Sorbonne. Hidden inside her corset, she smuggled a banned book—James Joyce's, *Ulysses*—through customs. Inadvertently she left the book on Papa's upstairs parlor table. He picked it up, and was idly thumbing through it when he came to the passage where the hero is evacuating. As he read the description and continued scanning the part about Bloom reading the ads in the mail-order book, tearing out the pages to use as "arse wipers," his rage mounted.

According to Mom, who was visiting at the time, Biddy came into the room looking for the book. "Who's reading this filthy book," Papa shouted. "Who brought this into my house?"

Biddy said, "I did, Papa. I brought it back from Paris which acclaims it as the best thing written today."

"I won't have such a filthy book in my home! And if contemporary literature is the description of bowel movements, then I know nothing of literature!"

With his adrenalin raging, he rushed from the room. Biddy kept the book. For some reason Papa didn't pursue the matter. Maybe he thought that if he was fool enough to send his daughter to Europe for further study, he deserved her avant-garde ideas.

Mom believed I would absorb from a book whatever I was ready to understand, and the rest would go over my head. She was right. When I was twelve I began serious reading. In Thomas Hardy I found the charming scene of a young couple making love in an open field, moonlight shining brightly on her blond under-arm hair. The fact of carnal love didn't disturb me. I knew it was unwise, but I also knew it happened in Atlantic. I read Mein Kampf, and understood, in the thirties, what kind of man Hitler was.

Aunt Biddy and Marquis Childs (by then a respected columnist and newspaperman based in Washington, D.C.), often entertained his colleagues. Biddy served them delicious lunches. During one of Mom's visits, Walter Lippman and another well-known newspaperman were the Childs' guests. The conversation cruised around the political, musical and literary worlds, touching on many topics.

Finally one of the men turned to Mom and asked, "Mrs. Shrauger, how on earth can you, coming from a small Iowa town, be so well informed?"

"I have eyes," she answered. "Newspapers, magazines, and books are available to Iowans as well as to all the other people in the United States who care to read them."

Sometime later I found this newspaper quote among Mom's papers:

"We do not outgrow literature as we outgrow the scientific knowledge. Literature of past generations, whether it was written yesterday or a thousand years ago, is always fresh. Literature is an expression of the changeless soul of man."

Mom, spent her life reading and learning, making up, I believe, for being made to study Home Economics in college. But actually, this was a desire always nurtured within her. She was boundlessly curious.

Everyone lives through losses in life, and in earlier days loss through death was quite common. I think, however, my Mom experienced more than her share. When she was eight, her baby brother, David, died on his first birthday; when she was twenty-six in 1922, her mother, Lue', died; a month later, her brother, Henry, died. In May 1931, when she was thirty-five, her father, Henry James, died. Two months later, on July 15, her sister, Lilian, died.

Lil's death is locked in my memory. On a hot and humid summer night, several of Mom and Dad's friends joined us in our backyard. Seated on blankets in a circle, we sipped ice tea and chatted, fruitlessly hoping for an elusive breeze. Above our heads the poplar leaves hung quietly. Stars spread in a great mass against the black of the night, the Milky Way taking precedence. This familiar sky created in me a sense of infinite peace; I felt serene and secure among the adults with whom I was growing up. Only the sound of our voices intruded upon the stillness of the night.

The telephone rang. Dad went to answer it. Silence fell over the group. Through the open windows, we could easily hear his voice.

"Yes, yes, this is Harold." There was a long pause.

"Just a moment. I'll call Cornelia."

Something in Dad's voice made us continue listening.

"Yes?" We heard the familiar deep tone Mom adopted when answering the phone.

Long silence. A piercing wail. Then uncontrolled sobbing poured out into the quiet of the night. I froze.

Dad came to the dining room window and said, "Cornelia's sister, Lilian, has drowned."

He returned to Mom. A collective sigh arose. We all knew how proud Mom was of Lil and how much she loved her. The condolences of our friends flowed as they told me to phone any time of the night if anything thing was needed. Dad stayed by Mom, and when the call was finished, he took care of her.

In later years when I was living in Rochester, New York, I'd call Mom just to hear her voice. She would never talk for very long. This puzzled and dissatisfied me. Eventually, because of her history, I realized long distance phone calls for her carried with them an aura of death. She'd preferred a chatty letter.

The accidental drowning had occurred on Racquet Lake, a small lake in the Adirondacks in New York State where relatives had a summer home. Lil, her two little girls, Cornelia Mary and Henrietta, along with the hostess's butler, Richard, and seven year old Taddy Bradley, Lil's nephew, were out on the lake for a ride on a large motor barge. Taddy's balloon got away from him, and in trying to catch it, he fell overboard. Richard jumped in to rescue him but was stricken with a heart attack. He called to Lil for help.

Because the barge contained no life preservers or rope, Lil dived in. Richard had disappeared. She managed to get hold of Taddy, but instead of swimming toward shore, which was quite close, probably thinking of her girls, she swam towards the drifting barge. All three—Taddy, Richard, and Lil—drowned.

Other friends in Atlantic didn't have to talk with us to find out what we knew; Mrs. Bell, the Central telephone operator, had stayed, listening, on the line. She spread the word.

Mom learned the complete story the next day. Not until a storm broke late in the afternoon did the rest of the family realize that the barge party hadn't returned. Guided by the screaming of little Cornelia Mary, age six, and Henrietta, age four, searchers found the barge. It had floated to the far side of the narrow lake. The little girls were safe, but motherless. By then it was too dark to look for the bodies, so the last sad news waited until the next day.

"Cornelia Mary, a remarkably level headed child," wrote Aunt Biddy to Mom a few days later, "was able to point out where she last saw her mother. Lil and Taddy were found in five feet of water. Richard was found two hundred yards away."

I'd never seen Mom so distressed. She, Hank, and Lil were so close in age that they were like triplets. They frolicked through their early lives often getting into trouble, sharing everything, forging their love for each other. Mom sparkled when telling me of their escapades. Now Mom, and her younger siblings, Biddy, and Bob, were the remnant of the Prentiss family.

I watched as Mom rose above her grief, not burying her sorrow, but talking about it, hearing details from Aunt Nettie and Mom's cousins who were vacationing at the lake with Lil. Mom was a wonderful example of how to live through a heartbreaking event, by accepting it and continuing to live.

Aunt Biddy said to me in later years, "Your mother's remarkable ability to rise above adversity was based on her habit of verbalizing her feelings."

I was one of her listeners. There seemed to be no end to her endurance. She was a survivor.

Because her Grandmother Bradley and mother, Lue', had both died near the age of fifty-four, Mom was convinced that she, too, would never see her fifty-fifth birthday.

She would say to us, "I have but one wish about my death: I hope that none of you children predecease me."

She had seen how her mother forever mourned her baby, Biddy's twin. Each year as Biddy's birthday came round, Lue' would review the event of little David's death and the cause of it. She'd talk about David, and wonder whether he and Biddy would have been as congenial as were Mom, Hank, and Lil. Mom knew he was always near the surface of Lue's thoughts.

I could sympathize with Mom's wish that we wouldn't predecease her. She had seen enough of early death in her family. But we three children were alive, and the future would bring what it would bring. She was surprised when her friends celebrated her fifty-fifth birthday in their usual way: a luncheon, little presents, and a bridge game. As each year succeeded itself, she continued to be surprised that she was still living.

When we were traveling in Spain and Portugal, as I introduced her to friends she often said gratuitously and in wonder, "I'm in my seventy-fourth year." Only I knew the weight behind that remark.

26

The last time I saw my Gramma, I was on my way to college for my first year. Dad was driving Cornie, Jeanne Howorth, and me to Iowa City. We stopped briefly to say goodbye to Gramma as she stood in the side-yard, gaunt and thin in her neat cotton dress, standing very straight, as she often admonished me to do, for I was now her height. She had stomach cancer but wouldn't see a doctor. Afraid of doctors, she refused to consult one.

Not long after we had departed she became too ill to take care of Grampa, so she allowed him to put her in the Atlantic Hospital. Mom, of course, visited her regularly.

"Cornelia," Sadie said to her one day. "I've never been happier in my whole life. All the nurses are so kind to me."

And Gramma smiled on Mom. She couldn't believe it.

Seven weeks later, the local paper said, in this—her last home—well taken care of by strangers, Gramma died.

In 1939, the Depression still upon us, the bank foreclosed on our La Vista Place home. Cornie was a senior in college and I was a sophomore. Mom later told me Dad could afford to pay only the interest on our mortgage since the market crash—all the years of our growing up—ten years.

Mom was in the hospital when the date came to move, and Dad simply carried many things to the burn pile. He dumped Grandpa Prentiss's plaster bust, the old Prentiss sofa, anything he didn't like or considered junk. I later noticed his stuffed pheasant that had gathered dust in the upstairs hall for years had also disappeared.

I didn't know about the move until it was accomplished. To my intense dismay I discovered that all my childhood treasures went up in smoke that day: my blue leather-covered diary given to me by Aunt Nettie—the record of my high school days; all my books; special toys; and a treasured music box—a dancer in pink tutu and on toe, who twirled to Tchaikovsky's music when the lid was taken off, a gift from Aunt Nettie when I was mad for dancing.

Their first rental house belonged to their friend Lucille Hammer. Dad drove us home from Iowa City at Christmas as usual. Inside the little white frame house, the annual festive cookie baking was in full swing. All Mom's friends who had time to spare filled the unfamiliar kitchen, washing batter bowls and baking pans, drinking coffee, eating cookies, and laughing along with Mom—a familiar sight in a strange kitchen. This wasn't my home.

Saturday night was the folks turn to have the Brawl,—their Saturday night get-together. A standing-rib roast sizzled in the oven, the delicious smell of it permeated the house. Dad oversaw its preparation, so that it was well done on the ends and pink in the middle. In Dad's house there was plenty to eat: meat, potatoes, vegetables, bread, salad, dessert, and coffee.

The doctors and dentists were the first to arrive; their wives, Peggy Petersen and Lucille Hammer, came early to help Mom with last minute preparations. Sam Marshall and Wally Bullock came from their clothing stores along with Hazel and Zora. Owen and Jenny Meredith arrived as Zora sat at Mom's baby grand and played popular music by ear. The tunes fell heavily on my ears; the routine was familiar, but, still, this wasn't my home.

By the next summer the folks had moved to another larger house across the street from Jackson School. All the familiar furniture was there, but, for me, this could never be home.

From this house Cornie's wedding to John Robert (Bob) Day took place. She and her bridegroom had graduated from the University of Iowa in May, 1940, and the date was set for July 28. Out of the great trunk came Grandmother Lue's satin wedding gown for alterations. Mom's friends came the day before and prepared sandwiches for the reception being held at home. I was asked by Mom to fill flower bowls with nasturtiums from the garden. Cornie asked me to sing at the wedding.

Just before we departed for the church, the local photographer came to take her formal wedding picture. In arranging her trailing veil, he unfortunately stepped on it, ripping a long gash.

"Never mind, never mind," comforted capable Lucille Hammer who was standing by to help out with unexpected emergencies. She quickly stitched up the long tear perfectly.

"It won't be noticed," she said, holding it to the light. She finished the mending just in time for us to depart for the church.

By the time the reception ended, Dad had worn seventeen different shirts during that hellish hot and humid July day. The temperature soared to over one hundred degrees, hotter in the church. It was apparent that the bride and bridegroom didn't seem to notice. And because of the high humidity in the church, my lovely white pique dress turned yellow with perspiration from my neckline to my hips.

During the week following the wedding, I was scheduled to have scar tissue removed from my throat. As an infant it had been necessary to excise my tonsils and adenoids.

"You won't feel a thing, Virginia," Dr. Montgomery told me confidently.

But I did, and I let him know! Mom helped me get through the ordeal by setting me up as a patient in a tiny bedroom on the second floor at the back of this strange house. It was just big enough for a single bed, a small table, and a straight chair. I owned nothing in the room but a few clothes.

A day or so later when Mom brought my breakfast, she said, "Dad received a terrible beating last night at the Elks Club from a much younger man. The two argued over the card game. A friend drove Dad home. He's horribly bruised and doesn't want you to see him."

I had no desire to see him. Shame spread within me like an amoeba. My father, in an ordinary fistfight!

A day or two later I was feeling better, so I decided to go downstairs for breakfast. As I walked down the hall, Mom came out of their bedroom carrying Dad's breakfast tray. The bed was placed so that as I walked toward their open door, I couldn't help but see Dad propped up on pillows. I was appalled at the mess that was my father's face—cut, bruised, red, black, blue—a mutilated face. I averted my glance and followed Mom down the steps. Whether or not he realized I'd seen him, I never learned.

This beating, probably a result of drinking, made me fully realize what Mom was living with. I tried not to think about it. But I never have been able to erase from my memory the vision of Dad's beaten face.

This was my last summer in Atlantic. The next two years of college, I returned only for Christmas. Since I was the last Shrauger in school now, it seemed a good idea for me to ride on the new streamliner, the Rocket. So, on my first ride in December of 1941, I packed my bag, put on my best dress, winter coat, hat, heels, purse, and gloves, and boarded at four in the afternoon.

It took five to six hours to get to Atlantic, so I dined in style. I sat alone. I enjoyed the pristine white table cloth, shining silverware, and ice cubes jiggling in a stemmed glass keeping time with the rhythm of the swaying train. I felt I was finally on my way to becoming an adult. The solid weight of the train, the pounding of the wheels on the tracks steadied me. I ordered from the menu. I saw myself reflected in the windows, and watched the other diners and their reflections, happy in this experiment, this rehearsal for my future life. Air travel, to come after World War II, would never give me the elegant feeling I had during those trips back and forth between Iowa City and Atlantic on the Rocket.

World War II was in full swing, and I was graduated in December, 1942. Mom came to witness the occasion. Dad, of course, "had to stay home at business."

Mom and I traveled home on the train. Dad met us at the station. He came up to me and kissed me on the mouth. I was shocked. He'd never done that—ever—or given me a hug or a kiss of any kind as I traveled to and from Iowa City. I suppose he felt my coldness, for he quickly turned away. I couldn't resist. I surreptitiously yielded to the impulse to wipe my mouth.

After New Years, I was to travel to Washington, D.C. where Cornie and Bob worked.

"Plenty of jobs here. Come and live with us," Cornie had written.

I accepted their invitation, happy at the thought of leaving a home that didn't seem like home anymore.

Because Mom was an inveterate letter writer, I knew she would continue writing me faithfully. From the time I left for college to the end of her life, I could count on two hands the number of weeks I didn't hear from her. She, of course, also wrote to my brother stationed in Albuquerque with the Army Air Corps, and to Cornie wherever Bob's duty took him until he was sent overseas. Her letters followed me to Washington, then to Mount Holyoke, Massachusetts, where I was trained to be a Woman Marine, and back to Washington, D.C. where I was stationed. Mom, of course, saved all the letters we wrote her.

In 1939, after Dad had established his own retail appliance business, Grampa's house came back on the market. Dad bought it. Again Mom's life changed.

Now she was in a gracious home which had plenty of space for us kids when we came to visit. The living room held a new sofa, the only one they'd ever had, and showcased her handsome Sheraton chairs, the French Secretary and Fire Screen. The claw-footed, marble and mirrored pier table raised the dining room to elegance, and her beloved baby grand piano was the centerpiece of the music room.

Mom was so pleased with her new home she decided to remove all the time-darkened finish from the oak trim in the dining room. As she'd never done house repairs of any sort, this was a sure show of joy to be living in Grampa's house. She devoted time and muscle to this messy, smelly job. In her letters she told me of her progress.

Dad furnished the kitchen with new appliances from his store, and he installed plenty of counter space and cabinets. What a change from Gramma Shrauger's meager kitchen!

They invited Grampa Shrauger to live with them, and he did so. Since the time he sold his house after he closed the doors of Shrauger and Johnson, he had been living with his younger son, Harlan and his family. Mom took good care of Dice in his last days, watching his diet carefully because of his diabetes. His bedroom was the one that had the adjoining cozy sitting room, the one he had used some years before because of Gramma's snoring.

During the war Harold had married Fran Kephart in March of 1943, and their daughter, Frances Cornelia, (always called Francie) was born on February 7, 1945. I had married Joe Allen Jones in May of 1944. Bob Day and Cornie had by this time been married five years. And in late August of 1945, we were all free to come to Atlantic at the same time. Mom and Dad planned a big reception.

Harold drove straight through from Albuquerque bringing Fran and their six-month-old-infant. Baby was to meet her grandparents and Great Grandfather Shrauger for the first time. Bob Day, closing his career in the Navy as a Lieutenant, came with Cornie from Washington, Iowa; and my husband, Allen, also a Naval Lieutenant and about to leave the Navy, traveled with me by train from Oklahoma where we first visited his uncle. I would remain a Marine until March of 1946.

For the reception, we military people appeared resplendent in our U.S. Navy, U.S. Army Air Force, and the U.S. Marine Corps uniforms. Members of our family, friends, and seemingly everyone Dad did business with greeted us. The adults we'd grown up among came dressed in their best. Mom radiated joy, proud of her children and their spouses. Dad was full of smiles.

The oak table was laden with sandwiches, fruit punch, cookies, and small cakes. The smell of coffee filled the rooms. Mom's good friends had 'pitched in' as usual, Mom told me, and helped with the preparations. We children stood with Mom and Dad in the receiving line, forever it seemed, as crowds trooped in to welcome us home.

Hiroshima and Nagasaki had been destroyed earlier in the month, and these terrible events were discussed quietly at this reunion of friends. That tragedy was the reason that my brother-in-law was being released from military duty. These devastating bombings made it certain World War II was coming to an end.

During my stay in Atlantic I had the pleasure of watching Grampa watch his Great Granddaughter after she'd been fed. Francie, six months old, lay on her blanket by the large windows, playing with her hands and bare feet. Short wisps of reddish hair were tied up with a pink ribbon on the top of her head. Gradually her eyes drooped as her motion button turned down: slowly they closed. Grampa sat in his chair by the fireplace, cane at his knee, a smile of utter joy on his face.

On November 20, 1945, while in Mom's care, he died in the house he had lovingly built. An editorial appeared regarding my Grampa which I quote:

> *Alantic owes much to the late D. E. Shrauger.*
> *There was nothing of the spectacular about him*
> *and he was not much in the public eye, but the work*
> *he did provided much for many in this community. There*
> *were dozens of families whose support through many*
> *years came from the business he brought to his*
> *city … Such men are true benefactors and deserve much*
> *more praise than they receive. This was not the only*
> *service performed by this man. For many years he gave*
> *his time and energy to the management of the city's*
> *light and water plant, and in no small way was he*
> *responsible for this outstanding institution. For such*
> *services, so often overlooked in the citizenry of any*
> *community, Atlantic owes a debt of gratitude to D. E*
> *Shrauger, a public servant in a very real sense.*

Later that same month, the Army Air Force discharged Harold. He left with the rank of Master Sergeant. As no houses were available in post WWII in Atlantic, it was decided that he and his family would live with Mom and Dad. Fran wrote that Mom fell into a contented period, living in a home offering grace and space, more like the one in which she had grown up. I thought Mom was settled there for the rest of her life and that Dad's eternal restlessness had quieted.

A "chance of a lifetime" for Mom occurred in 1951. She took Sam Marshall's place who was unable at the last minute to accompany his wife, Hazel, on a five-week trip to Europe. Ordinarily Mom wouldn't have been able to afford the required $500; but she had "squirreled away" dimes for some time, first to buy voice lessons for me at the University; then, out of habit, she kept on saving; miraculously she had almost the exact amount.

The channel passage from England to France was exceptionally rough. Mom was playing bridge; a huge German gentleman passing by her table lost his balance as the boat tilted and he stepped on Mom's right foot. Luckily no bones were broken. She "never missed a thing" because she donned her stretchy slipper, fashionable that year, on her bruised foot and wore it during the entire tour.

She was carrying rosaries, requested by Dad's hired man, hoping to have the Pope bless them. The effort became the highlight of her trip. Mom and Hazel arrived in St. Peter's Square early. They stood along the roped aisle through which the Pope would be carried. The crowd soon became a solid body.

"How will I ever get these rosaries blessed, Hazel. I can hardly keep on my feet what's more attract the Pope's attention."

"Madame, excuse me, but I think I can help you."

The deep voice came from behind her. Turning, Mom saw a tall man, obviously an American, looking down on her.

He continued. "When the Pope approaches us, have the rosaries ready. I'll cry out 'Viva la Papa'! Immediately, with the rosaries dangling from your hand, stretch your arm high toward the Pope. I'm sure he'll turn toward us and bless your rosaries."

At that moment the Pope's entourage entered the square. Voices of thousands melded into a deafening roar.

"It was thrilling," Mom told me. "I felt I was rising aloft on the sound of humanity. I glued my eyes on the Pope as the procession made its way slowly toward us. He nodded to each side of his litter, hand extended, blessing the throng. He was magnificent in his red robes, his tall hat—he was truly a religious King.

"As he approached us, from behind came the deep bass voice crying, 'Viva la Papa! Viva la Papa.' On cue, I stretched my arm high, the rosaries dangling—and the Pope turned, leaned over, and actually touched my hand as well as the rosaries! I felt a tremor rush through my body—and indeed—not only were the rosaries blessed, but so was I. Virginia, at that moment, I could have become a Catholic!"

After living with Mom and Dad for a year and a half, Harold and Fran bought the once fire-ravaged, but rebuilt, McDermott house on its four-acre lot near La Vista Place. Harold worked with Dad for nine years, and then moved on to another business opportunity, eventually settling in Le Mars, Iowa. Dad bought the little house from Harold and rented it out for a year or two. But he had another dream.

He loved the view the McDermott house offered from its site overlooking the rolling hills of southwestern Iowa.

"This is my vista!" I am sure he said to himself.

Here was plenty of space for him to garden near the house, and there was a fine strawberry bed in a far corner. He dreamed that eventually he could subdivide the four acres and make money.

Never one to resist dreams, and needing cash as usual, he sold Grampa's house without consulting Mom and moved the household belongings when she was away from Atlantic. Fran wrote saying Dad's action was a terrible blow to Mom. Being forced to move from the big Shrauger home to the tiny, inconvenient house depressed her. Having lived through the traumas of her marriage—gambling, alcoholism, lack of money, loss of the La Vista Place home, the bouncing from house to house—now she found herself robbed of living a gracious old age. The little house had temporarily served Harold's family nicely, but proved a grossly inadequate replacement for the home she loved. Now, when many of her friends were building their large and gracious post-war homes, she felt she was moving backwards.

The house contained no decent storage space. Sometimes snakes slithered into the tiny, dank, dirt-floored basement. Since the kitchen was too small for her lovely dishes, Dad stored them in sealed boxes on shelves in the basement. Yes, there was the vista from the small windows, but that didn't cancel daily discomfort and the absence of any semblance of her former life.

Still, in her usual way, she knuckled under and made her adjustments. She accepted the vicissitudes of her life with Dad as her responsibility, maybe, I sometimes wondered, her punishment. She never complained to me in the weekly letters, but I knew her feelings. She obviously loved Dad, and in his way he loved her. She took good care of him, and managed to erase from her conscious mind all the disturbing events that happened because of him.

Her large chartreuse living room rug that had brought color to Grampa's living room was cut to fit both the miniature living room and the separate dining room where the oak dining table occupied most of the space. The Prentiss silver service sat on her antique tea cart crammed into one corner near the table; her dictionary and stand crowded beside it in front of the small rear window. The ornate pier table was against the inner wall. Fran and Harold, who came to help her arrange the furniture, found place for the rest of the lovely antiques in the cramped living room. For lack of space, her piano had to be sold. The one bedroom and bath was at the top of the open, steep and narrow stairway under the slant roof. Still, she managed her routine duties, and entertained her bridge club when it was her turn; but she became quieter, and her gaiety submerged.

In 1961 Dad made another change. Mom was sixty-five, and he was sixty-seven when he established a Norge Dry Cleaning business in a small white cinder-block building on East Seventh Street with the financial assistance of his son-in-law, Bob, who by now had a successful legal practice in Washington, Iowa.

Mom and Dad ran the business together, the first time she had worked a full-time job.

With her usual external ebullience, she was up, dressed, and had breakfast waiting for Dad when he returned from the shop having by then cleaned the chemicals and prepared the machines for the day's business. After breakfast, off they'd go to the plant.

Most of the time, Mom greeted the customers, took in their soiled clothes, treated them with spot removers, and fed them into the cleaning machines.

She wrote, "Many of the women's slacks smell of urine and are often bloody, but I've gotten used to that, and now I don't mind."

Dad was in and out all day in his usual style, taking over at lunchtime when Mom drove home to prepare their soup and sandwiches, ate hers, and returned so Dad could go home for his.

In her weekly letters she gave me a report.

"Not many customers have come in today which worries me, but at least I can dash this note off to you. But then, yesterday was pretty busy so I guess it all evens out. We aren't living high, but we're getting along."

She had resigned from all her clubs, no longer played the organ at church, but still enjoyed bridge with her oldest Atlantic friends. She was the only one who drove, so she picked up the others and they went as a group to the hostess's house.

They also resigned from the Golf Club. "Dad is slowing down, and we really can't afford that now."

She continued writing her many letters and read when business was slow.

However, she gained a bonus that filled her needs. Many residents of Atlantic and nearby farms and towns whom she hadn't known before became customers. Since her warmth encouraged confidences, she enjoyed these new acquaintances. Together Mom and Dad worked six days a week and housecleaned on Sundays.

My parents celebrated their fiftieth wedding anniversary, August 23, 1965 in their little house. Biddy, and husband, Mark Childs, came from Washington, D.C., her brother, Dr. Robert Prentiss, with his wife, Alice, came from San Diego, and all of us children, spouses and grandchildren converged on Atlantic. Many friends from Washington, D.C. to California swelled the guest roster. The evening before the reception, family and out–of–town friends gathered in the shaded backyard of the little house for a picnic supper.

The next day the reception was held at the Whitney Hotel. The grandchildren took part: registering the guests, interviewing them, and acting as junior hostesses. A formal dinner followed for family and out-of-town guests. Dad's brother Harlan, long estranged from Dad but now reconciled, attended the occasion with his wife, Gladys. It was the last time Mom, her sister, Biddy, and brother, Bob, were together.

My Uncle Bob, upon refreshing his memory as to what items of Bradley furniture Mom was enjoying in the little house, asked for the two Sheraton chairs and the French fire-screen as an even trade for a cash advance he had made to Dad some years before. Since I was the designated heir of those pieces, Mom asked my permission to do this, which I freely gave. The difficulties of the father fall heavily upon his progeny.

A few years later, Biddy, always a heavy smoker, died of lung cancer. Then in 1971 Alice Prentiss died, and the following year, on March 8, 1972, Bob Prentiss died. Mom, the oldest Prentiss child, had survived her entire family.

27

The End of an Era

In 1974, when Dad was almost eighty, Dad began to draw Social Security payments. Mom told me they were both weary, and welcomed retirement.

Encouraged by Bob Day, Mom and Dad drove the two hundred miles to Washington, Iowa to inspect Halcyon House, a home for the elderly now being built on land he and Cornie once owned. Bob helped establish Halcyon House.

Liking the two-bedroom apartments, and realizing that they could afford the payments, they found comfort knowing Cornie and Bob would be only five minutes away. Dad signed the papers. Mom never told me how she felt about moving away from Atlantic, their home since marrying in 1915.

Even though it was late fall, luck hadn't deserted Dad. He readily sold his little house and acreage and scheduled the move for late December. My younger son, Prentiss, and I drove from Rochester to help. Cornie and Bob brought a large U-Haul from Washington.

After breakfast the day before the move, I was cleaning the kitchen, and Dad said, "I'll take this trash to the burning pile. I'll do this little job of work."

Bundled in his heaviest jacket, wool hat, warm gloves, and wearing a white mask against the bitter cold to protect his ailing lungs, he looked like a leprechaun in winter garb.

As he slowly returned to the house, he stopped at the bottom of a small incline. I watched him as he turned toward the glittering snow-covered Iowa hills, drinking in his favorite view.

I thought, "Perhaps he's considering his failure to develop the acreage, his final chance to 'make his ship come in', his last idle dream."

He walked another ten feet, turned again, now rocking back and forth on the heels and soles of his Hush Puppies, staring once more toward the hills, his beloved vista. Then he came into the house.

We spent the day loading the van with most of the household things. Before we left Atlantic the next day, we would finish. The weekend before, Harold and

Fran had driven from Le Mars and boxed Mom's dishes and all the odd shaped serving things. Bob, with his many years experience of loading at the University of Iowa and in the navy, expertly engineered packing the van. A strong man, brought up on an Iowa farm, Bob did most of the carrying assisted by Prentiss and, somewhat, by Dad and me.

Mom's good friend, Kay Finkbine, served us dinner that night. Dad didn't eat much, but he did enjoy her homemade bread. She came along with us the next morning when we gathered for breakfast at a downtown motel for our last Atlantic meal. Dad ate nothing, saying he wasn't hungry.

Finally Bob stuffed the last two items into the U-Haul, a broom and a kitchen mop, and forced the door shut. As we cheered, I stared at the closed U-Haul, and thought of the family history witnessed by the things stored in that van, the life of almost sixty years of the Harold Shraugers in Atlantic, Iowa.

We gathered in the tiny living room, now empty, so Dad could find the papers Bob needed as he drove the U-Haul back to Washington. Opening his jacket, Dad sat on the floor, leaned against a wall, and began to sort through his pockets and rifle through his wallet. As he looked first at one paper, then another, I wondered if he'd find the right one. He looked like an elf with his little round belly, soft black cap, and gray wool jacket open down the front showing his inevitable red and grey plaid flannel shirt. The cap was askew, pushing wisps of graying hair out in front of his ears, his upper lip slightly raised as had become his habit when concentrating. I became aware of his labored breathing. Finding the paper, he gave it to Bob who helped him to his feet.

Dad and Mom headed toward Des Moines in their Oldsmobile sedan while Bob and Cornie followed in the U-Haul. Prentiss and I turned northwest to visit Harold and Fran for a day or two in Le Mars, Iowa.

Snow began to fall about four-thirty just as Dad turned southeast at Des Moines to drive the last leg to Washington. Immediately a white snow sheet spread over the road and the stubbled cornfields. Then the fine snow turned into a screen of huge roiling flakes that the car's headlights couldn't pierce. Dad drove steadily on, followed by Bob and Cornie.

Mom later told me she could see the side of the road from her opened window. She became Dad's second pair of eyes. They traveled this way for over two hours. Cornie told me that when they could see Dad's car at all, he was perilously weaving down the road. Luckily there were no oncoming cars.

Dad collapsed as soon as he pulled into the Day's driveway. Cornie rushed into the house and called the Washington, Iowa hospital, just a block down the street. Within ten minutes Dad was in intensive care. His heart attack, the doctor said, was brought on because of his failing lungs. How like him to will himself and Mom safely to Washington before collapsing. In his own way, he always took care of her.

Cornie called Harold in Le Mars. He met Prent and me as I pulled into his driveway. I decided to leave the next morning for Washington.

After Dad was stabilized, he and Mom moved into Cornie and Bob's "barn", as they called the huge room above their three-car garage. For a few weeks, until the Halcyon House apartments were completed, this was their home. (In July, Cornie had a small dinner party in the barn in celebration of Dad and Mom's sixtieth wedding anniversary, Dad in the apartment, of course; we took his dinner to him.)

Once more Harold and Fran came to arrange Mom's furniture in the first apartment Mom and Dad had ever lived in. It was a pleasant place, small but well planned, and Mom felt settled once more living among her familiar things. She began her final job, taking care of Dad.

They lived together in this cheery apartment for two years. A large window in the living room let in the morning sun. Again, green was the predominate color, and all the furniture spoke of rooms past. Mom became an attentive nurse leaving Dad only to attend church on Sundays and visit the YMCA for a weekly bridge game. Mrs. Green, also a resident of Halcyon House, visited Dad while Mom was gone.

I came to Washington often. During the early days of Dad's illness, when he felt strong enough, he told me about his life and friends in Exira, Iowa.

"I could drive by the time I was twelve or thirteen, before we moved to Atlantic. My Dad let me drive our Ford around our meadow when I was eleven. He had the first Ford in town.

"My friends had strange names, Turd, for one, Harry Hash, another, a boy who was half Indian. There was Walter Marietta, who had an aura of mystery about him because he disappeared from town from time to time—then mysteriously reappear. He never said anything about where he'd been. All of my cronies ended up doing time in jail except for me."

He told me about the summer day his gang overheard businessmen in town saying they expected the local bank to be robbed. They were setting up a trap.

"All the men had armed themselves. We boys," Dad said, "had the confidence of men. We got our rifles. We knew how to use them for we were trained hunters. We made a stakeout up the road from town near the railroad tracks and lay quietly on our bellies in tall weeds, rifles at the ready; finally we gave it up as nothing happened.

"The next day we went back to our stakeout and found grass flattened just fifty Yards from it. It turned out that the robbers had stolen a railroad handcar and come up to Exira on the new tracks. But somehow they were scared off. We boys and all the men in town played vigilantes to no avail."

He nodded his head slowly, a slight smile on his face as he remembered this long-ago incident.

Dad told me how a lifetime friend of his who cleaned one of the Atlantic banks at night retrieved World War II gas ration stamps from the wastebaskets.

"He always gave me plenty, so I didn't have to limit my driving."

As for me, at that time living in the nation's capitol, I took the trolley and walked a lot.

This was the only adult conversation, if it was a conversation, I ever had with my Dad. We had talked together when I was a little girl, but when or why those times stopped, I don't know. Now I remained silent; but I listened.

One morning after we three were finished with breakfast, Dad needed to go to the bathroom. He was comfortable in his upholstered chair in front of the television, and Mom and I, having a second cup of coffee, were still in our nightclothes. I stood in front of him and put my arms under his armpits as Mom drew up the wheel chair. At this time, he could still move from his chair and into the wheelchair, but he couldn't walk at all. I lifted. As he tried to stand, he crumpled, and in slow motion simply sat down on the floor taking me with him. He was sitting on my nightie and robe.

"Mom, I can't get up. Call Bob," I said. "I'm sure he hasn't left for work yet." She did.

While we tried to make light of the difficulty, Dad sat quietly on the floor leaning against his chair with his eyes closed.

"Don't worry, Harold," said Mom. "Bob is on his way."

Bob arrived, removed his Russian fur hat, took in the situation and addressed us cheerily, "Well, well, well, what have we here?"

He marched over to Dad, stood in front of him, put his hands under Dad's armpits, and in one easy heave lifted him to his feet, turned him, and got him settled in the wheelchair. I moved out of the way the moment Dad's weight lifted from my robe.

Bob left, saying, "I'll be by again at noon." He made all of us feel good.

Now and then I was Dad's sitter while Mom would go out for some much needed recreation. I knew how tirelessly she tended him. Every morning she bathed him, helped him into his clean pajamas and robe, wheeled him into the living room and settled him into his chair. Then she turned the television to the news and brought him his breakfast tray. She saw that his every need was taken care of. Then she'd busy herself making up their beds, gathering the laundry together, and doing whatever else needed to be done.

When I stayed with them, I did the grocery shopping which Cornie usually did for her, cooked the meals, did the dishes, the laundry, and whatever else was necessary. When she was out, the only requirement besides talking to him if he wanted to talk and getting his lunch at noon, was taking care of any unforeseen eventuality. That came soon enough.

He needed to use the toilet. By now he now always sat in his wheelchair. I wheeled him into the bathroom, and had him hold onto my shoulders after I'd undone his pajama bottoms. As he half stood, I swung him around so he could sit on the elevated toilet seat. I left the room while he took care of his needs.

When he called me, he was looking unusually pale and breathing heavily because he was disconnected from his oxygen tank. It wasn't possible to trundle the five foot tank into the bathroom. Perspiration covered his brow. I dried his face, and the sight of this man, my father, his huge frame drooping forward, brought tears to my eyes.

Mom told me to be sure he was really clean after he had used the toilet, so I took the washcloth she had laid out for me, wet it, and soaped it. As Dad leaned forward I cleaned him and then wiped off the soap.

"This isn't too bad," I said to myself.

After toweling, I took the can of talcum she had told me to use and patted the powder puff around his large, smooth bottom.

I thought, "This is just like cleaning up my boys' bottoms when they were babies—only it's a larger territory."

Somehow this intimacy made me feel closer to Dad, although if I could have chosen, I would have preferred another kind of intimacy built up through the years. But I snatched at crumbs.

From time to time during the last year and a half of Dad's life, I drove a triangle, from Rochester, where two of my children lived, to West Virginia, where I made my home, and to Iowa where I helped Mom. The first winter I stayed with my parents and took two classes at the University of Iowa. I thought I was there to relieve Mom, since Dad was failing rapidly. But afterwards I came to believe I also was hoping to make a positive connection with my father. When the chance came to do this, I didn't recognize it.

As I put my books into my book-bag, ready to drive to Iowa City, Mom came to my bedroom with a question.

"Virginia," she asked hesitantly, "Dad wants to know if you remember the day during lunch when he hit you in the face?"

Instantly I was boiling with anger. "Of course I do," I blurted. Hearing the question was like being hit in the face again.

Grabbing my book-bag, I rushed out of the apartment, absolutely unable to consider, then, or for many months, why he had asked. I once more pushed that incident deep inside myself.

Soon Dad was doing nothing but breathing oxygen through the long tube that connected him to a huge, green tank. When I was with them, Mom gave me the larger bedroom, and she slept in the guest room on a cot next to Dad's hospital bed.

"I prefer being there," she said, "for then I'll know if he's all right. I like being nearby to help if he needs anything."

As he continued to fail, the cot was her permanent sleeping place. After he was ready for the day, I wheeled the oxygen tank out into the living room.

Harold and Fran came to Washington for Dad's last Thanksgiving. I had returned to the east to celebrate the holiday with my children. Harold and Fran, not having been with Dad for a while, could immediately see that caring for Dad was now too much for Mom. A family conference decided it was necessary to move him to the Halcyon House infirmary. Dad would be eighty-two December sixth, and Mom would be eighty the end of the next January.

Dad didn't protest this move, Mom told me later. When I came back the following week, he lay quietly in his bed, head elevated, oxygen tube protruding from his nose, eyes closed. He held his folded hands on his still-large belly, looking like an unsmiling, reclining Buddha.

Mom stayed with him all day every day. He wasn't hungry anymore. I sat with him from time to time to give Mom a chance to get some fresh air or smoke a cigarette.

She never stayed away long, "for in my heart, this is where I am needed, and this is where I want to be," she said.

She'd stay with him every night until about nine o'clock; then she felt she had to go to bed. My Mom was a sterling example of devotion: devotion to her husband and devotion to duty.

One afternoon as I watched him, he lay still, maybe sleeping, looking peaceful.

"He's given up," I thought. "He's slept beside Mom for over sixty years. Now he sleeps alone. He doesn't like that. He's coasting to a stop."

Events in my family in the east again took me away, and I didn't see Dad again. He died December 13, 1976 at two in the morning.

For some reason the nursing staff didn't call Mom when they discovered Dad was dead. Instead they called Cornie and Bob who came immediately across their back yard to the infirmary. Without telling Mom of Dad's death, they had Dad's body removed.

After the funeral director departed with Dad's body, Cornie and Bob went to Mom's apartment, wakened her, and told her of Dad's death.

"Where is he? I want to see him."

"Oh, he's gone."

"What do you mean?"

"His body has already been sent to Mr. Eden's funeral home. He'll send it right on to the crematorium."

The day of the memorial service, Mom took me aside and said, "I never will get over regretting that I didn't stay with your father that last night before he died. I was surprised that he was hungry, and I spoon-fed him the Jell-O and whatever else he wanted from the tray. I thought that he was better, that maybe he wouldn't die just yet. He went to sleep. I sat there until about nine o'clock, and then I went upstairs. If only I had remembered that sometimes those who are dying want to eat a last dinner. Why didn't I remember? Why didn't I stay the night?"

She never complained about not being notified by the staff about Dad's death, or that Cornie and Bob sent his body away without calling her.

The Memorial Service was held in the Halcyon House parlor. His brother, Harlan, and his cousin, Graham Wallace, drove the two hundred miles from Atlantic, as did a few of his remaining lifetime friends. His ashes were buried immediately after the service at the Elm Grove Cemetery nearby.

Cornie had planned who was to ride in each car, and exactly which seat they'd occupy. As I went to my appointed place in the funeral director's car, old friend Hazel Marshall, chewing gum as usual, stumped about in her humped, awkward way, fussing about the seat to which Cornie had assigned her.

"I am sorry, Hazel, you can't go in the family car."

"Well, I'm almost family. I've known Cornie and Harold since we were nineteen years old."

This was a fact, but it didn't affect Cornie's decision. And Hazel, true to her form, was trying to squeeze in and have things her own way. But she had to reckon with my sister. As I listened to the last of that conversation, I slid under the driver's wheel of the funeral director's car to the place in the middle where I had been assigned. My shoes scraped over metal. I looked down to see what was there. It was a small, green box. The realization came in a flash—Dad's ashes! Here was my Dad, what was left of him, right under my feet. The father who had caused me misery, who influenced the way I felt about men, who had, I thought, never loved me, never supported me in my endeavors, never, never, never. Here he was: in a little metal box!

I regret to say a small smile momentarily flickered across my face.

In the days to come, mail flooded into Cornie's house. People I had never heard of wrote condolence notes to Mom: people my Dad had quietly helped along life's way, lifetime friends whose names I didn't know, younger people who respected him—whom he had influenced to register and vote when the twenty-sixth amendment allowed them to at age eighteen—when he was the Exalted Ruler of the Elks Club. (Mom joked and called him the Exhausted Rooster.) Also we heard from people whose appliances he had cleaned and restored with no charge after the Nishnabotna Creek flooded Atlantic. Who was this man they were referring to? I didn't know him.

As Cornie and I went over these notes, I realized that no one begins to know all there is to know about any person, a father, a mother, or oneself. This out-pouring of words made me feel better about Dad, for I now saw that he had a rich life completely unknown to me, a life of kindness, of helping, and of being a good friend.

It was much later that I came to understood why Dad had sent Mom to ask me if I remembered that long-ago day when he had struck me across my face. A good friend came to visit me in West Virginia. As he talked about his concern for his children, his loving and forgiving nature showed itself. His sensitivity triggered my buried, hopeless yearning for such a father.

I told him what my Dad had wanted to know: whether I remembered that sad day at lunch in the long ago past.

"Why did he bring that up?" I asked. "I was so full of buried anger, all I could do was explode and leave."

"Perhaps your father wanted to make amends," my friend said.

Yes. Too late. Too late. Too late I realized that Dad had carried for years a deep guilt, a full weight, for striking me. Having little to do in his dwindling days but review past events, he evidently mulled over the crucial event that separated us and, through Mom, hoped to bring the happening into the open. But I didn't given peace to my Dad. I couldn't hear him. Now I had no peace. Now I was the guilty one. My friend comforted me while I wept bitterly, mourning that lost last chance—my one opportunity to bring closure to that ancient incident.

After Dad died I came as often as I could to visit Mom. When Cornie and Bob vacationed, I sometimes house-sat for them. A few times Mom became my traveling companion as we visited Cape Cod, Florida, and Spain and Portugal. She resumed a full schedule of church, cards and clubs. Bob and Cornie included her in their entertainments. Now and then visitors from Atlantic would drive to Washington.

I couldn't believe that Mom had never been in a grocery store. Cornie had taken over the shopping after the move from Atlantic took place. So Mom and I grocery shopped one day.

Her excitement at what she saw was a wonder and pleasure for me. The size of the store and the variety of products amazed her; the kinds of frozen foods astonished her. She enjoyed touring about the store as I selected what we needed. As far as I know, that was her first and last grocery shopping expedition.

She told me at age eighty-six, "not a day goes by but that I think of Dad."

Her apartment building was connected by hallways, through a parlor, and past the dining room to the entrance door. The dining room was available to her; she preferred her own kitchen. When we went out to lunch or dinner, I noticed as we passed the open French doors to the dining hall where the assembled white haired "inmates" (her word) were eating, her pace would accelerate; she was silent. She never glanced into that door. I felt she feared the day when she might have to eat there. As we walked to the foyer, all we could hear was the clickety clack of cutlery on ceramic. She called the whole place "The Martin House."

The smoking habit she acquired at the age of fifteen limited her life. At age eighty-six, because of poor circulation, she developed gangrene in her right foot necessitating amputation. While Cornie and I were having her admitted to the university hospital, she sat in her wheelchair in the hall and tried to bum cigarettes from passersby. Her doctor had previously forbidden her to smoke; she had gone cold turkey.

Later, in discussing her canvassing in the hall, she told me, "I failed in my enterprise."

During Grampa Shrauger's last days, his doctor had forbidden cigar smoking. This was during the WWII when I was sending him his favorite William Penn cigars from the Navy Exchange.

Dice protested saying, "Doc this is the only pleasure I have now. I won't give them up."

Mom, who supervised his care, sided with Dice and Dad, and Grampa kept on smoking. But Mom was kept from smoking by her militant, rule-following daughter, Cornie.

Mom was admitted to the hospital; two days of tests were begun. Soon Cornie and I realized Mom had begun to hallucinate. The staff discovered her thyroid medication hadn't appeared on the list sent to the hospital by her Washington doctor. Her whole system had become disorganized, and several more days were required to get her stabilized. Meanwhile the gangrene crept past her ankle, thereby causing her surgeon to remove the leg above the knee.

She made a good recovery and soon moved to the infirmary at Halcyon House with expectations of returning to her apartment. I watched her obediently and easily do leg-lifts for the Physical Therapist who had been assigned to help her with her prosthesis, but she couldn't adjust to the device. Finally she resigned herself to life in a wheelchair. Also, she was now tethered to an oxygen supply, like Dad, but technology had reduced the tank.

For a few months, an aide followed her with a portable oxygen tank as she rolled down the hall to meet her faithful bridge partners who came to Halcyon House to play.

Eating in the Halcyon House dining room was now necessary. Mom embraced this new life in her positive way, "rising to the occasion" as she would say. When I was with her, we sat together with other inmates and the nurse who was assigned to their table for the day.

After lunch one day, the nurse took me aside and said, "I love it when I'm assigned to the table where your mother is. She talks, and makes jokes, and we have fun!"

Cornie brought family pictures of Mom's Mama and Papa, of Dad, Harold, Fran and Francie, and of herself, and hung them on the wall across from the foot of Mom's bed where she could see them when she awakened. Mom told me she felt happier having the faces of some of her loved ones on the wall looking at her.

Slowly, however, her interest in life deteriorated: the TV became dark, newspapers lay unread, books became a part of her past. But she'd wake from her snoozing when the aids came to help her, making jokes, "so they would feel at home," she told me.

Just a few days before she died, Bob came to visit her at noon, as was his habit. It was a bitter cold February day, and he was wearing his heavy, black winter coat and Russian fur hat.

Well," greeted Mom, "I see the Czar of Russia has come to visit me."

Two or three days later the head nurse called Cornie to say Mom was dying. We all gathered, I, driving from West Virginia, and Harold and Fran from Le Mars. Cornie sat all night with Mom the night before we arrived. I sat the following night. I listened all night to her imaginary conversation with her old friends, the Montgomerys.

Harold, on the third night, read aloud her favorite Bible passages.

On Friday, Cornie again took the vigil. She told me that during the night Mom roused and said to her, "I think I'm dying, Cornie."

At seven the next morning, Cornie called. "Mom just died. Come over."

Fran awakened Francie and granddaughter, Jenny, who had driven in from Chicago late the night before. As we gathered to say goodbye, we realized it was Francie's birthday. Mom lay in the characterless room facing the photographs of her parents, her husband, and her children. The moment, always a surprise, had come. She was on her back, her arms on top of the coverlet, her eyes closed, jaw dropped. I brought her jaw up into place, my fingers feeling the heat of her still warm chin. It fell again as I took my hand away. She, the eldest and last living child of Lue' Bradley and Henry James Prentiss, had now joined them.

The nurses came, wrapped her in a sheet, and trundled her off on a gurney to be cremated in the custom of her family. Mom had lived three weeks over eighty-nine years, thirty-five years more than she thought she would live.

Two days later we buried her ashes beside Dad's at Elm Grove Cemetery, in Washington, Iowa. It seemed sad to me that their ashes would lie forever in Washington, and not in Atlantic where the richness and variety of their lives had spun out. But, I was comforted knowing that their ashes lay next to each other.

We held a Memorial Service at the United Presbyterian Church. I couldn't believe so many people came—half the large church was filled. Many of Cornie's and Bob's friends were there, and many were friends Mom had made in the nine years since Dad had died, proof of her love of people.

Her life was over. I had one consoling thought. She'd achieved her often-repeated wish that none of her children predecease her.

Sometime later I found this statement among Mom's papers:

"In reading about my relationship with Papa, I am appalled at the picture I gave of him! It is all true, the incidents described—but in later years when I spent a week of every month with Mama and Papa (during their last illnesses), the eighteen months she was invalided with cancer of the hip, he was friendly with me—in fact, as I look back at the time when Son and I lived in Iowa City with them (WWI, and I paid for our board and room) I was pregnant with Cornie, and he was very kind to me to see I wouldn't fall down while walking to town with me.... Then Mama died—and

(later) he had a stroke and Bennett acted as his valet, though a medical student. He would send train fare so I could be with him for a week, as I did with Mama. He also sent me a check for $30 for spending money. So I feel in his later days he developed an affection for me which he couldn't feel while I was growing up since he considered me a problem child.

*"I forgive all the **unfair** discipline, recognizing he wanted the best for me—but the two episodes—the terrible beating at Aunt Emma's because of the sex incident and the push he gave me knocking me out when my head hit the brass bedstead—when Bobbie cut himself on his hand because I was reading and neglecting my duty as baby sitter—I can't forgive."*

AFTERWORD

The soul of my maternal line is, in part, laid bare with everyone's approval. My four children were lucky to have Cornelia Prentiss Shrauger as a baby sitter now and then; but we lived far apart, the children in Rochester, New York, Mom in Atlantic, Iowa. Nevertheless they had the experience. Mom nursed two of them through measles. Angela, my eldest, inherited the family's independent and doggedness genes and has now retired from her self-built Occupational Therapy Clinic which dealt with youngsters born with various physical problems. She now lives in Maui with her husband Steven. They have two grown sons, Zachary and Shane. Dennis, my first son, loves contemporary popular music, has a great curiosity about many things, and is using eBay to dispose of his collection of instruments at present. He lives in Pittsford, N.Y. Our last Cornelia, my second daughter, is a PhD psychologist working with veterans at Fort Sill. In her free time she breeds and raises Rottweilers near Lawton, OK. Son number two, my youngest, Prentiss, is a talented pianist and computer operator, and lives with his partner in Willis, Texas. I am now writing a prequel to STRONG WOMEN—FOUR GENERATIONS. After that I plan a memoir concerning my years living in the mountains of West Virginia.

For the continual interest and love my four children Angela, Dennis, Cornelia, and Prentiss have shown me during the many years of the assembling of **STRONG WOMEN—FOUR GENERATIONS** I am deeply indebted.

Virginia S, Jones

Virginia S. Jones has tackled one of the most basic, yet one of the most elusive and challenging subjects any writer can confront: unraveling the mysteries of the human heart. She cares deeply about her characters with such conviction that we, too, quickly learn to care for them. She has a first-rate story to tell, and tells it with grace and sensitivity. All in all, she has crafted a remarkably accomplished family memoir, one that will reward the reader on several levels. I look forward to reading more from this talented author, and I think that, when you finish this book, that you will feel the same.

William R. Trotter, author of the nonfiction trilogy *The Civil War in North Carolina* and recent novels *Winter Fire, The Sands of Pride, The Fires of Pride*, and, soon to be released, *Warrener's Beastie*.

Employing her photographic memory of events, great understanding of and empathy for her characters, and a free-flowing writing style evocative of Helen Hooven Santmyer's ... And Ladies of the Club, Virginia S. Jones has produced an amazing family saga featuring strong women who liberated themselves in a society far less tolerant than today's. Ms. Jones' wide-ranging life experiences, meticulous research, and untiring devotion to portraying the maturation of her characters guarantee a memorable reading experience. Older readers will revel in the waves of nostalgia Jones' words evoke; younger readers may well yearn for a time when simple events brought lasting friendships and unimagined pleasures.

Having shared a long-term "pen-pal' relationship with this intelligent, perceptive, and inspiring author, I can only hope that Strong Women, Four Generations, 1858—1982 achieves the success it deserves. I highly recommend Virginia S. Jones' delightful, thought provoking memoir.

Col. Kenneth L. Weber, USAF (Ret.), author of *What the Captain Really Means and A Life Not Long But Wide*

978-0-595-36675-0
0-595-36675-9

Printed in the United States
91290LV00005B/125/A

9 780595 366750